NDI OLIVER BAXTER TERESA WILLIAMS BAYLESS LINDA WARREN BERGI
LAUREEN DIX BRESSLER KERIN BLASINGAME BRITTON GINGER CAGLI
JD JANICE HOLLOMBE COBB TRICA MILLER COFFMAN
KAHN COOPER KATHLEEN COOPER LUCY CO
KAREN TOSTENSON DAIGLE SUE STOCKIRD DAV
MAN EATON CAROL COELHO EDDE KATHR ERIKSE
N JANE BENNETT FORTUNE ANNE WOLF FRAN DEBORAH CROSS FREMMIN
ELLEN EASTON GIBSON KRISTI CLARK GIGUIERE RITA DIBELLA GLADDIN
MCLEAN HARRIS AUDREY HAUGE PATRICIA JACKSON HAU
ASON ANDREA TUNNEL INDART JOANN DOUGLASS JOHNSEY JILL JOHNSO
ON JONES ELAINE ZIMMERLI JORDAN JESSICA BARNETT KAISER JOAN CRESALIA KAR
CKIRD KLEIN LINDA HIGHTOWER KNOTT MARY JEAN PELOUS KRONBETTE
ACMICHAEL KAREN BONADELLE MCCAFFREY PATRICIA PICKLE MCCAN
LL KNAPP MCLAUGHLIN KATHERINE SPERRY MCMULLEN LINDA MORGAN MELL
ONEY ELIZABETH MOORE JANE KOLIGIAN MOOSOOLIAN SUSAN CARLTON MOOSOOLIA
FER NEWBY WINIFRED NISHIMINE CHRISTINE BACLAWSKI OBERTI CATHY OLSE
NDA JONES PEARSON JUDY WEST PERACCHI MARYCLAIRE ALLAN POLACE
ISENBERRY MARY RANDRUP CATHY STARK REITZ KAREN ACCORD ROBINSO
T HAIRE SANDER HALLY SHELLEY SCHAFFER MARGE SIMONELLI SCHOENBUR
EKOYAN NANCY DEYAGER SIMPSON SUSAN SAITO SMITH TERRI STIERS STEPHENSO
GERI AGHASHIAN TAHAJIAN CANDACE BRAGG TALLEY JEANNE TEFFT TARTE
MARGARET BYDE THORNHILL ROSAMOND THORP FARINSKY JOY COOK TOLLADA
VAN VLEET BARBARA BERBERIAN VARTAN SANDRA PAVLOVICH VUCOVIC
URST THERESA GIVENS WIEBE PAT FRYE WITZANSKY KAY KENDRICK WYAT
ADOLPH LYNNE AYERS ASHBECK PENNY EVERSON BAXTER KATHLEEN YAZIJIAN BOON
DONNA TAYLOR DUCKWORTH SUSAN LIBBEY EMIGH ROSEMARY FARRA
BARBARA WHITE LOYD DEBRA SHERR OSTROW ANITA BISHOP RENNE
YRNE BETTY OLSEN ALLER ANGELA GATES ANDERSON GLENNA MULLER ANDRAR
NES FOX ANTRIM NANCY PENNYCOCK ARNOLD NANCY BRADFORD ASBUR
KATHRYN BECK BARIEAU JANE HUSTED BARNETT MARION DOW BARSTOV
JOYCE HASWELL BIRD JEAN SNIDER BISCEGLIA PHYLLIS HALL BLANKENBECKLE
LEY RODDER BLUM JANE WILLIAMS BORNEMAN KATHLEEN WILLARD BOYC
LEY HARNISH BRINKER JACQUELYN CAMPBELL BROWN MARILYN SMITH BROW
SHIRLEY POTTER BURNS DONNA ARCELUS CANNON JEAN WALTERS CARTE
OBURN JOAN HUBBARD COLLINS WENDY REINERS CORDS JULIA HORNADY CORYEL
G CROCKET BARBARA MATTHEW DAHLGREN BEVERLY DANIELS CAROL EASON DA
IETRICH SUZANNE DIETRICH ELNA MAGNUSSON DIMOCK PAMELA DOLLA
RFEY JEAN ELLEN EASTON VIRGINIA STAMMER EATON JOAN NOBLE EGA
DWAY EWELL KAY GILLIS FARMER SUE ANN POWELL FEW LYNN JOHNSEY FINC
IRMA HOLLINS FRANSON KAY SWETT FRASE VIRGINIA THOMASON FRY
RGINIA NISWANDER GRANZ BEVERLY BERNHAUER HACKER RANDI JEAN HAL
CYNTHIA GRIFFIN HANSEN MARJORIE MARVIN HARKNESS ELANOR BLACK HARRI
RICIA HORNBECK HENDERSON LORIS WILLIAMS HENRY GEORGINA SHARP HICKMA
E FARRIOR HOLMES MARGARET DAVIDSON HOME PATRICIA ERICSON HOPPE
MARGARET RATCLIFFE JAMISON MARLO GRIFFIN JOHNANSEN NANCY ALWINE JONES
RY DEAN INDART KING MARY MARTIN LAFOLLETTE PAULA BEATTY LANCASTE
SCARBROUGH LAVAL SHARON SOROKIN LEVY CONSTANCE CANNON LEWI
BECCA MOORE LYLES VALERA WHITFORD LYLES CAROL MCGILL MACKECHNI
SS MARSELLA MICKEY BIDEGARY MATHIESEN CHARLOTTE GOODWIN MCAULIFF
ARON MAGEE METZLER SALLY STEVENS NAGLE ANNETTE GOERLICH NEWMA
T OSBORNE ANN RUTTER OWEN JODY PALMER SHARI PETERSON PALOUTZIAN
A DREW PETERS JERRIE HILL PETERS MARY PHILLIPS MARY RENNING PHILLIPS
E TRUXAW QUINLISK JO ANN QUINN CAROLIN HANSEN RANDALL CAROL LEV REB
GORDON RODGERS CHRIS JOHNSON ROGERS DOROTHY TRACEY ROHLFIN
UMBLEY MARY LOU RUMBLEY JODELL LORD RYAN KARLENE LOWE RYA
GARET STRATTON SANDER ROY ALLYN ANDRIS SAULSBURY ELVA CAINE SA
NN MORGAN SHAW JUDY TEMPLETON SHEHADEY CHARLENE HALLAIAN SHEKOYAN
SMITH CONNIE CHEDESTER SMITH BARBARA PERRY SNELL JANE PARIS SPAULDIN
ERLING LYNN WILLIAMSON STOREY ANNALEE ROBINSON STRACHA
NGUEVILLE STUBBLEFIELD MONA JO BUIE TELLES BARBARA HOSTETTER THOMA
WHEELER THORP BARBARA TAYLOR THRELKELD LYNDA WILLIAMS TIPTO
K VAN ROZEBOOM SUSAN HELMS VILDOSOLA MURIEL PAPAC WALTO
A BARBEAU WISWALL SHIRLEY KINER WITHAM BARBARA SUMMERS WIT

A COOKBOOK

California Treasure

Recipes
from
The Junior League of Fresno

Wimmer Brothers Books
P.O. Box 18408
Memphis, TN 38181-0408
"Cookbooks of Distinction"™

Photo Credit:

Misha Langer, Fresno, California

Photo Text:

Joan Aller Crossman
Ladean Quinlisk McCormick

Consulting Editor:

Carolyn J. Hewitt, B.S., Consulting Home Economist
Hewitt's Custom Cookery, Fresno, California

Library of Congress Catalog Card Number 85-080736

ISBN: 0-9615379-0-6

Design by Joan Aller Crossman

"The Junior League of Fresno, Incorporated has no reason to doubt that recipe ingredients, instructions, and directions will work successfully. The recipes in this book have been collected from various sources, and neither The Junior League of Fresno, Incorporated nor any contributor, publisher, printer, distributor, or seller of this book is responsible for errors or omissions."

California Treasure
P.O. Box 16278
Cardwell Station
Fresno, California 93755

The purpose of the Junior League is exclusively educational and charitable and is to promote voluntarism; to develop the potential of its members for voluntary participation in community affairs; and to demonstrate the effectiveness of trained volunteers.

The profit realized by the Junior League of Fresno, Incorporated, from the sale of *CALIFORNIA TREASURE* will be used to support community projects that we undertake in the Central Valley area. It is to this community involvement, and to the Junior League volunteers who participate in that involvement, that we dedicate this book.

Acknowledgements

The Junior League of Fresno, Incorporated, would like to thank the many people who contributed to this book. The members and friends of Junior League who donated recipes; the test kitchens; the underwriters; and the cookbook committee:

Chairman: Ladean Quinlisk McCormick
Vice-Chairman: Darla Babcock Anton
Research Chairman: Sandy Speers Stubblefield
Recipe Chairman: Carol Smith Kempen
Format Chairman: Joan Aller Crossman
Marketing Chairman Deborah Cross Fremming

The Committee:

Kathy Boome Angelillo
Lynda Blake Biggs
Nancy Choolijian Boghosian
Kathleen O'Hare Coit
Faye Turnbaugh Coyle
Karen Tostenson Daigle
Janis Helmick Donaghy
Nancy Driver
Marge Browne Freeman
Gaye Madden Giffen
Cheryl Zimmerman Heberger
Janet Johnson Johnson
Elaine Zimmerli Jordan
Susan Houghton MacMichae
Elizabeth Rowland Meux
Christine Baclawski Oberti
Cathy Olsen
Florence Bisceglia Olsen
Sally Stocking Porter
Roy Allyn Saulsbury
Hally Shelley Schaffer
Charlene Hallaian Shekoyan
Michelle Gamber Strachen
Terry Falke Zuber

Contents

SECURITY BANK

Fulton Mall
Fresno

Once a busy street and "main drag", the Fulton Mall was opened to the public in September of 1964. This area, the first outdoor mall in the country, is now home to beautiful shade trees, birds and the strolling public. Everywhere one looks there are works of art to delight the eye and the imagination. There are fountains by Charles Owen Perry, George Tsutakawa, Bruno Groth, J. Newton Russell, and Hans Sumpf. Bronzes by Clement Renzi, Bernard Rosenthal, Francois Stahly, Peter Vouzkos, and a copy of La Grande La Veuse by August Renoir. Sculpture by Ramondo Puccinelli, Gordon Newell and Clare Falkenstein. Mosaics by Joyce Aiken, Jean Ray Laury and Stan Bitters, and a clock tower by Jan De Swaart.

In 1851, the United States Army built a fort in the area of Rootville, and Fort Miller became the seat of the government. The town's name was soon changed to Millerton. In 1874, the county seat was moved to the present location and named Fresno. Fresno, pronounced "Frez-no", is the Spanish word for ash, and was named for the Oregon ash trees native to the area.

Fresno County today is a thriving, active community with a population of 558,600. The city is a designated Port of Entry with every form of transportation available. It is the only place in the nation just one and one-half hours from three National Parks, and is within one hundred and thirty miles from the nearest seaport.

Fresno County is the home of one of three Junior Leagues in the great Central Valley. Along with the Junior League of Bakersfield, to the South, and the Junior League of Sacramento, to the North, the Junior League of Fresno represents the best in community involvement and voluntarism. Since 1948, the members, their husbands, children and friends, have demonstrated just how valuable voluntarism is to constructive and healthy change in a community.

A forward thinking community with its pulse on its citizens, Fresno is described as "A great place to raise a family."

Introduction

To the visitor flying over the Central Valley of California, the Landscape must look like a large patch-work quilt; the colors in shades of green and brown, with ribbons of bright blue water, reflecting the clear sky above, winding their way throughout. The "calico" patches are the miles of cotton fields, acres of orange and almond groves, the cattle, sheep and dairy farms, lemon groves, oil fields, acres of grape vines, rice fields, melon and wheat fields, and rows of furrow. The bindings for the quilt are the Coast Range mountains on the West and the Sierra Nevadas on the East.

However, this is no simple country quilt . . . this great Central Valley . . . this San Joaquin. Nestled amongst the millions of acres of farm land are large cities, small hamlets, and towns. Like clusters of stars at night, the cities and towns burst forth across the landscape. Each one different from the rest, and each one a cradle of the history of the Valley. The Soldiers, the Bandidos, the Mountain Men, the range wars, the scandals and the successes, all add to the color of the area. But most importantly, there are people. The people of the San Joaquin Valley represent every race, ethnic background, culture and religion. Perhaps no where else on Earth will one find such a harmonious, yet diverse population. It is a "far cry" from the Valley that the first Europeans explored in 1772.

By the late Pliocene age, about forty million years ago, the sea which covered the San Joaquin Valley had retreated, leaving the Valley looking much as it does today. There were some fifty tribes of Yokuts and Miwok Indians living throughout the area when Francisco de Ulloa, the Spanish explorer, reached the lower region in 1539. Legend has it that he gave California its name. There is no direct translation from the Spanish, but in the romantic tradition of the time, Francisco named the region after a fictional utopian island in a story written in the 1500's by the Spanish author Montalzo.

In 1805, Color-Sergent Gabriel Moraga, accompanied by Father Pedro Muñoz, explored the banks of the San Francisco River, named thirty years before by his father, José Joaquin Moraga; and re-christened the river the San Joaquin. Some say that the change was to honor his father, and others, that it came from the Catholic tradition of biblical names: San Joaquin (Saint Joachim), the name of the father of the Virgin Mary. And so, as logic would decree, the Valley of the San Joaquin River became the San Joaquin Valley.

In the last three hundred years, California has enjoyed three separate governments; the Spanish, the Mexicans, and finally the Americans, until 1850, when California joined the United States. It is the influence of these governments, and the pioneer spirit of the people who came to call California their home that gives the state the flavor and colorful lifestyle that it represents today.

The great Central Valley, this San Joaquin, can best be described by the following, written by John Charles Fremont, American explorer, army officer and politician, in 1844: ". . . One might travel the whole world over, without finding a Valley more fresh and verdant — more floral and sylvan — more alive with birds and animals — more bounteously watered — than we had left in the San Joaquin . . ."

This collection of recipes is a reflection of our diversity, our history, and our love of the land.

Please enjoy . . . this, our gift to you . . . our California treasure.

Appetizers & Party Punches

Cheese Ball with Strawberry Preserves

(Great for large groups — men love this.)

Yield: Serves 8 to 10

4 cups (1-pound) grated sharp Cheddar cheese
1 cup mayonnaise
1 cup chopped pecans
1 small onion, chopped
1 cup strawberry preserves, preferably homemade

In a bowl, combine cheese, mayonnaise, pecans, onions and cayenne. Form mixture into a ball with a well or indentation in the center. Place ball on a serving plate surrounded by fresh parsley sprigs. Fill well or indentation with strawberry preserves and serve with assorted crackers.

California Peach Cheese Spread

Food Processor

Yield: 3 cups

1 (16-ounce) can peach slices in light syrup
2 (8-ounce) packages cream cheese, softened
2 tablespoons minced green onion
2 teaspoons garlic salt
1 teaspoon dried dill weed
Crisp crackers or party rye bread

Thoroughly drain liquid from peaches, reserving 2 tablespoons of the juice. Chop peach slices finely and set aside. In food processor bowl or small mixing bowl, combine softened cream cheese, reserved peach juice, onions, garlic salt and dill. Blend until smooth. Fold in chopped peaches. Turn into an attractive serving bowl or ramekin and chill well. Serve with crisp crackers or party rye bread.

Macadamia Cheese Spread

(Make day before — great for summer parties) Yield: Serves 15 to 20

1 (8-ounce) package cream cheese, softened
¼ cup butter or margarine, softened
2½ cups (10-ounces) shredded sharp Cheddar cheese
¼ cup chutney, finely chopped
1 cup macadamia nuts, chopped

In a small mixing bowl, beat cream cheese and butter or margarine together until smooth. Add Cheddar cheese and beat. Stir in chutney and nuts. Chill overnight. Serve with assorted crackers.

Fluffy Fruit Dip

(Great dip sauce for fresh fruit) Yield: 2 cups

1 cup sugar
⅔ cup light corn syrup
½ cup hot water
2 egg whites, stiffly beaten
Dash of salt
¼ teaspoon vanilla
¼ cup mayonnaise
1 tablespoon shredded orange or lemon peel

Combine sugar, corn syrup and hot water in medium saucepan. Heat slowly, stirring until sugar dissolves, then boil without stirring to the firm ball stage (248 degrees on candy thermometer). Very slowly, beat hot syrup with stiffly beaten egg whites. Add salt and vanilla. Cool to room temperature; fold in mayonnaise and orange or lemon peel. Serve as a dressing for fresh pineapple, fruit salad, or as a dip for strawberries or other fresh fruit wedges.

Horseradish Dip

(For an unusual container for this easy-to-make dip, hollow out the center of a small red cabbage so that a small plastic drinking glass can be inserted to hold the dip.)

Yield: 2 cups

2 cups (1-pint) dairy sour cream
1½ teaspoons dried horseradish
¼ teaspoon garlic salt
½ teaspoon ground pepper
1 tablespoon paprika
1 tablespoon green onion, minced
1 teaspoon salt
1 teaspoon dried tarragon, crumbled
1 clove garlic, crushed

In a small bowl, combine sour cream, horseradish, garlic salt, pepper, paprika, green onions, salt, tarragon and garlic. Chill for several hours to allow flavors to mellow. Serve dip with fresh vegetables such as carrots, celery, cucumber, cauliflower and bell pepper.

Hot Crab Dip

Yield: Serves 15 to 20

1 tablespoon milk
1 (8-ounce) package cream cheese, softened
2 tablespoons finely chopped chives
¼ teaspoon prepared horseradish
¼ teaspoon salt
Dash of pepper
1 (6½-ounce) can fancy Alaskan King crab
⅓ cup almonds, blanched, chopped and toasted

In bowl, mix milk, cream cheese, chives, horseradish, salt and pepper until well blended and smooth. Stir in crab. Pour mixture into an ovenproof serving dish and bake in a preheated 375 degree oven for 15 minutes. Remove from oven and sprinkle with almonds. Serve hot with crackers.

Microwave Clam Dip

Yield: Serves 8 to 12

2 slices bacon
1 (8-ounce) package cream cheese
¼ cup finely chopped onion
2 tablespoons grated Parmesan cheese
2 tablespoons chili sauce
2 tablespoons milk
½ teaspoon dried basil, crumbled
¼ teaspoon garlic salt
⅛ teaspoon pepper
1 (7½-ounce) can minced clams
Crackers and vegetable dippers

Place bacon in a 1-quart non-metal casserole between layers of paper toweling. Microcook on High until bacon is crisp, about 2 minutes. Remove bacon and paper toweling; crumble bacon and set aside. Place cream cheese in same casserole. Microcook, covered, on High just until cheese is softened, about 1 minute. Blend in onion, Parmesan, chili sauce, milk, basil, garlic, salt and pepper. Drain clams and stir into cheese mixture. Microcook, uncovered, on High until dip is heated through, about 3 minutes, stirring after each minute. Stir in crumbled bacon. Serve warm with crackers and vegetable dippers such as celery, carrots, zucchini and green pepper strips.

Valley Shrimp Dip

(Very light appetizer—perfect for large group)

Yield: Serves 10 to 12

1 (32-ounce) bottle catsup
1 (12-ounce) bottle chili sauce
Juice of 1 lemon
2 (3-ounce) cans tiny shrimp or 6 ounces fresh shrimp
⅓ cup fresh parsley, chopped
8 green onions, chopped
1 (6-ounce) can chopped chiles
8 celery hearts, chopped

In large bowl, combine catsup, chili sauce, lemon juice, shrimp, parsley, onions, chilies and celery hearts. Refrigerate and chill well. Serve dip in a large round, shallow dish. Serve with Armenian cracker bread or assorted crackers.

Hot Beef Hors D'Oeuvres

(Lovely served in quiche dish surrounded by Melba rounds)

Yield: Serves 10

- 1 (8-ounce) package cream cheese
- 1 cup (8-ounces) dairy sour cream
- 1 (2½-ounce) package dried beef
- ¼ cup grated onion
- 1 green pepper, chopped
- 1 (6½-ounce) can sliced water chestnuts
- ½ cup chopped walnuts

In a saucepan over low heat, melt cream cheese and sour cream together. Snip dried beef with scissors; add to the cream cheese mixture along with the grated onion, green pepper and water chestnuts. Mix well. Pour mixture into an attractive dish and sprinkle with chopped walnuts. Serve hot dip with Melba rye rounds.

For unexpected guests:

Grate together 1 pound Monterey Jack cheese
1 pound Cheddar cheese

Add 1 (4-ounce) can diced green chiles and mix together. Pour into a buttered 8x11-inch pan. In a separate bowl beat 5 eggs and pour over chile mixture. Bake at 350 degrees for 45 minutes or until set. Cut into squares and serve.

ATLANTE de TULA

Atlante De Tula
Fresno

Courthouse Park: Replica of a Toltec Sculpture, circa 900 A.D. The atlantean figure, the only sculpture of its type in North America, represents the bond between the pre-Columbian culture of Mesoamerica and the modern Mexican American community; and is "Donated to the Mexican American Community of the San Joaquin Valley and to the County and the City of Fresno, California by the people and the Government of the State of Hidalgo, Mexico. October 1980."

The history of Spanish rule in the Americas reflects a long and romantic era. "They came in search of empire and brought with them the culture of European centuries." Yet the qualities which had decreed Spain a great empire were the very qualities which brought about her downfall.

In 1823 the revolution in Mexico brought freedom from Spain and put California under Mexican rule.

Many of the ranchers in the San Joaquin Valley, during the Mexican days, were men of uncommon ability. The first "white" man to establish a home in the Valley, in 1836, was a native of Spain, José Noriéga. Mexican ranchers followed with their vaqueros (cowboys) and cattle brought into Mexico from Spain; and the ranchos sprang up along the rivers of the Valley. Men with names like Arias, Hernandez, Gomez, Higuera and Rica helped turn the once hostile land into a fertile valley. Don José Y. Limantour, French by birth and a Mexican by choice was the owner of one of the largest ranchos in the area. His was one of the illustrious early families in the Valley. One of his sons became Secretary of the Treasury under Presidente Porfirio Diaz and shares with Alexander Hamilton the honor of being one of the two greatest financial wizards in North America. This son was also the first Mexican elected to the French Academy.

The history of the Mexican in California is a long and a rich one. From the very beginnings of the Valley, the Mexican people have contributed to the overall well-being of the community. From the José Noriéga family of the 1800's to the Angel Lopez family of today, the traditions of the past live with the promise of the future.

Compliments of **Gottschalks**

French Fried Artichoke Hearts

Yield: Makes 24

2 (16-ounce) cans artichoke hearts, drained
6 whole fresh eggs, beaten
1 cup flour
1½ cups bread crumbs
½ teaspoon salt
¼ teaspoon pepper
⅛ teaspoon garlic powder
Oil
1 tablespoon butter or margarine
Juice of 2 lemons
Dash Worcestershire sauce
California dry white wine

Drain artichoke hearts. Beat the eggs and then dip the artichoke hearts into the eggs. In a small bowl, mix the flour, bread crumbs, salt, pepper and garlic powder. Drain the eggs from the artichoke hearts and dip them into the flour-crumb mixture. Deep fry until golden brown. Remove and drain. Melt the butter in a medium frying pan and sauté the artichoke hearts with a little dry white wine. Squeeze the juice of the lemon over the hearts and add a dash of Worcestershire sauce. Remove from pan. Serve hot with cocktail sauce or mayonnaise.

Cucumber Boats with Caviar

Cucumbers—as many as needed
Italian-type salad dressing
½ cup dairy sour cream
1 (3½-ounce) jar salmon caviar
Sprigs of parsley
Lemon wedges or slices

Peel cucumbers, if desired, and slice lengthwise. Hollow out the center of each half with the tip of a spoon, removing seeds. In a shallow bowl, marinate cucumber boats with Italian-type salad dressing for approximately one hour; refrigerate. Meanwhile, combine sour cream and caviar; chill until ready to use. Remove cucumber boats from marinade and pat dry; fill hollow with sour cream-caviar mixture. Cut each boat into serving pieces and top with a sprig of parsley. Serve on a chilled plate with small wedges or slices of lemon.

Avocado Frosted Cauliflower

Yield: Serves 15

1 head cauliflower

Steam cauliflower until tender but still firm. Place in a large bowl.

Marinade:

6 tablespoons vegetable oil
3 tablespoons white distilled vinegar
Salt and freshly ground pepper to taste

Combine oil, vinegar and seasonings and mix well. Pour over warm cauliflower and chill overnight.

Frosting:

3 medium ripe avocadoes, peeled and pitted
1 small onion, finely minced
3 tablespoons of the above marinade
Dash of nutmeg
Dash of salt
1 teaspoon lemon juice
½ cup toasted sliced almonds

In medium bowl, mash avocados with fork. Add onion, marinade, nutmeg, salt, lemon juice and mix well. Frost cauliflower completely with mixture. Sprinkle with toasted almonds. Serve frosted head on a large platter surrounded by assorted crackers accompanied by a small knife for cutting.

Baked Japanese Eggplant Appetizer

Yield: Serves 8

8 Japanese eggplants
Salt
1 cup mayonnaise
¼ to ⅓ cup finely chopped scallions
20 round, buttery-type snack crackers, rolled into crumbs

Peel eggplant; cut into ½-inch thick slices. Lay on platter and sprinkle with salt; let stand 20 minutes. Rinse slices thoroughly in cold water and pat dry on both sides with paper toweling. Mix mayonnaise and scallions together. Spread mixture on both sides of eggplant slices. Dip eggplant into crumbs and place coated slices on a non-stick baking sheet. Bake in a preheated 375 degree oven for 15 minutes. Turn slices and bake an additional 15 minutes. Sprinkle baked appetizers with salt to taste. Serve hot.

Note:
Grated Parmesan cheese may be sprinkled on the eggplant slices for a different flavor.

Bleu Cheese Stuffed Mushrooms

Microwave

Yield: 24 appetizers

1 pound (about 24) medium-sized fresh mushrooms
1 (8-ounce) package cream cheese, softened
½ cup dairy sour cream
2 teaspoons onion powder
2 ounces bleu cheese
¼ cup walnuts, chopped

Rinse and pat dry mushrooms; remove stems and save for other uses. Set caps aside. In a medium bowl, combine cream cheese, sour cream and onion powder; beat until smooth. Press bleu cheese through a sieve; stir into cream cheese mixture. Spoon into a pastry bag fitted with a star tube. Pipe into mushroom caps; sprinkle with chopped walnuts. Place on a microwave-proof dish and cook on High for 5 to 6 minutes. Place mushrooms in chafing dish to keep warm or serve immediately while hot.

Deep Fried Mushrooms

Yield: Serves 10 to 15

3 pounds mushrooms
½ cup flour
Salt and pepper to taste
2 eggs
2 tablespoons milk
3 cups vegetable oil
½ cup cornflake crumbs

Clean mushrooms. Mix flour, salt and pepper together in a plastic bag. Put clean mushrooms, a few at a time, into bag with flour and shake to coat well. In a bowl, mix eggs, milk and 2 tablespoons of the oil. Dip floured mushrooms into egg mixture, then roll in cornflake crumbs. In large pan add the remaining oil and heat to 375 degrees. Deep fry the mushrooms in small batches, until crisp. Transfer to a dish lined with paper towels. Mushrooms may be done ahead of time and reheated in a microwave before serving or kept warm in a conventional oven. Serve with your favorite dipping sauce.

Note:
May substitute cheese-cracker crumbs.

Mushrooms Stuffed with Escargots

Yield: 18 mushrooms

½ cup soft butter
1½ teaspoons minced shallots
1 large clove garlic, finely minced
1½ tablespoons minced parsley
½ tablespoon grated celery
¼ teaspoon salt
Pepper to taste
18 mushrooms with caps of 2-inch diameter
18 canned snails - drained

Cream 6 tablespoons of the butter with the shallots, garlic, parsley, celery, salt and pepper. Cut and discard the stems from the mushrooms making the cut at the base of the cap. With a sharp knife, hollow out a ¾-inch depression in top of each cap. Sauté the mushrooms in the remaining 2 tablespoons of butter for five minutes. Place a small amount of herbed butter in the depressions that were cut, then a snail, and then a little more butter. Bake in a preheated 375 degree oven for 15 minutes.

Stuffed Snow Peas

Yield: 50 appetizers

50 snow peas or Chinese pea pods
1 pound Boursin cheese
½ to ¾ cup half and half or light cream

Wash pea pods and blot dry. Trim ends from pea pods; strip away any side strings. Set aside. In a small bowl, mix ½ cup half and half with Boursin cheese, adding more if necessary to achieve a creamy consistency. Put cheese mixture into a pastry bag, fitted with a star tip, and force mixture in a decorative pattern on the flat surface of the pea pods. Refrigerate pods until slightly firm. Serve on a plate lined with fresh chicory, if desired, and decorated with cherry tomatoes.

Crab Cream Stuffed Cherry Tomatoes

Yields: 36 appetizers

1 cup shredded crab meat, fresh or canned
¼ cup fresh lime juice
1 (3-ounce) package cream cheese, softened
¼ cup heavy cream
2 tablespoons mayonnaise
1 tablespoon minced onion
½ teaspoon minced garlic
1 teaspoon dill weed
2 drops Tabasco
1 teaspoon Worcestershire sauce
Salt to taste
36 cherry tomatoes

Marinate crab meat in lime juice for an hour. Mix together cream cheese, cream and mayonnaise until smooth. Add onion, garlic, dill, Tabasco, Worcestershire and salt. Fold in crab meat. Makes about 2 cups. Spoon the mixture into the hollowed-out cherry tomatoes. Chill well before serving.

Antipasto

Yield: Serves 12 to 15

1 (29-ounce) can tomato purée
1 (16-ounce) bottle catsup
1 (6-ounce) can sliced black olives, drained
2 (6½-ounce) cans small shrimp, drained
1 (4-ounce) can sliced mushrooms, drained
1 (6½-ounce) can crab meat, drained
1 (6-ounce) jar marinated artichoke hearts
1 (6-ounce) can minced clams, drained
1 (4-ounce) can diced green chiles
1 tablespoon sugar
4 dashes vinegar
Garlic powder to taste
1 tablespoon minced onion

In a large bowl, combine all ingredients and chill well for several hours. Serve with crackers.

Notes

Caponata

Yield: Serves 8

½ cup olive oil
2 small eggplants, peeled and diced
2 onions, thinly sliced
1 cup celery, diced
2 cups fresh Italian tomatoes or 1 (16-ounce) can Italian type tomatoes, undrained
2 tablespoons capers, drained
1 tablespoon pine nuts
8 black Italian olives, pitted and chopped
2 tablespoons sugar
¼ cup red wine vinegar
½ teaspoon salt
Pinch of pepper

Heat oil in large skillet; fry the eggplant until soft and lightly browned. Remove the eggplant from pan with a slotted spoon and reserve. Add onion and celery to frying pan and sauté until soft and slightly golden. Combine tomatoes, that have either been puréed or forced through a sieve, the onions and celery and simmer for 15 to 20 minutes. Add the capers, pine nuts, olives, sugar, wine vinegar, salt, pepper and the reserved eggplant. Cover skillet and allow mixture to simmer for about 20 minutes, stirring occasionally. Allow Caponata to cool and then chill in refrigerator. Serve with thinly sliced French bread as a first course or hors d' oeuvre.

Deep Fried Won Ton

(A simplified version of a Chinese classic)

Yield: makes 50 won ton

1 pound lean ground beef
¼ cup finely chopped green onions
6 to 8 finely chopped water chestnuts
1 teaspoon cornstarch
1 teaspoon soy sauce
½ teaspoon salt
⅛ teaspoon pepper
⅛ teaspoon garlic powder
1 teaspoon sesame oil
1 egg slightly beaten
1 package Won Ton skins (about 40 to 50)
Oil for deep fat frying

Combine lean ground beef, chopped green onions, chopped water chestnuts, cornstarch, soy sauce, salt, pepper, garlic powder, sesame oil and egg; mix together lightly. Take a generous teaspoonful of the meat filling and roll it into a cylinder between the palms of your hands. Place the filling approximately 1-inch from one of the points of the won ton skins. Cover filling with the nearest point and roll to the opposite corner. Moisten this corner with a drop of water, and seal. The completed won ton will be tube-shaped with open ends. Place assembled won ton on a waxed paper-lined tray. Cover tray with waxed paper and refrigerate until ready to fry. Deep fry (8 to 10 won ton at a time) in hot oil (375 degrees) for 2 minutes or until crisp and golden. WARNING: Cooking too much cold food at one time will lower the fat temperature drastically and make the food soft and greasy tasting instead of giving it a crisp, light flavor. Drain cooked won ton on a cooling rack placed over paper towel-lined tray or baking sheet. Serve hot won ton plain or with sweet-sour, mustard and/ or plum sauce.

Note:
Fried won ton may be kept warm for an hour or so in a 250 degree oven, or reheated for 5 minutes in a 450 degree oven. Fried won ton may be frozen and reheated at 450 degrees for 15 to 20 minutes. For best results when reheating, place them on an elevated cooling rack over a rimmed baking sheet.

Simple Sweet-Sour Dipping Sauce: Yield: 2¼ cups

1 (20-ounce) can crushed pineapple
½ cup catsup
½ cup brown sugar
¼ teaspoon salt
2 tablespoons cider vinegar
Dash or two of Tabasco sauce

In the blender, process the crushed pineapple. Add the catsup, brown sugar, salt, vinegar and a few dashes of Tabasco sauce, if desired. Blend well. Pour into a saucepan, and heat over moderate heat until warmed through. Serve hot.

Potato Skins

Yield: Serves 6

6 medium-sized baking potatoes
½ cup butter or margarine
12 slices bacon, crisply fried and crumbled or 3 to 4 ounces real bacon bits
Minced onion, enough to sprinkle on each appetizer
8 ounces shredded Cheddar cheese
1 (8-ounce) package dairy sour cream
4 green onions, chopped fine
1 avocado, mashed
½ teaspoon lemon juice

Scrub potatoes; dry and pierce with a fork in several places. Arrange on a baking sheet and bake in a preheated 375 degree oven for 1½ hours or until tender. Let stand until cool enough to handle. Cut potatoes in half lengthwise and scoop out centers, leaving a ¼-inch thick shell. Cover; chill shells up to 2 days. (You may use the centers for mashed potatoes if you wish.) When ready to use, melt the butter and brush potato shells inside and out. Place cut side up on a baking sheet. Sprinkle with minced onion and bake in a preheated 425 degree oven for 20 minutes or until brown and crisp. Sprinkle some cheese and bacon into each shell. Bake just until cheese melts. Serve hot. Serve the sour cream and avocado-lemon mixture in separate dishes to be put on individually, or put a dab on each skin before serving.

Guacamole Pinwheel

Food Processor

Yield: Serves 12 to 16

1 (0.25-ounce) envelope unflavored gelatin
¼ cup cold water
1 cup mashed ripe avocado (2 to 3 fruits)
2 tablespoons lemon juice
1 (0.6-ounce) package dry Italian salad dressing mix
2 cups (1-pint) dairy sour cream
3 tablespoons chopped green chiles
¼ teaspoon onion powder
2 to 3 dashes of Tabasco sauce
2 to 3 drops green food coloring
Various toppings such as: chopped green onions, green peppers, cucumbers, ripe olives, tomatoes and cooked baby shrimp
Tortilla chips or assorted crackers

Oil, or spray with cooking oil spray, a 9 to 10-inch quiche dish, pie plate or tart pan with a removable bottom. Set aside. In a small pan, sprinkle gelatin over cold water. Let stand for 5 minutes to soften. Heat mixture just to the boil to dissolve gelatin. In a large bowl or food processor work bowl, fitted with metal blade, blend avocado, lemon juice, salad dressing mix, sour cream, chiles, onion powder and Tabasco. Add dissolved gelatin and mix thoroughly. Add green food coloring, if needed to obtain the desired color. Pour mixture into prepared mold. Cover with plastic wrap and refrigerate until firm. Pinwheel may be refrigerated up to 2 days, but do not freeze. If using a quiche or pie plate, it is not necessary to unmold. If using a tart pan, unmold before serving on an attractive platter. To serve, surround with tortilla chips or assorted crackers. Garnish with one of the various toppings listed above.

Cheese Puffs

(Perfect to keep in freezer for unexpected guests)

Yield: 60 puffs

- 2 (3-ounce) packages cream cheese, cut into 1-inch pieces
- ½ pound medium Cheddar cheese, diced into ½-inch pieces
- ½ pound butter or margarine, cut into 16 pieces
- 4 egg whites, beaten stiff
- 1 loaf French bread (soft crust)

In the top of a double boiler over simmering water, combine cream cheese, Cheddar cheese and butter. Melt slowly and stir until well blended. Fold cheese sauce into beaten egg whites. Cut bread into irregular pieces and then dip each piece of bread into the cheese mixture and place on a cookie sheet.* When ready to use, take directly from freezer and place on a foil-lined cookie sheet. Bake in a preheated 425 degree oven for 10 minutes. Serve hot.

* Place in freezer until puffs are frozen, then remove from cookie sheet and store in freezer bags until ready to use.

Cheese and Mushroom Canape

Yield: 2½ dozen

- ¼ pound fresh mushrooms, chopped
- 1 tablespoon butter or margarine
- 1 (8-ounce) package cream cheese, softened
- 1 teaspoon minced onion
- Salt to taste
- Pepper to taste
- ¼ teaspoon chopped fresh basil or pinch of dried basil
- ½ teaspoon California dry sherry
- Small rounds of bread
- Butter

Clean and chop mushrooms. Sauté mushrooms in butter. Combine cream cheese, minced onion, salt, pepper, basil and sherry. Add mushrooms and stir together. Toast bread rounds on one side; turn them over and lightly butter. Spread the mushroom-cheese mixture on the buttered side and refrigerate or freeze the canapes until ready to use. At serving time place under the broiler until light brown.

Flaky Crab Puffs

Yield: 36 appetizers

1 (6 to 8-ounce) package frozen Alaskan crab, thawed
2 tablespoons butter or margarine
¼ cup sliced green onions
1 cup chopped fresh mushrooms
1 cup grated Monterey Jack cheese
1 (3-ounce) package cream cheese, softened
⅓ cup mayonnaise
2 tablespoons minced parsley
¼ pound phyllo dough
½ cup melted butter

Break crab meat apart and blot dry on paper toweling. Melt butter in skillet; add onions and sauté for 1 minute. Add mushrooms and sauté 1 minute longer. Combine mixture with crab meat, Jack and cream cheeses, mayonnaise and parsley. Unroll phyllo dough and place 2 sheets on work surface (keep remainder covered with waxed paper and damp towel to prevent drying). Cut each group of 2 sheets into strips approximately 2x10-inches. Brush each strip with melted butter. Place a scant tablespoon of the crab filling at one end of each strip. Fold over to form a triangle, then continue folding like a flag. Brush end with a little butter and carefully tuck into fold to seal. Place triangle, seam side down on ungreased baking sheet. Repeat with remaining phyllo and filling. Bake in a preheated 350 degree oven for 25 to 30 minutes or until crisp and golden. Serve warm or at room temperature.

Note:
For freezing instructions, see Cheese Boeregs recipe (page 364).

Vegetarian Hye Roller

Yield: Serves 5 to 6

1 large round of Armenian cracker bread
4 ounces herbed cream cheese
3 tablespoons mayonnaise
½ grated carrot
4 mushrooms, sliced
1 large tomato, sliced very thin
3 ounces marinated artichokes (½ of 6-ounce jar)
½ ripe avocado, sliced and dipped in Fruit Fresh
1 ounce sliced black olives
Shredded lettuce or alfalfa sprouts (optional)

Soften crisp cracker bread by spraying with warm tap water. Spray both sides of the bread. Cover with dampened tea towel or put in plastic bag and allow the round of bread to soften for 15 to 20 minutes. You may also use the pre-softened cracker bread (available in some areas). While the bread is softening, blend your herbed cream cheese with the mayonnaise and spread herbed cream cheese over the entire surface of the cracker bread. Cover the round of cheese-covered bread with the grated carrots, mushrooms, tomato, marinated artichokes, avocados and olives. Start at one end and roll the bread as tightly as you can (jelly-roll fashion). The Hye Roller can be served immediately or you may cover the entire roll with plastic wrap and refrigerate for later use.

Cover a serving platter with butter leaf lettuce or large green leaf lettuce. Slice the sandwich roll into ½ to 1½-inch slices. Each sandwich roll will make from 10 to 24 slices depending on thickness. This makes a beautiful tray of appetizers.

Hot Mushroom Crescents

Food Processor | Yield: 4½ dozen appetizers

- 4 (3-ounce) packages cream cheese, softened
- 10 tablespoons unsalted butter or margarine, softened
- 1½ cups unbleached all-purpose flour
- 1 medium onion, quartered
- ½ pound fresh mushrooms, cleaned and stems trimmed
- ½ teaspoon dried thyme
- Freshly ground black pepper
- 1 large egg

Use the metal blade of a food processor; mix 3 packages of the cream cheese with 8 tablespoons of the butter, pulsing 3 times and then allowing the machine to run for 1 minute, stopping twice to scrape down the work bowl. Add the flour, ½ cup at a time, to the work bowl, pulsing 6 or 8 times after each addition or until the flour is blended. Carefully remove the dough from the work bowl and flatten it into a disc. Wrap the dough in plastic wrap and refrigerate for at least 30 minutes. Using the metal blade, chop the onion, pulsing 10 to 12 times until finely chopped. Remove the onions from the work bowl and set aside. Repeat chopping process with mushrooms. Melt the remaining butter in a medium skillet over moderate-high heat. Add the reserved onion and cook, stirring often, until the onion is lightly golden. Add the mushrooms and cook, stirring, until the moisture from the mushrooms has evaporated.

Reduce the heat to moderate-low; add the remaining cream cheese and stir constantly until thoroughly mixed. Stir in the thyme and pepper to taste and remove the pan from the heat. Let the mixture cool to room temperature. Preheat the oven to 400 degrees. On a lightly floured surface pat or roll out half of the dough to a ⅛-inch thickness. Cut out rounds with a floured 2½-inch cutter. Pat together the scraps of dough, flatten to a ⅛-inch thickness and cut more rounds. Place about ½ to 1 teaspoon of the mushroom filling on each round. Fold in half and crimp the edges firmly together with a fork, prick tops for steam vents. Place on an ungreased baking sheet. Repeat with the remaining dough and filling.

In a small bowl, beat the egg with 1 teaspoon of water and brush the mixture over each of the crescents. Bake in the lower third of the preheated oven for 15 minutes or until golden brown. Cool on a wire rack for about 10 minutes before serving. The cooked crescents may be frozen and reheated in a preheated 300 degree oven for 20 minutes.

Crab-Bacon Rolls

Yield: 20 rolls

1 egg, beaten
¼ cup tomato juice
½ cup fine bread crumbs
1 tablespoon chopped parsley
1 tablespoon lemon juice
¼ teaspoon salt
¼ teaspoon Worcestershire sauce
Pepper to taste
1 (7½-ounce) can or 1 cup of crab meat
10 slices of bacon, cut in half crosswise

In medium mixing bowl, beat egg and tomato juice together. Add bread crumbs, parsley, lemon juice, salt, Worcestershire sauce, crab and pepper. Mix thoroughly. Divide mixture into 20 equal parts and roll into "fingers" about 2-inches long. Wrap each roll with ½ slice of bacon and fasten with a toothpick. Place on cookie sheet and broil in oven for about 10 minutes, turning often to brown evenly. Serve hot.

Chiao-Tzu
(Chinese Pot Stickers)

(Time consuming to make unless commerically-made Shao-mai or wonton skins or wrappers are available)

Yield: 50 to 60 appetizers

- ⅔ cup boiling water—see note
- 2½ cups all purpose flour—see note
- ⅓ cup cold water—see note
- ¾ pound ground pork (not too lean)
- 4 ounces shelled raw shrimp, cut into small pieces
- 3 dried Chinese black mushrooms, soaked in boiling water until soft, drained and chopped
- 2 tablespoons soy sauce
- 2 tablespoons sesame oil
- 1 tablespoon green onion, chopped
- 2 teaspoons salt
- 1 teaspoon finely chopped ginger
- 10 ounces Chinese cabbage or fresh spinach
- 6 tablespoons peanut oil
- ⅔ cup water

Add boiling water to flour, mixing well with chopsticks; stir in cold water. Knead dough until smooth and elastic. Let stand, covered, for at least 15 minutes. Meanwhile cook ground pork until it loses its pink color and crumbles; drain. Combine pork, shrimp, mushrooms, soy sauce, sesame oil, green onion, salt and ginger. Mix thoroughly until well blended. Blanch cabbage or spinach in boiling water for about 2 minutes; remove and immediately plunge into cold water. Remove from water and squeeze dry. Chop finely and squeeze dry again. Add to pork-shrimp filling mixture and blend well. Set aside. Remove dough to floured board. Knead again until smooth. Divide dough into 60 pieces. Remove one piece of dough to work surface and cover rest. Flatten each piece with hand and roll into a very thin 2½-inch pancake; use a 2½-inch cookie cutter, if desired, to make a perfect circle. Place a tablespoon of filling in center of dough. Moisten one-half of outer edge of dough circle with cold water. Fold dough over filling to make a half circle and pinch edges together. Carefully stretch filled circle to elongate slightly. Pot stickers may be frozen at this point if desired. To cook, heat a flat frying pan until very hot and add about two tablespoons of the peanut oil. When oil is hot, add enough pot stickers to cover bottom of pan without overlapping (approximately 18 to 20 to a 10-inch pan). Cook until bottoms are golden, about 1 to 3 minutes. Add ⅔ cup water, reduce heat slightly, cover and cook until water has evaporated, about 5 minutes. Add 1 tablespoon oil to side of pan and fry another half minute. Place a preheated serving plate over frying pan and invert pan quickly. Cover pot stickers and keep warm in low oven. Repeat cooking process for remaining portions. If pot stickers are frozen, all cooking times will need to be increased. Serve hot pot stickers with a dipping sauce made with ¼ cup soy sauce, 2 teaspoons sesame oil and 2 tablespoons white distilled or rice vinegar.

Note:
If the round Shao-mai skins or wrappers are not available, good results can be achieved by simply cutting a square wonton skin or wrapper into a circle.

Brandied Chicken Wings

Yield: 14 to 28 drumettes

¼ cup butter or margarine
1½ cups brown sugar, firmly packed
½ cup soy sauce
1 cup California brandy
2 tablespoons dry mustard
14 to 28 chicken drumettes (chicken wing drumsticks)

In a medium saucepan, melt the butter. Add brown sugar, soy sauce, brandy and dry mustard and heat until sugar is dissolved. Put drumettes in shallow, foil-lined pan; cover with sauce. Bake in a preheated 275 degree oven for 3 to 4 hours.

Glazed Sausage Balls

Yield: 60 sausage balls

⅓ pound bulk pork sausage
¾ pound ground pork or beef
½ teaspoon salt
½ teaspoon dry mustard
½ teaspoon coriander
¼ teaspoon ground allspice
1 egg, slightly beaten
¼ cup fine dry bread crumbs
¼ cup green onions, thinly sliced
½ cup apple jelly
½ cup chutney, finely chopped
1 teaspoon lemon juice

In a large mixing bowl combine the sausage and the ground pork or beef. Add the salt, dry mustard, coriander and allspice to the meat and mix. Beat the egg and add to the mixture. Add bread crumbs and green onions and mix well. Shape into 1-inch balls and refrigerate or freeze if made in advance. To cook, place thawed meatballs on jelly roll pan (or cookie sheet with rim) and bake in a preheated 500 degree oven for 6 to 8 minutes or until well browned. Drain well. In large skillet over low heat, combine the apple jelly, chutney and lemon juice. Stir until jelly is melted. Add meatballs and simmer for 8 to 10 minutes or until well glazed. Transfer to a chafing dish and keep hot. Serve with cocktail picks.

Baked Clams Oregano

Yield: 24 clams

24 Cherrystone clams
4 slices day old bread, finely crumbled
1 clove garlic, minced
¼ cup chopped parsley
½ teaspoon oregano
1 teaspoon salt
½ teaspoon pepper
Olive oil to moisten
¼ cup Parmesan cheese

In a large pan put a small amount of water and bring to a boil. Drop clams into boiling water and cook until done. They are done when they begin to open. Remove clams from water and discard any clams that have not opened. Remove clams from shells reserving juice and finely chop clams. Save the shells for restuffing. In a bowl combine bread, garlic, parsley, oregano, salt and pepper with enough olive oil to moisten. Stir clams and reserved juice into mixture. Place a little mixture in one half of clam shells and bake in a preheated 350 degree oven for 15 to 20 minutes. Sprinkle with Parmesan cheese before serving.

Poached Salmon with Dill Sauce

(The salmon may also be served hot as an entree.)

Yield: Serves 6 to 8

Poached Salmon:

1 whole salmon, 5 to 7 pounds, filleted
½ cup dry vermouth
2 to 3 lemons, sliced
3 cups chopped fresh parsley

Place filleted salmon on enough foil to wrap completely with pinched, folded edges. Stuff the inside of the salmon with a layer of lemon slices topped with the parsley. Pour dry vermouth over the top of the salmon. Close foil tightly. Bake in a preheated 325 degree oven for ½ to 1 hour depending on weight of the fish. Do not overcook. Salmon flesh should be pink and moist. Chill thoroughly. When cold, carefully remove the skin on the top of the fish. Decorate salmon with lemon slices and fresh dill. Serve on a chilled platter accompanied by dill sauce.

Dill Sauce:

1 (16-ounce) carton dairy sour cream
2 tablespoons to ¼ cup mayonnaise, according to preference
Peel from 2 to 3 lemons, grated
Lemon juice to taste (about 1 large lemon)
3 to 4 teaspoons dried dill weed
Few shakes celery salt
Dash Worcestershire sauce

Mix sour cream, mayonnaise, lemon peel, lemon juice, dill weed, celery salt and Worcestershire sauce thoroughly. Chill. Serve poached salmon with the dill sauce and crackers.

HARLAND'S Mesquite Grilled Prawns and Japanese Eggplant with Ginger Butter

(A favorite Fresno appetizer)

Yield: Serves 4

Ginger Butter:

4 tablespoons butter, preferably unsalted, softened
1 teaspoon finely chopped shallots
½ teaspoon finely chopped garlic
1 teaspoon freshly grated ginger
Juice of ½ lemon
3 to 4 sprigs parsley
Dash cayenne pepper

Combine butter, shallots, garlic, ginger, lemon juice, parsley and cayenne in a blender jar or processor work bowl fitted with metal blade; blend until a smooth butter is formed. Store flavored butter in refrigerator until needed. Double this recipe if desired as it keeps well and is an excellent seasoning for vegetables, chicken or fish.

Appetizer:

Ginger butter
High quality olive oil
4 small Japanese eggplants, halved lengthwise with stems intact
Salt and pepper to taste
12 large raw prawns, deveined and butterflied

Just before serving time, bring ginger butter to a creamy consistency by placing it in a warm spot or in the microwave for a few seconds. Start charcoal in an outdoor barbecue, using mesquite charcoal if available. When coals are nearly ready, start eggplant by heating a large skillet over high heat. When pan is hot, add 2 tablespoons olive oil and sauté eggplant halves, cut side down, until golden brown. Turn halves over and continue cooking another minute; remove to a platter. When charcoal coals are ready, dip the prawns in a little olive oil and arrange them along with the partially cooked eggplant on the grill for 1½ to 2 minutes on each side. Serve 3 prawns and 2 eggplant halves per serving, on warmed plates, around a generous spoonful of the softened ginger butter.

HARLAND'S
Sautéed Prawns with Garlic and Pernod

Serves 4

1 tablespoon unsalted butter
1 tablespoon olive oil
12 large raw prawns, peeled, deveined and butterflied
2 teaspoons finely chopped garlic
¼ cup Pernod liqueur
¼ cup dry white wine
½ cup heavy or whipping cream
Juice of ½ lemon
Salt and pepper to taste

Heat butter and olive oil in a 12-inch frying pan over high heat. Add the cleaned prawns and garlic to the pan and allow to brown for just a few seconds before adding the Pernod. (Careful—Pernod ignites immediately.) When the flames die down, turn the prawns and add the wine and continue cooking another minute or so until the liquid in the pan has mostly evaporated. Remove the prawns to a warm platter. Add the cream to the pan liquids and cook until the reduced sauce coats the back of a spoon. Add lemon juice and salt and pepper to taste. Strain the sauce over the cooked prawns and serve immediately.

Seafood Croustades

Yield: 32 appetizers

32 slices of thinly sliced sandwich bread
6 to 8 tablespoons butter or margarine, melted
1 cup mayonnaise
⅓ cup grated Parmesan cheese
⅓ cup shredded Swiss cheese
¼ to ⅓ cup chopped onions
½ teaspoon Worcestershire sauce
3 drops Tabasco sauce
2 ounces cooked baby shrimp, chopped
2 ounces cooked crab meat, flaked
Paprika

With rolling pin, flatten slices of bread. Using a 2½-inch cookie cutter, cut a round from each bread slice. With a pastry brush, lightly brush each side of the bread round with melted margarine. Press each round into a 1½-inch miniature muffin tin. Bake at 400 degrees for 10 minutes or until golden brown. Remove from oven and cool in pans. You may make toast cups in advance and freeze them empty. Meanwhile, prepare filling: soak shrimp in ice water for 10 to 20 minutes to remove salty taste and improve texture. Remove shrimp from water and blot well on paper towels; chop. If canned crabmeat is used, soak and blot as for the shrimp. In a medium bowl, combine mayonnaise, Parmesan, Swiss cheese, onions, Worcestershire and Tabasco. Mix well. Carefully stir in shrimp and crabmeat. Fill each croustade with filling. Sprinkle tops with paprika and place on baking sheet. Place under broiler or in hot oven to heat to serving temperature. May serve immediately or cool and freeze. May store frozen for 2 to 3 months.

To serve frozen croustades—reheat in a preheated 450 degree oven for 7 to 10 minutes.

Acapulco Seafood Empanadas

Food Processor Yield: about 2 dozen

Dough:

2 cups all-purpose flour
1 teaspoon salt
⅔ cup chilled lard, cut into small pieces
5 tablespoons warm water
Oil for deep-fat frying

Place flour, salt and lard in a processor work bowl fitted with a metal blade. Process with on/off bursts until lard is cut into pea-sized pieces. Sprinkle water over dry ingredients and process mixture until mixture begins to form a ball. Remove dough from work bowl and divide. Roll out ½ at a time on a lightly floured surface. Cut into 3-inch circles. Set aside.

Filling:

½ pound (8-ounces) halibut or crab
2 tablespoons chopped onion
½ clove garlic, minced
2 tablespoons vegetable oil
Dash of California dry white wine
2 teaspoons all-purpose flour
½ teaspoon salt
¼ teaspoon pepper
1½ tablespoons fish or chicken stock
2 teaspoons minced green onions
1 tablespoon finely minced, toasted, blanched almonds

Chop fish or shred crab into small pieces and sauté with onion and garlic in oil until partially cooked. Add a dash of wine; blend in flour, salt and pepper. Stir in stock. Remove from heat and add green onions and almonds.

Method:
Put about 2 teaspoons of filling on one side of each circle. Lightly moisten the edge and fold over filling into a crescent shape. Seal with the tines of a fork. Fry a few of the empanadas at a time, in oil preheated to 400 degrees, until golden brown. Drain on paper toweling.

Shrimp Arnaud

Yield: Serves 6 to 8

2 cloves garlic
¾ cup olive oil
1 teaspoon fresh chervil or ½ teaspoon dried chervil
1 teaspoon fresh tarragon or ½ teaspoon dried tarragon
¼ cup Dijon mustard
3 tablespoons prepared mustard
5 green onions, chopped
3 tablespoons horseradish
Juice of 1 lemon
1½ tablespoons paprika
1 teaspoon salt
¼ teaspoon pepper
¼ teaspoon red pepper flakes
2 pounds cooked, peeled shrimp

In a small mixing bowl, combine pressed cloves of garlic and oil; mellow overnight at room temperature. The following day, with mortar and pestle, crush fresh chervil and tarragon leaves, adding them along with the mustards, green onions, horseradish, lemon juice, paprika, salt, pepper and red pepper flakes to the garlic-oil mixture. Mix well and pour over the prepared shrimp and marinate in the refrigerator for a minimum of 3 hours (all day is even better). Serve as a first course with thinly sliced French bread to catch the marinade.

Bay Shrimp with Braised Leeks

Yield: Serves 6

White parts only of 3 leeks
2 cups chicken broth, preferably homemade
Salt and white pepper
1½ pounds small, raw bay shrimp
2 tablespoons unsalted butter
2 tablespoons olive oil
1 cup heavy or whipping cream
3 tablespoons minced fresh parsley

Quarter leeks lengthwise; cut them into 1-inch lengths and wash well. Place chicken broth in a saucepan; add leeks and cook over moderate heat for 10 minutes or until tender. Drain leeks well; season with salt and pepper and keep warm. Stock may be saved for another use. In a skillet, cook shrimp in butter-oil mixture over moderate heat for one minute, stirring constantly. Add cream and 2 tablespoons of the parsley to the shrimp and cook one minute longer. Divide leeks among 6 pre-warmed plates. Transfer shrimp, with a slotted spoon, to the plates and keep warm. Reduce the sauce remaining in skillet over high heat. Spoon the thickened sauce over the shrimp and garnish with the remaining parsley.

Deviled Shrimp

Yield: Serves 10 to 12

2 pounds medium to large raw shrimp
1 lemon, thinly sliced
1 medium red onion, thinly sliced
1 cup pitted black olives, well drained
2 tablespoons chopped pimiento
¼ cup vegetable oil
2 cloves garlic, minced
1 tablespoon dry mustard
1½ teaspoons salt
½ cup lemon juice
1 tablespoon red wine vinegar
1 bay leaf, crumbled
Dash of cayenne
Chopped parsley

Shell and devein shrimp. Bring 1 quart salted water to a boil; add shrimp and cook for a scant 3 minutes. Drain at once, rinse in cold water, drain again and set aside. In a bowl, combine lemon slices, onion, black olives and pimiento and toss well. Combine oil, garlic, dry mustard, salt, lemon juice, wine vinegar, bay leaf, cayenne and parsley and add to the lemon mixture. Arrange shrimp on a serving dish and pour marinade over them. Cover and chill no longer than 3 hours. Serve with toothpicks.

Chinese Shrimp Toast

Food Processor Yield: Serves 12

(Food Processor makes this formerly complicated dish fast and easy. It has more flavor if made the day before.)

½ pound raw, shelled, cleaned shrimp
1 tablespoon minced, blanched pork fat or bacon
8 water chestnuts
1 egg white
1 tablespoon minced green onions, white part only
1 tablespoon California dry sherry
1½ tablespoons cornstarch
1 teaspoon minced fresh ginger root
¼ teaspoon sugar
1 teaspoon salt
1 tablespoon chopped cilantro (optional)
15 slices (2-day old) bread, crusts trimmed, each cut into 4 triangles
2 cups peanut oil

Blend shrimp with pork fat and water chestnuts in processor until a smooth paste forms. Beat egg white with green onions, sherry, cornstarch, ginger, sugar, salt and optional cilantro. Add to shrimp mixture and mix well. If time permits, cover and refrigerate overnight. Just before serving, spread shrimp paste generously on bread triangles. Heat oil in a wok or deep fryer to a temperature of 375 degrees (use candy thermometer). Fry bread triangles in hot oil, paste-side down, for 1 to 2 minutes. Turn and fry for a few seconds more. Remove with slotted spoon; drain on paper toweling. Serve immediately.

Note:
Shrimp toast may be fried ahead of time and refrigerated or frozen, then reheated—no thawing necessary. Set on a baking sheet lined with brown paper and place in a preheated 350 degree oven for 8 to 10 minutes or until crisp.

Chicken Liver Mousse

(This is very rich and wonderful!)

1 pound chicken livers
4 tablespoons butter or margarine
1½ teaspoons flour
½ medium onion, minced
1 clove garlic, crushed
2 tablespoons Madeira wine
½ teaspoon seasoned salt
Pepper to taste
1 (.25-ounce) envelope unflavored gelatin
½ cup chicken broth
1 cup (2-sticks) butter or margarine, softened
½ cup heavy cream, whipped

In a skillet over medium heat, brown chicken livers in 2 tablespoons of the butter. Sprinkle with 1½ tablespoons flour when brown. In a separate skillet sauté onion and garlic in 2 tablespoons of butter until softened. Add to chicken livers. Add Madeira wine, seasoned salt and pepper to taste to chicken livers. Put mixture in a blender and purée. In small bowl, dissolve gelatin in chicken broth. Pour chicken liver mixture from blender into mixing bowl. Add gelatin and mix, then let cool. When cool, beat in ¼ pound softened butter and then fold in cream. Chill for several hours. Serve on sweet French bread rounds.

Chutney Chicken Pâté

Food Processor Yield: Serves 15

2 cups cubed, cooked chicken
¼ cup minced onion
1 large sweet pickle, minced
½ cup minced parsley
1 teaspoon dried oregano, crumbled
1 teaspoon dried thyme, crumbled
3 tablespoons chopped toasted almonds
½ teaspoon salt
Pinch of pepper
½ cup mango chutney
¾ cup mayonnaise
Crusty French or sour dough bread

In food processor, using metal blade, mince chicken by pulsing several times. Transfer to bowl and stir in onion, pickle, parlsey, oregano, thyme, almonds, salt, pepper, chutney and mayonnaise. Pack into a crock or small casserole, smooth top and chill, covered, overnight. Serve with thinly sliced French or sour dough bread.

Country Pâté

(Make a day ahead.) Yield: Serves 10 to 12

½ pound bacon
2 tablespoons butter
1 bunch green onions, chopped
1 pound ground pork
1 pound ground veal
2 eggs, well beaten
½ pound chicken livers, chopped
½ cup Calvados or apple brandy
¾ cup fresh bread crumbs
⅓ cup milk
1½ teaspoons salt
½ teaspoon nutmeg
½ teaspoon pepper

Preheat oven to 350 degrees. Line bottom and sides of 9x5x3-inch loaf pan with bacon strips. Reserve 3 strips to top. In small skillet, melt butter; add onions and sauté. Transfer to large bowl. Add pork, veal, eggs, chicken livers, Calvados, bread crumbs, milk, salt, nutmeg and pepper and mix well. Pack mixture firmly into the lined loaf pan and place reserved bacon strips on top. Cover tightly with foil and bake 1 hour. Remove foil and bake 45 minutes more, or until meat thermometer inserted in center reads 170 degrees. Remove pâté from oven and drain off all fat. When cool, remove from pan and wrap tightly in foil and refrigerate overnight.

Curried Sherry Pâté

Yield: Serves 10

2 (3-ounce) packages cream cheese, softened
1 cup grated Cheddar cheese
½ teaspoon curry powder
½ teaspoon garlic powder
¼ teaspoon salt
4 teaspoons California dry sherry
1 cup mango chutney
½ cup green onions, chopped

In a medium bowl, mix cream cheese, Cheddar cheese, curry powder, garlic powder, salt and sherry. Remove from bowl and shape into a flat-topped round and place on serving plate. Cover round with chutney and top with green onions. Chill. Garnish with fresh parsley if desired and serve with crackers.

Russian Punch

(Non-alcoholic)

Yield: about 50 servings

24 cups (6-quarts) water
Juice of 6 oranges
Juice of 3 lemons
1 gallon apple cider
2 cups sugar
2 teaspoons whole cloves
2-inch stick cinnamon
5 tablespoons tea leaves

In a large pot, combine water, orange and lemon juices, apple cider, sugar, cloves and cinnamon, and bring to a boil. Remove from heat and add tea. Allow mixture to steep for 5 minutes, and then strain through cheesecloth into a punch bowl. Serve hot.

Amaretto Tea Punch

(A light and refreshing drink for a summer luncheon or brunch)

Yield: 2 quarts

1 tablespoon sugar
1 quart "sun" tea or weak brewed tea
¼ cup fresh lemon juice
1 cup Amaretto di Saronno
¼ cup fresh lime juice
1 (6-ounce) can frozen orange juice, thawed
1 (12-ounce) bottle club soda, chilled
Ice cubes
Mint sprigs

In a large pitcher combine sugar, sun tea, lemon juice, Amaretto, lime juice and orange juice. Mix together and place in refrigerator until thoroughly chilled. When ready to serve, add the ice and soda. Pour into glasses and garnish with the mint sprigs.

Always use ripe fruit in milkshakes and other blender drinks which include milk. Under-ripe fruit will cause the milk to curdle.

Christmas Punch

(Very good—but very potent!)

Yield: 48 cups

1 quart California brandy
1 quart California dry sherry
1 cup lemon juice
⅔ cup powdered sugar
½ cup Curacao
4 quarts California pink champagne
2 quarts club soda
½ cup grenadine
Ice cubes or ice ring

In a large punch bowl, combine brandy, sherry, lemon juice, powdered sugar, Curacao, champagne, club soda and grenadine.

Sangria Cooler

Yield: 8 cups

1 small orange
1 small lemon
¼ pint strawberries
1 (750 milliliter) bottle
  California dry red wine
  (about 3¼ cups)
3 cups orange juice
¼ cup California brandy
¼ cup sugar
1 (16-ounce) bottle club soda
1 tray ice cubes

Early In Day:
Thinly slice orange and quarter. Thinly slice lemon and halve. Hull strawberries; cut each in half. Set aside. In a large pitcher, combine wine, orange juice, brandy and sugar. Stir until sugar is dissolved. Stir in fruit mixture. Cover and refrigerate.

Just before serving, stir club soda into sangria. Pour sangria into glasses over ice cubes, making sure to place some fruit in each glass.

Hot Spiced Wine

Yield: Serves 15 to 20

4 cups (1-quart) water
3 cups sugar
12 whole cloves
2 sticks cinnamon
6 whole allspice
½ teaspoon powdered ginger
Peel of 1 orange
Peel of 1 lemon
2 cups fresh orange juice
¾ cup fresh lemon juice
1 fifth bottle California
  Burgundy or Claret wine

In a medium saucepan, combine water, sugar, cloves, cinnamon, allspice, ginger, orange peel and lemon peel. Slowly bring to a boil, stirring constantly until sugar is dissolved. Simmer 10 minutes, and remove from heat; allow to stand for 1 hour. Strain. Return to heat once more; add orange juice, lemon juice, and wine. Heat gently do not boil. Serve hot.

Spiced Percolator Punch

Yield: 17 cups

2 (32-ounce) bottles cranberry juice cocktail
1 (46-ounce) can unsweetened pineapple juice
1 cup brown sugar, packed
4 teaspoons whole cloves
12-inch stick cinnamon, broken
¼ orange peel, cut into strips
3¼ cups (1 fifth) light rum
Lemons, sliced and quartered for garnish

In a 24-cup percolator combine cranberry juice, pineapple juice and brown sugar. Place the cloves, stick cinnamon and orange peel in the coffee maker basket. Assemble coffee maker; plug in and percolate. Just before serving, remove basket and discard its contents. Stir in rum and keep hot. Float a quartered lemon slice in each cup for garnish.

Yellowbird

Yield: Serves 6 to 8

2 cups (16-ounces) fresh orange juice
2 cups (16-ounces) pineapple juice
1¼ cups (12-ounces) light rum
1 cup (8-ounces) Galliano
¼ cup (2-ounces) Crème de Banane
Ice
Garnish—pineapple cubes, orange slices, cherries

Combine orange and pineapple juices, light rum, Galliano and Crème de Banane. Mix well. Fill tall glasses with ice and pour liquid over ice. Place pineapple cubes, orange slices and cherries on toothpicks or skewers and place into glasses.

Merced River
Yosemite

The beautiful Merced River (River of Mercy), flows through Yosemite Valley and out through deep gorges and steep canyons into the San Joaquin Valley. This magnificent river runs with icy-cold mountain water, and when one stands on its banks, the whole body becomes one with this treasure of nature. The subtle trembling of the ground as the river passes, the sheer majesty of the view and the cool breeze against the face leave the momentary visitor struck with the wonder of it all.

In 1848, a little flattened piece of gold about the size of a gold dollar was found near Sutter's Mill and sent to the Smithsonian. The "gold rush" was on! Beginning in early 1849, would-be millionaires flocked to the area from nearly every country in the world, each working claims along the rivers.

Although the era has been romanticized in song and fable, the life of the "49er" was far from romantic. Just to reach the "Mother Lode", and have the privilege of living in tents with no food, working side by side with strangers, ever watchful for bandits and claim-jumpers; a miner had to cross the Rocky Mountains. In 1849, Joe Miller, prominent pioneer business man, told of his adventures at the age of nineteen, while traveling to California. "In crossing the Colorado River, we met a large party of Indians who had a raft which they used as a boat to get people across the river. The provisions were all put on the raft and I was put in charge of them and as many Indians as the raft would carry across and they were expected to return for the others..." The rest of his party was left on the shore to swim the animals across the river, but the Indians swam the animals downstream. (The story continues) "...The Indians that were with me picked up all of the provisions and clothing and ran away with them. We were practically destitute and had a hard tramp to the nearest settlement. I was bound to get to the mines and finally got to Agua Fria, half-starved and half-naked."

By 1859 the old California miners began to leave for other fields. Some left for the gold fields of British Columbia, and others for the farm fields of the Valley. Like the early Spanish, the miners came in search of riches and left the heritage of pioneer strength and spirit.

Compliments of **San Francisco Floral Company**

Wedding Punch

(A festive punch for weddings or other celebrations)

Yield: Serves 70

- 1 gallon California dry white wine
- 1 quart gin
- 1 pint dark rum
- 1 (8-ounce) can peach nectar
- 2 (12-ounce) cans frozen orange juice concentrate, thawed and undiluted
- 2 (12-ounce) cans frozen unsweetened grapefruit juice concentrate, thawed and undiluted
- 1 (20-ounce) can unsweetened pineapple juice
- 1 quart ginger ale, chilled

In a large punch bowl, combine wine, gin, rum, peach nectar, orange juice concentrate, grapefruit juice concentrate and pineapple juice, and chill. At serving time, add a molded ice ring and the chilled ginger ale.

Ice Ring

(Can be made up to 1 month ahead of time)

Yield: 1 ring

Basic Ice Ring:

Use a metal round salad mold with a hole in the middle, or you may use a plastic salad mold. Put a small amount of water or fruit juice in the bottom of the bowl (just enough liquid to cover bottom of pan). Let freeze. Add decoration to make it pretty, and add flavor to the punch. Add fillings and liquid at different intervals or layers. This will take most of the day, as the addition of the liquid must be in small amounts. The more frozen ice you have, the more liquid can be added.

Orange Ring:

2 medium-sized oranges, thinly sliced
1 large lemon, thinly sliced
2 cups fresh orange juice

Alternate sliced oranges and lemons, with juice and ice in ring.

Summer Bounty Ring:

4 small bunches California white seedless grapes, washed with stems attached
4 small bunches California red seedless grapes, washed with stems attached
Bunch mint sprigs (amount depends on your creativity)

Alternate grapes according to color, with mint leaves placed so that ring has appearance of grape bunches surrounded by "leaves".

Wedding Ring:

Bunch of leather-leaf fern, washed well and cleaned
Bunch of maiden-hair fern, washed well and cleaned
Daisy blossoms, washed well and cleaned (the amount depends on you)
Violet blossoms or small rose buds, washed well and cleaned

Arrange blossoms and ferns to resemble small bouquets. When ring is unmolded, it will be a beautiful addition to a punch bowl.

Soups

Red Bell Pepper Soup

(A lovely colorful soup to serve in the fall)

Yield: Serves 8

6 red bell peppers, diced
4 cups chicken stock, preferably homemade
1 small potato, peeled and diced
1 small onion, diced
½ cup (1-stick) butter
1 to 2 cups evaporated milk or half and half
Salt and pepper to taste

In large saucepan, boil bell peppers, chicken stock, potato, onion and butter together until tender. Add vegetables to a blender or food processor and puree. Strain mixture and place into a large saucepan. Add milk, stirring frequently until soup reaches serving temperature. Season with salt and pepper to taste and serve.

ERNA'S ELDERBERRY HOUSE

Green Pepper Soup with Fresh Figs

Yield: Serves 4 to 6

4 ripe figs
1 tablespoon butter
1 medium onion, finely chopped
2 tablespoons finely chopped green pepper
2 cups + 2 tablespoons chicken or veal broth, preferably homemade
Juice of ½ lemon
3 tablespoons California dry sherry
Salt and pepper
1 egg yolk
¼ cup whipping cream or heavy cream
1 teaspoon green peppercorns
Freshly chopped tarragon

Peel the figs and reserve one. Coarsely chop the rest of the figs and set aside. In a saucepan, melt butter and add onion and green pepper. Sauté until the onion is translucent, then add the chopped figs and cook for 1 additional minute. Remove from heat and add enough of the broth to make puréeing possible in a blender or food processor. Return purée to the pan and add the remaining broth, lemon juice, sherry, salt and pepper. Bring mixture just to the boil; remove from heat. Meanwhile, beat egg yolk with cream; add some of the hot soup mixture to the egg mixture to warm it before it is whisked into the soup. Slice the reserved fig. Garnish each serving with sliced fig, green peppercorns and fresh tarragon.

Chilled Avocado-Clam Soup

Yield: Serves 4 to 6

1¼ cups peeled and diced ripe avocado
½ cup half and half or light cream
1½ cups chicken broth
1 (7½-ounce) can minced clams, undrained
½ teaspoon salt
3 dashes Tabasco sauce
Chives and paprika for garnish

Puree avocados, using a sieve, blender or food processor. Transfer the pureed avocados to a large bowl and slowly beat in the cream and chicken broth. Beat until smooth. Stir in the clams, salt and hot pepper sauce. Chill soup thoroughly. Serve with a sprinkling of chives and a dash of paprika.

Store washed greens in airtight containers in refrigerator.

Cold Zucchini Soup

Food Processor Yield: Serves 12

4 medium zucchini, sliced and quartered
2 (14½-ounce) cans chicken broth
1 bunch green onions, chopped
1 teaspoon salt
1 teaspoon white pepper
1 teaspoon dill seed
2 (8-ounce) packages cream cheese with chives
1 cup dairy sour cream
Chopped chives or lemon slices for garnish

Place zucchini, chicken broth, onions, salt, pepper and dill seed into a saucepan and cook until vegetables are tender (about 20 to 30 minutes). Blend the cream cheese, sour cream and zucchini mixture in a blender or food processor. Chill soup overnight (this mixture must be very cold). Serve in small bowls and sprinkle with chopped fresh chives or top with thin slices of lime or lemon.

Icy Gazpacho

Yield: Serves 8

1 cup finely chopped, peeled tomatoes (fresh or canned)
½ cup finely chopped green pepper
½ cup finely chopped celery
½ cup finely chopped cucumber
¼ cup finely chopped green onions
1 tablespoon finely snipped parsley
1 small clove garlic, finely minced
2 to 3 tablespoons tarragon vinegar
2 tablespoons olive or vegetable oil
½ teaspoon salt
¼ teaspoon lemon pepper
1 teaspoon Worcestershire sauce
2 cups tomato juice
Dash of Tabasco sauce

Combine tomatoes, green pepper, celery, cucumber, onion, parsley, garlic, vinegar, oil, salt, lemon pepper, Worcestershire sauce, tomato juice and Tabasco in a stainless steel or glass bowl. Chill until soup is icy cold. Taste and adjust seasonings. Serve the soup in small glasses or punch cups with an ice cube in each, if desired. Cooked baby shrimp may be added to gazpacho for a more hearty presentation.

Tear greens into bite-sized pieces. Do not cut with a knife.

Vichyssoise

Food Processor

Yield: Serves 12

4 leeks, sliced thinly
1 medium onion, chopped
¼ cup butter or margarine
5 medium potatoes, peeled and sliced
3 (14½-ounce) cans chicken broth
3 cups milk
2 cups heavy or whipping cream
Salt and pepper to taste
Chives for garnish

In a large stockpot, sauté leeks and onion in butter. Add the potatoes and chicken broth; simmer until potatoes test soft. Puree mixture in blender or food processor and return to stockpot. Add milk and 1 cup of the cream. Bring soup to a boil and then puree mixture again. Chill thoroughly. Before serving, stir in the second cup of cream. Serve in chilled bowls; sprinkle with chopped, fresh chives.

Cream of Almond Soup

Yield: Serves 6

½ cup butter or margarine
4 tablespoons all-purpose flour
2 tablespoons instant chicken bouillon
1 quart boiling water
1 cup finely ground, blanched almonds
⅛ teaspoon freshly ground pepper
1 cup heavy or whipping cream
Salted whipped cream (optional)
Ground toasted, blanched almonds (optional)

In a large saucepan over low heat, melt butter or margarine; add flour. Cook, stirring for 2 to 3 minutes. Dissolve bouillon in boiling water; gradually add to the flour mixture. Stir mixture constantly until smooth. Add the ground almonds and pepper. Cook for 10 minutes. Slowly add cream and continue to cook until heated through. Do not boil! Pour soup into blender or food processor and process until smooth. If desired, individual servings may be garnished with salted whipped cream and toasted ground almonds.

Cream of Broccoli Soup

Food Processor

Yield: Serves 4

1 bunch broccoli (1¼ to 1½-pounds), washed, trimmed and cut up
1 small onion, finely chopped
3 cups chicken broth, preferably homemade
2 tablespoons butter or margarine
1 teaspoon salt
½ teaspoon curry powder
⅛ teaspoon fresh ground pepper
⅛ teaspoon dry mustard
4 tablespoons all-purpose flour
1 cup half and half
Minced chives or thin lemon slices for garnish

Combine broccoli, onion and broth in a large stockpot. Bring to a boil and then simmer for 10 to 15 minutes. Place mixture into blender or food processor and purée. Return puréed mixture to stockpot. Add butter or margarine, salt, curry powder, pepper and mustard; stir and simmer on a low heat. Meanwhile, mix flour and half and half together into a smooth paste; add to soup mixture. Cook until hot and thickened, but do not boil. Top each serving with chives or thin slices of lemon.

Cream of Mushroom Soup

Yield: Serves 4

4 tablespoons butter or margarine
½ pound fresh mushrooms, sliced
1 medium onion, chopped
1 cup lightly packed minced parsley
1 tablespoon all-purpose flour
1 can (about 14-ounces) regular-strength beef broth
1 cup dairy sour cream
¼ cup California dry sherry

In a wide frying pan over medium heat, melt butter. Add mushrooms, onion and parsley. Cook, stirring often, until mushrooms are soft and liquid has evaporated. Stir in flour; then remove from heat and blend in broth. Bring to a boil, stirring constantly. Purée mixture with sour cream and return to pan. Add sherry and heat through.

Highly perishable vegetables should be washed, drained thoroughly, and placed in the refrigerator in plastic bags or in the vegetable compartment.

Cream of Peanut Soup

Food Processor Yield: Serves 10 to 12
(This soup is also good served icy cold.)

1 medium onion, chopped
2 stalks celery, chopped
¼ cup butter or margarine
3 tablespoons all-purpose flour
2 quarts chicken stock, preferably homemade
2 cups creamy style peanut butter
1¾ cups light cream or half and half
Chopped parsley for garnish

In a large stockpot, sauté the onion and celery in the butter until soft, but not brown. Stir in the flour until well blended. Add chicken stock, stirring constantly, and bring to a boil. Remove from heat and purée soup mixture in a blender or food processor. Return to stockpot and add peanut butter and cream, stirring to blend thoroughly. Heat slowly over low heat until just hot, but do not boil. Serve garnished with parsley.

Creamy Zucchini Soup

Food Processor Yield: Serves 6 to 8
(This soup may be served hot or cold.)

5 medium zucchini, thinly sliced
1 medium onion, chopped
¼ cup butter or margarine
2 (14½-ounce) cans chicken broth
¼ teaspoon nutmeg
¼ cup heavy or whipping cream
Salt and pepper to taste
Grated Parmesan cheese or dairy sour cream

In a large saucepan, sauté onion and zucchini in butter. Add broth and simmer for 15 minutes. Purée small portions of the soup mixture, at a time, in a blender or food processor. Add cream and blend until mixed. If soup is to be served hot, heat slowly to serving temperature and sprinkle Parmesan cheese on individual portions. If to be served cold, chill thoroughly and top each serving with a dollop of sour cream.

Less-perishable vegetables may be stored unwashed in a cool, dry place.

Springtime Cream of Asparagus Soup

Yield: Serves 4 to 6

3 tablespoons butter or margarine
2 tablespoons finely chopped onion
2 tablespoons finely chopped bell pepper
1 large clove garlic, minced
½ teaspoon celery salt
½ teaspoon Beau Monde seasoning
Pinch dried basil
½ teaspoon chopped parsley
Salt and pepper to taste
3 tablespoons all-purpose flour
1½ cups half and half or light cream
3¼ cups milk
2 (15-ounce) cans asparagus, drained; or 2 pounds fresh asparagus cooked
4 chicken bouillon cubes
⅓ cup cubed Velveeta cheese

In a large stockpot sauté onions, green pepper and garlic in melted butter. Add the celery salt, Beau Monde, basil, parsley, salt and pepper. Blend in the flour; slowly add the half and half and 3 cups of the milk. Purée the asparagus in a blender or food processor with the remaining ¼ cup milk and add it along with the cheese, the bouillon cubes, and asparagus mixture to the stockpot mixture. Simmer together for about 15 minutes, stirring occasionally.

Swiss Cream of Potato Soup

Yield: Serves 4 to 6

4 medium potatoes, peeled and diced
2 slices bacon, diced
¼ cup finely minced onion
2 tablespoons butter or margarine
1 tablespoon chopped parsley
2 teaspoons salt
½ teaspoon nutmeg
Pinch cayenne pepper
¼ teaspoon dry mustard
1 teaspoon Worcestershire sauce
3 cups milk
½ cup grated Swiss or Cheddar cheese

Cook potatoes until tender in just enough water to cover, drain. Meanwhile in a large pan, sauté the bacon and onions over low heat, stirring, until soft and slightly golden. Mash ½ of the potatoes, or all of them, depending on the soup texture you wish. Add the potatoes, butter, parsley, salt, nutmeg, cayenne pepper, mustard and Worcestershire to the bacon-onion pan. Mix well. Stir in the milk and heat over low heat. DO NOT ALLOW TO BOIL. Stir. Sprinkle with cheese just before serving.

Carrot Soup

Food Processor
(The secret to this soup is to cook it very slowly.)

Yield: Serves 8 to 10

4 tablespoons butter or margarine
2 medium onions, chopped
2 pounds carrots, peeled and chopped
4 cups chicken broth
1 cup fresh orange juice
Grated peel of one orange
Salt and white pepper to taste

Melt butter in a large 3-quart pot. Add onions and cook on low heat for 30 minutes. Add carrots and broth to the onions. Cook for 45 minutes on medium heat. Purée this mixture in a blender or food processor. Return the purée to the pot and add orange juice, grated orange peel, salt and pepper to taste. Simmer for 10 additional minutes.

Cauliflower Soup

Yield: Serves 4 to 6

1 medium head cauliflower, washed and broken into florets
1 medium yellow onion, finely diced
3 medium potatoes, peeled and diced
4 tablespoons (1/4 cup) butter
12 cups chicken stock, preferably homemade
1/4 cup California dry sherry
1 cup heavy or whipping cream
Pinch of garlic
Salt and white pepper to taste

Sauté cauliflower, potatoes and onions in butter for 20 minutes. Add chicken stock and simmer for 20 minutes, or until potatoes and cauliflower test tender. Remove from heat; purée mixture in small batches, in a blender or food processor. Return puréed mixture to pan; add sherry, cream, garlic, salt and pepper and heat to serving temperature. Taste and adjust seasonings if necessary.

Crab Spinach Soup

Yield: Serves 4 to 6

3 tablespoons butter or margarine
½ cup chopped onions or ¼ cup chopped shallots
1 bunch fresh spinach, stemmed, washed, dried and chopped
¼ pound fresh mushrooms, sliced
2 tablespoons all-purpose flour
2 cups chicken broth
2 cups half and half or light cream
Salt and freshly ground pepper to taste
⅛ teaspoon freshly ground nutmeg
½ pound fresh crabmeat (canned crabmeat may be substituted if necessary)
¼ pound Parmesan cheese, grated
¼ cup Bourbon (optional)

Melt butter or margarine in a heavy saucepan; add onions or shallots. Cover and sauté over low heat until tender and translucent, about 20 minutes. Increase heat and add spinach and mushrooms, stirring constantly, until spinach wilts. Sprinkle flour over vegetables and cook 2 minutes, stirring constantly. Gradually add chicken broth and heat to boiling, still stirring. Add cream, salt, pepper, nutmeg, crab and cheese. If desired, add Bourbon for zippier taste. Simmer about 10 minutes or until crab is heated through. Be careful not to let mixture boil or crab will toughen.

Dill Weed and Tomato Soup

Yield: Serves 6

10 large ripe tomatoes
1 large onion, sliced
2 cloves garlic, minced
3 tablespoons butter or margarine
5 tablespoons all-purpose flour
5 cups chicken broth
1½ teaspoons tomato paste
¾ cup heavy cream
4 tablespoons minced fresh dill or 2 tablespoons dried dill weed
Dairy sour cream
Salt and pepper to taste

Wash and core the tomatoes. Reserve 2 tomatoes and chop the remainder. In a large stockpot, sauté the onion and garlic in melted butter or margarine. Stir in ½ of the chopped tomatoes and cook over high heat for 3 minutes, stirring constantly. Remove from heat. Blend the flour with some of the broth into a paste. Add this, the remaining broth and tomato paste to the stockpot and bring to a boil. Lower heat and add the rest of the tomatoes; simmer for 15 minutes. Strain soup and discard what remains in the colander. Return to pan and stir in the heavy cream. Peel, seed and chop the reserved tomatoes. Add the tomatoes and the dill to the soup. Heat to serving temperature. Season to taste with salt and pepper. Serve hot topped with dollops of dairy sour cream.

Greek Lemon Soup
An old Fresno recipe from our Greek pioneers

(This light soup is wonderful to serve on a hot day.)

Yield: Serves 8

8 cups chicken broth, preferably homemade
2 cups cooked rice
½ cup butter or margarine (1 cube) melted
1 teaspoon chicken stock base or seasoning
½ cup California Sauterne wine
3 egg yolks, well beaten
Juice of 2 lemons
2 lemons, thinly sliced, for garnish

In a large pan, place chicken broth, rice, butter, chicken stock base and wine. Simmer for 30 minutes. In a small mixing bowl beat egg yolks and stir in juice of 2 lemons. When ready to serve, slowly mix 1 cup of the hot soup into the lemon-egg mixture. Then add this mixture to the rest of the soup and mix well. Serve immediately, garnished with thin slices of lemon and a sprinkle of chopped parsley. This soup can be made into a meal by adding pieces of cooked chicken, more rice, etc. . . .

Lemony Mushroom Soup

Food Processor

Yield: Serves 4 to 6

(A very special rendition, richly flavored with duxelles and lemon.)

1 pound fresh mushrooms, chopped
Juice of ½ lemon
1 tablespoon butter or margarine
2 tablespoons minced shallot
½ dried bay leaf
¼ teaspoon dried thyme
2 cups whipping or heavy cream
1½ cups chicken stock
1 teaspoon salt
½ teaspoon freshly ground pepper
1 teaspoon cornstarch dissolved in 1 tablespoon water
1 tablespoon chopped fresh parsley (garnish)

Chop mushrooms with lemon juice in processor. Melt butter in large skillet over medium heat. Add shallot and sauté lightly. Add mushrooms, bay leaf and thyme and cook, stirring frequently, until liquid is completely evaporated, about 10 minutes.

Blend in cream, chicken stock, salt and pepper and bring to boil. Reduce heat and simmer 20 minutes. Add dissolved cornstarch and simmer 10 minutes longer. Adjust seasoning. Ladle into heated bowls and sprinkle with parsley.

French Onion Soup

(This must cook very slowly to achieve a wonderful blend of flavors . . . great for a dinner party)

Yield: Serves 6 to 8

4 large yellow onions, peeled and thinly sliced to make about 5½ cups
4 tablespoons butter or margarine (½ stick)
½ teaspoon paprika
1 bay leaf
½ teaspoon salt
½ teaspoon pepper
¼ cup all-purpose flour
½ cup dry white wine
3 (14½-ounce) cans beef broth
Slices of French bread, buttered and toasted lightly
½ cup shredded mozzarella or Swiss cheese

In a large covered pot, cook onions in butter over very low heat for 1½ hours until golden. Stir frequently. Add paprika, bay leaf, salt and pepper. Add flour a little at a time, stirring while you add; cook for 3 minutes. Add wine and stir until well blended; cook for 5 minutes. Add broth and stir until mixed and simmer for 1 hour more. Ladle into broiler-proof soup bowls; add slice of toasted bread on the top of each bowl and place 1 tablespoon or more of cheese on top of each slice. Broil until cheese melts.

Homemade Chicken Soup

Yield: Serves 6

2 stalks celery, cleaned and cut into 3-inch pieces
1 large carrot, peeled and cut into 3-inch pieces
1 large leek, cleaned and cut into 3-inch pieces
6 sprigs fresh parsley
1 bay leaf
2 whole cloves
1 large onion, peeled
9 cups water
1 (5 to 6-pound) baking hen, washed
1 tablespoon salt
8 whole peppercorns

Place celery, carrot, leek, parsley and bay leaf into a cheese cloth bag. Stick cloves into the whole onion. Place cheese cloth bag and onion in a large stockpot. Add water, hen, salt and peppercorns. Simmer for 2½ hours on low to medium heat. Remove chicken; cool and separate bones and meat. Strain broth through a colander and discard vegetables. Cool and skim off fat and discard.

Homemade chicken stock (from recipe above)
2 (10-ounce) cans of chicken broth
1 cup chopped carrots
½ cup diced celery
½ cup diced onion
⅓ cup uncooked rice or ½ cup uncooked noodles
1 (10-ounce) package frozen peas
½ teaspoon salt
¼ teaspoon pepper
¼ cup fresh chopped parsley for garnish

In a large stockpot, add the cans of chicken broth to the broth made when the chicken was cooked. Add the carrots, celery and onions to the broth. Simmer 10 minutes. Add the cut-up chicken pieces, rice or noodles, peas, salt and pepper. Cook 15 to 20 minutes or until rice or noodles are cooked. Adjust seasonings. Sprinkle fresh parsley on the top of each serving.

Lentil Soup

Food Processor
(A nutritious low-fat meal.)

Yield: Serves 6

2 carrots, peeled and finely minced
1 small onion, finely minced
1 small clove garlic, minced
1 stalk celery, chopped
1 cup dried lentils, rinsed in cold water
5 cups water
1 to 2 small ham hocks
⅛ teaspoon dried thyme
⅛ teaspoon dried oregano
Salt and pepper to taste
½ cup chopped tomatoes (canned or fresh)
1 (8-ounce) package small macaroni shells, cooked al dente
Grated Parmesan cheese (optional)

In a blender or food processor, finely mince carrots, onion, garlic and celery. Add to large stockpot, along with the rinsed lentils, water, ham hocks, thyme, oregano, salt and pepper. Bring to a boil; reduce heat and simmer for 2 hours or until lentils are tender, stirring frequently. Remove ham hocks from soup mixture; cool and separate meat from bone. Finely mince ham by hand or machine and return to stockpot along with tomatoes and cook over low heat for 30 to 45 minutes. Cool and remove from heat and add macaroni shells; mix and store in refrigerator overnight to allow flavors to blend. Before serving, return to stove and cook until soup is warm and macaroni shells are soft; approximately 15 to 20 minutes on medium heat.

Mexican Black Bean Soup

Yield: Serves 6

2 cups dried black beans
1 ham hock
8 cups water
4 cups beef broth, preferably homemade
Salt and pepper to taste
2 tablespoons olive oil
½ onion, chopped
1 clove garlic, minced
1 small tomato, diced
½ cup diced cooked ham
1 tablespoon white wine vinegar
Dash of Tabasco sauce

Wash beans and place in large soup pan; cover with water and soak for 2 hours. Drain. To the beans, add ham hock, water, broth, salt and pepper; bring to a boil. Lower heat and simmer for 1½ hours. Remove ham hock from soup, allow to cool and remove meat from bone. Reserve. Place mixture back in soup pan and set aside. In a small skillet, heat the oil; add the onion, garlic and tomato and sauté for 4 minutes. Add the diced ham, vinegar and Tabasco sauce to onion mixture and stir. Add mixture to the soup and bring to a boil. Serve while hot.

Split Pea Soup

(A cold weather friend; great with corn bread or muffins.)

Yield: Serves 4 to 6

2 to 3 carrots, peeled
1 stalk celery
1 small onion
5 cups water
1½ cups dried split peas, rinsed in cold water
1 to 2 ham hocks
Salt and pepper to taste

In a blender or food processor, finely mince carrots, celery and onion. Add to stock pot, along with water, split peas and ham hocks. Cook over low to medium heat for 1½ to 2 hours or until peas are tender, stirring frequently. Remove ham hocks from soup mixture; cool and separate meat from bone. Finely mince ham by hand or machine and return to stock pot. Simmer soup for an additional 30 minutes. Season with salt and pepper according to taste.

Pacific Seafood Gumbo

(The seafood in this recipe is subject to your individual preferences, the availability of the seafood and your pocketbook.)

Yield: Serves 10 to 12

6 to 8 strips bacon
10 tablespoons all-purpose flour
2 onions, chopped
1 large green pepper, chopped
2 cups chopped celery
2 cloves garlic, minced
2 (16-ounce) cans stewed tomatoes
1 (8-ounce) can tomato sauce
1 (4-ounce) can sliced mushrooms, undrained
1 to 2 pounds frozen okra, sliced
1 quart or more of chicken or turkey stock, preferably homemade
Raw or canned shrimp, quantity as desired
Crab meat, quantity as desired
Oysters, undrained, quantity as desired
Tabasco sauce to taste
Salt and pepper to taste
1 bay leaf
½ cup chopped parsley
Water as needed
½ cup California dry sherry
Cornstarch, if desired for thickening

In a heavy, large skillet, fry the bacon until browned. Remove the bacon and all but 6 to 8 tablespoons of the drippings. Crumble bacon and reserve. Add flour to the bacon drippings to make a roux or paste; brown roux but be careful not to burn. Add onions, green pepper, celery and garlic. Sauté for a few minutes, stirring constantly. Transfer mixture to a large stockpot. Add tomatoes, tomato sauce, mushrooms and okra. Simmer for a few minutes or until the vegetables are partially cooked. Add the broth, crumbled bacon, shrimp, crab, oysters, salt, pepper, Tabasco sauce, bay leaf and parsley. Add water if needed to thin. Bring liquid to a slow boil. Stir in sherry, cover and simmer for several hours, stirring occasionally. Add additional seasonings, if needed, to taste. Thicken with cornstarch mixed with a small amount of water, if necessary. Remove from heat and allow gumbo to mellow for an hour or so. Reheat. Serve in soup bowls over steaming cooked rice.

Best Clam Chowder

Yield: Serves 4 to 6

4 slices bacon
3 green onions, sliced
5 medium potatoes, peeled and diced
1 stalk celery, finely chopped
1 carrot, shredded
1 clove garlic, minced
2 cups water
1 teaspoon salt
¼ teaspoon pepper
Pinch dried thyme
Pinch dried dill weed
1 teaspoon Worcestershire sauce
2 cups chopped clams with liquid
1 pint half and half
Enough all-purpose flour or cornstarch to make a paste (optional)

In a large stockpot, cook bacon until crisp. Add onions, potatoes, celery, carrot, garlic, water, salt, pepper, thyme, dill weed and Worcestershire. Cover and simmer about 15 minutes. Slightly mash the potatoes with a fork or potato masher. Add clams, clam juice and half and half. Thicken chowder if desired with a paste made of flour or cornstarch and water; stirring constantly while adding and heating to serving temperature.

Cabbage Patch Soup

(A thick, hearty soup—almost stew-like.)

Yield: Serves 4 to 5

1 pound lean ground beef
½ pound bacon, chopped
1 large onion, peeled and chopped
1 to 1½ cups chopped celery
1 (14½-ounce) can stewed tomatoes, undrained
1 (15½-ounce) can kidney beans, undrained
1 (10¾-ounce) can tomato soup
1 tablespoon chili powder
1 tablespoon garlic powder
4 to 6 cups water
Salt and pepper to taste
1 small head of cabbage, shredded

Sauté the beef, bacon, onion and celery in a large saucepan. Drain off excess fat. Add the tomatoes, beans, soup, chili powder, garlic powder, water, salt and pepper. Simmer over low heat for 3 to 5 hours, if time permits; stirring frequently. Just before serving add the cabbage and simmer for another ½ hour. If the soup is too thick add water according to your own taste.

Italian Sausage Soup

(A hearty meal-in-a-bowl soup.)

Yield: Serves 8 to 12

- 1½ pounds Italian sausage (¾-pound mild, ¾-pound spicy), cut into ¼-inch thick slices
- 2 cloves garlic, pressed
- 2 onions, chopped
- 2 pounds tomatoes, peeled, cored and quartered
- 1½ to 2 cups dry red wine
- 5 cups regular-strength beef stock or broth
- ½ teaspoon dried basil
- ½ teaspoon dried oregano
- 3 tablespoons chopped parsley
- 1 medium green pepper, chopped
- 2 medium zucchini, sliced
- 2 cups small elbow-type macaroni or other small pasta
- Salt and pepper to taste
- 2 carrots, peeled and sliced (optional)
- Grated Parmesan cheese

Cook sausage in a large frying pan. Remove from pan and pour off all but 3 tablespoons of the drippings. Sauté garlic and onions in the drippings until soft. Add tomatoes, sausage, wine, stock, basil and oregano. Simmer, uncovered for 30 minutes. At this point, soup mixture may be cooled and refrigerated for a day. Skim fat from top, then reheat. Add parsley, pepper, zucchini, macaroni, salt, pepper and optional carrots. Simmer for 25 minutes or until pasta and vegetables are tender. Serve with freshly grated Parmesan cheese.

Minestrone Soup

Yield: Serves 8 to 10

1½ to 2 pounds lean beef stew meat
1 cup coarsely chopped onion
1 teaspoon minced garlic
1 teaspoon salt
¼ teaspoon pepper
2 tablespoons olive oil
1 (1½-ounce) package Au Jus gravy mix
2 (14½-ounce) cans beef broth
4 cups water
1½ teaspoons Italian mixed herbs
1½ cups thinly sliced carrots
1 (1-pound, 12-ounce) can tomatoes, undrained
1 (15-ounce) can kidney beans, undrained
1¾ cups pitted ripe olives, plus 1 cup of the liquid
1 cup small shell macaroni
2 cups thinly sliced zucchini
Grated Parmesan cheese to taste

Cut the beef into 1-inch cubes. In a large Dutch oven, mix together the meat, onions, garlic, salt and pepper. Add the olive oil and stir to coat the meat evenly. Brown the meat uncovered in a preheated 400 degree oven for about 40 minutes, stirring once or twice. (May substitute range-top browning if you desire.) Remove browned meat from oven or range. Add gravy mix, beef broth, water, Italian herbs and carrots and bring to a boil on top of the range. Reduce heat to simmer; cover and cook for one hour or until meat is almost tender. Add the tomatoes, beans, olives, olive liquid and macaroni. Sprinkle zucchini on top. Cover and simmer for 40 minutes or until vegetables and macaroni are tender. Serve with grated Parmesan cheese. (Entire cooking may be done in a preheated 350 degree oven but the cooking time must be extended.)

Tortilla Soup

(Fantastic, different soup! Be sure to serve very hot so cheese melts.)

Yield: Serves 6 to 8

- 2 onions, chopped
- 3 cloves garlic, pressed
- 6 cups chicken broth or stock, preferably homemade
- 2 (4-ounce) cans diced green chiles
- 4 tomatoes, finely chopped or puréed
- ¼ teaspoon cayenne pepper
- ½ teaspoon cumin or comino
- ½ cup heavy cream, whipped
- ½ cup dairy sour cream
- 2 cups grated Jack cheese or Jack pepper cheese
- 6 corn tortillas, cut into wedges and fried until crisp

In a large, heavy stockpot, sauté onions and garlic until tender. Add broth, chiles, tomatoes, cayenne pepper and cumin. Simmer for 30 to 40 minutes or more—the longer the better. Meanwhile, whip cream and fold it into sour cream. Place a handful of the tortilla wedges in bottom of each soup bowl and top generously with cheese. Ladle hot soup over them. Add a large dollop of the cream mixture to the top of each bowl.

Wimpy's Hamburger Soup

(Add garlic bread and a green salad for a hearty but easy family supper.)

Yield: Serves 4 to 6

3 tablespoons butter or margarine
1½ pounds lean ground beef
1 (18-ounce) can tomatoes, drained
2 (10½-ounce) cans beef consommé
1 (10½-ounce) can onion soup
4 carrots, peeled and sliced ¼-inch thick
1 (8-ounce) can corn, drained
¼ cup chopped celery tops
¼ cup chopped parsley
1 bay leaf
½ teaspoon dried oregano, crumbled
Salt to taste
¼ teaspoon freshly ground pepper
½ cup macaroni, bow ties or shells
4 to 6 tablespoons grated Parmesan cheese

Melt butter in a large stockpot. Add beef, cook, stirring, over medium heat for 5 minutes or until browned. Drain off all fat. Add tomatoes, consommé, onion soup, carrots, corn, celery, parsley, bay leaf, oregano, salt and pepper. Stir to blend. Heat to boiling, then reduce heat and simmer for 30 minutes. Discard bay leaf. Meanwhile, cook the pasta in a separate saucepan according to directions. Drain. Place some macaroni in the bottom of each bowl. Ladle soup into the bowl and stir. Sprinkle with Parmesan cheese.

Breads

Blue Ribbon Bread

(A wonderful recipe with many breadmaking hints and suggested variations)

Yield: 3 loaves

- 3 packages active dry yeast
- 2¼ cups warm water (110 degrees)
- ½ cup honey or molasses
- ⅓ cup vegetable oil or melted butter
- 1 tablespoon salt
- 1 cup powdered instant non-fat dry milk
- 4 eggs
- About 10 cups flour (see directions)

When making a light dough for rolls or cinnamon bread, use honey and all unbleached white flour.

When making a mixed grain or whole wheat bread, use honey or molasses and whatever variety of flours that suit your fancy.

When using flours other than wheat, rye, etc., use no more than 3 cups of non-wheat flours out of a total 10 cups called for, because grains other than wheat do not have gluten in them. It is this gluten in wheat flour that gives bread dough its elasticity. This elasticity is what enables the dough to rise and keep its shape.

To make this recipe, dissolve the yeast in warm water in a large mixer bowl. Add honey or molasses, oil or butter, salt, powdered milk, eggs and 5 cups of the flour. If using some whole wheat flour and some unbleached white flour, all of the whole wheat flour goes in now. If using less than 5 cups of other than wheat flour, it all goes in now with enough of the wheat flour being used to make up the 5 cups. (Different flours absorb liquid at different rates and it is necessary to let that absorption happen before all the flour is added to the dough.) Beat this mixture at a medium speed for 4 or 5 minutes, until dough is very elastic and sticks to itself. This is the gluten developing stage, and the more non-white flour being used, the more important this beating is. Work in enough of the remaining flour to make a manageable dough. This may be done with a heavy duty mixer or by hand. Knead the dough on a lightly-floured board, adding more flour as necessary, until the dough is smooth and elastic (10 to 15 minutes). Place dough in a lightly oiled bowl, turning once to oil top.

Cover and let rise in a warm place until doubled. Punch down dough and let rest while preparing the baking pans. This amount of dough will make three 9x5x3-inch loaves or 3 to 4 dozen rolls or some combination of loaves and rolls.

Grease the baking pans. Divide and shape the dough and place in pans. Let rise until double, about 45 minutes. Bake in a preheated 375 degree oven for 40 minutes. Rolls bake at 400 degrees for about 20 to 25 minutes or until rolls test done.

Variations:

Jewish Challah:

Omit the instant non-fat milk and use the honey and all unbleached white flour. To form Challah, divide the dough into two equal portions. Set one aside while working with the other. Divide each portion into 3 pieces. Roll each piece into a long rope, about 15 to 18 inches long. Braid the ropes together, pinching the ends tightly together so it won't come apart. Place on a greased cookie sheet, cover and let rise until double. Just before baking, brush on an egg wash made by mixing 1 egg yolk and 1 tablespoon water. Bake as for a loaf of bread.

Mixed Grain Bread:

In place of 10 cups of flour use:

½ cup quick cooking oatmeal
½ cup yellow cornmeal
½ cup wheatgerm
1 cup rye flour
3 cups whole wheat flour
4 to 5 cups unbleached all-purpose flour

Re-read the instructions to know when to add the flours. Add the oatmeal, cornmeal, wheatgerm, rye flour and whole wheat flour to the first mix.

Herb Bread:

Using all whole wheat flour for the recipe, add the following herbs to the first mixture:

⅓ cup chopped fresh parsley
2 tablespoons dried basil leaves, crumbled
2 tablespoons chopped fresh chives
2 teaspoons dried oregano
1 teaspoon dried thyme

Raisin Bread:

Using all unbleached all-purpose flour in master recipe, add 1½ cups raisins to the dough before adding the second addition of flour.

Seed Bread:

In the master recipe, use 5 cups whole wheat flour and enough unbleached all-purpose flour to finish. Before adding the all-purpose flour add:

½ cup raw, unsalted, shelled sunflower seeds
¼ cup hulled millet seed
¼ cup flax seed

For a "lightly floured board," use about 1 tablespoon of flour from each cup of flour in the recipe.

Cheese and Beer Wheat Bread

Yield: 2 loaves

1½ cups (12-ounces) beer
⅔ cup water
½ cup vegetable oil
1½ cups whole wheat flour
4½ to 5 cups all-purpose flour
½ cup sugar
½ cup wheat germm

2 teaspoons salt
2 packages active dry yeast
1 egg, room temperature
2 cups (8-ounces) Cheddar cheese, cut into ½-inch cubes

In a saucepan, heat beer, water and cooking oil until very warm (120 to 130 degrees). In a large mixer bowl, combine warm liquids, whole wheat flour, 1 cup all-purpose flour, sugar, wheat germ, salt, yeast and egg; beat 2 minutes at medium speed. By hand, stir in remaining all-purpose flour. On well-floured surface, knead dough until smooth and elastic, about 5 minutes. Place in greased bowl, turning to grease top. Cover; let rise in warm place until light and doubled in size, 1 to 1 hour + 15 minutes. Line 2 (1-quart) casseroles or 2 (9x5x3-inch) loaf pans with foil; generously grease (no oil). Punch down dough. On well-floured surface work cheese cubes into dough, ½ at a time, until evenly distributed. Shape into 2 loaves. If any cheese cubes are on the surface of the loaf, remove them to avoid excess browning. Place loaves in greased casseroles or loaf pans. Cover, and let rise in a warm place until light and doubled in size, 45 to 60 minutes. Bake in a preheated 350 degree oven for 40 to 50 minutes or until loaf sounds hollow when lightly tapped. Immediately remove from pans.

Two-Way Cheese Loaf

(Very unusual and very good!)

Yield: 1 loaf

- 1½ cups all-purpose flour, sifted
- 2¼ teaspoons baking powder
- 1 teaspoon salt
- ¼ teaspoon baking soda
- ½ cup whole wheat flour
- ⅓ cup shortening
- ⅔ cup sugar
- 2 eggs
- ⅓ cup California rosé wine
- ⅓ cup milk
- ⅔ cup coarsely chopped walnuts
- ¾ cup shredded sharp Cheddar cheese
- ½ cup crumbled bleu cheese
- 2 teaspoons poppy seeds
- 2 teaspoons sesame seeds

In a large bowl, resift flour with baking powder, salt and baking soda. Stir in whole wheat flour, and set aside. In a large mixing bowl, cream shortening with sugar; beat in eggs, one at a time. Add wine, milk and flour mixture; stir just until blended. Add nuts. Divide dough in half. Add the Cheddar cheese to one portion and mix lightly. Blend the bleu cheese into the second portion. Spoon dough into a greased 8-inch tube pan, placing Cheddar dough on one side of pan, bleu cheese dough on the other. Sprinkle poppy seeds over Cheddar dough, sesame seeds over the other. Bake on the lowest rack setting in a preheated 350 degree oven for 1 hour or until bread is browned and tests done. Let stand 10 minutes, then turn out onto a wire rack to cool. Serve plain or with butter, or whipped cream cheese.

Winter To Spring
Yosemite

On June 25, 1864, President Lincoln signed a bill which set aside, under the protection of the State of California, a huge tract of Sierran land which included the Yosemite Valley and the Mariposa Big Trees. This tract of land, the first federally mandated park, is some thirty-six miles long and forty-eight miles wide. Yosemite Valley lies in the heart of this area, and has remained protected and virtually untouched since the first "white" man discovered it in 1833.

Yosemite is the Indian word for grizzly bear, and was the name of the tribe who lived on the Valley floor.

The first "white" man to see Yosemite was Mountain Man Joseph Reddeford Walker. In 1833, while on a fur-trapping expedition into the San Joaquin Valley, Walker led his men from Nevada, through the Sierras, toward the Valley. His men were frozen and starving when they finally reached the edge of Yosemite Valley. Its grandeur completely escaped the men. They needed food, not scenery.

During the 1840's, the Indians began to make raids on the "white invaders" in the mining camps and towns. In 1850, Major James D. Savage formed a volunteer Company, known as the Mariposa Battalion, to deal with the situation. In March, 1851, Major Savage and his Company entered the Indian stronghold and officially discovered Yosemite. The Indians were dispersed and the Valley was named "Yosemite" out of respect for the strength of the natives.

Men like Galen Clark, John Muir and Captain John Charles Fremont followed, and the rest, as they say, is history.

In 1871, while sitting on the porch of the Hutchings Hotel, Ralph Waldo Emerson is remembered to have stated, "This Valley, is the only place that comes up to the brag about it, and exceeds it."

Cranberry Wheat Germ Bread

Yield: 1 loaf

1 egg, slightly beaten
½ cup orange juice
¼ cup warm water (110 degrees)
2 tablespoons vegetable oil
2 cups all-purpose flour
1 cup sugar
2 teaspoons baking powder
½ teaspoon baking soda
1 teaspoon salt
3 tablespoons grated orange peel
½ cup chopped walnuts or pecans
1 cup raw cranberries, coarsely chopped
½ cup toasted wheat germ

In a large bowl, beat egg, orange juice, warm water and oil together. Sift flour, sugar, baking powder, soda and salt together and add to liquid ingredients, stirring just to combine. In a separate bowl, toss orange peel, nuts, cranberries and wheat germ together and fold gently into batter. Spoon into a greased and lightly floured 9x5x3-inch pan. Bake in a preheated 350 degree oven for 50 to 60 minutes or until loaf tests done. Remove from pan and cool completely before slicing.

Whole Wheat Granola Bread

Yield: 2 loaves

4½ cups warm water
3 packages active dry yeast
¾ cup honey
1 egg
1½ cups granola (See "Whole Wheat Granola" recipe, pg. 320)
1½ cups wheat germ
½ cup + 2 tablespoons vegetable oil
5 teaspoons salt
5½ cups whole wheat flour
5 cups white flour

In an 8-quart mixing bowl, dissolve the yeast in the warm water. Add the honey, egg, granola, wheat germ, vegetable oil, salt and whole wheat flour. Beat at medium speed for 4 to 5 minutes until dough is very elastic. Add white flour, gradually working in enough to make a manageable dough. Knead dough on a lightly floured board, adding more flour if necessary, until dough is smooth and elastic: 10 to 15 minutes. Place dough in an 8-quart greased bowl, turning dough over to grease both sides. Cover with plastic wrap and let rise in a warm place until doubled. Punch dough down; divide into 4 equal parts and shape into loaves. Place in greased 9x5x3-inch loaf pans. Cover and let rise in a warm place until almost double. Bake in a preheated 350 degree oven for approximately 45 minutes. Turn out of pan onto cooling racks. Let cool completely and store in plastic bags.

Dilly Casserole Bread

Yield: 1 round loaf

1 package active dry yeast
¼ cup warm water (105 to 115 degrees)
1 cup creamed cottage cheese
2 tablespoons sugar
1 tablespoon instant minced onion
1 tablespoon butter, melted
2 tablespoons dill seed
1 teaspoon salt
¼ teaspoon soda
1 egg
2¼ to 2½ cups all-purpose flour

In a large mixing bowl, sprinkle yeast over warm water; stir to dissolve and allow to proof. Heat cottage cheese in a saucepan until lukewarm (110 to 115 degrees). Add warmed cottage cheese, sugar, instant onion, butter, dill, salt, soda and egg to bowl and beat well. Add flour, a little at a time, beating well after each addition to make a stiff batter. Cover and let rise in a warm place until doubled, 50 to 60 minutes. Stir dough with 25 vigorous strokes. Turn into well-greased 1½-quart round (8-inch) casserole. Cover and let rise in a warm place until light, 30 to 40 minutes. Bake in a preheated 350 degree oven for 40 to 50 minutes. During the last 15 minutes of baking, cover with foil if necessary to prevent excessive browning.

For really spectacular biscuits, use butter in place of shortening and add two eggs to your recipe. NOTE: Decrease amount of milk when adding eggs.

Great Ideas For "Store-Bought" Bakery Breads

Hot Cheese Bread:

½ pound shredded sharp Cheddar cheese
½ pound softened butter
1 small clove fresh garlic, mashed
Paprika or dried parsley
1 loaf French bread, sliced

In a small mixing bowl, combine cheese, butter and garlic and mix with a fork. Spread on bread slices and broil until bubbly. Sprinkle with paprika or dried parsley for color. Serve hot.

Herb Bread:

1 large loaf unsliced white bread
1 cup softened butter
¼ teaspoon dried summer savory
¼ teaspoon garlic salt
¼ teaspoon ground thyme
1 tablespoon dried parsley

Cut off all crusts of bread EXCEPT bottom crust. Slice in half lengthwise from top to bottom (vertically), not side to side (horizontally), then slice crosswise into pieces, but DON'T slice through bottom crust. In a mixing bowl, combine butter, summer savory, garlic salt, thyme and parsley. Spread all uncrusted sides of bread with the butter mixture. Wrap bottom half in foil to catch drips. Bake in a preheated 400 degree oven for 12 to 14 minutes.

Cheese-Topped French Bread

Food Processor
(Double recipe for a whole loaf of bread)

5 ounces sharp Cheddar cheese
1½ tablespoons California dry sherry
½ teaspoon Dijon-style mustard
¼ teaspoon Tabasco sauce
Either onion or garlic powder
1 loaf French bread

Insert shredding disc and process Cheddar cheese, making about 1¼ cups of grated cheese. Insert plastic blade and process cheese with the dry sherry, mustard, and ¼ teaspoon Tabasco sauce until smooth. Cut French bread in half horizontally. Spread half loaf with softened butter, then spread cheese mixture over buttered surface and dust lightly with either onion or garlic powder. Place bread on a foil-lined baking sheet. Bake in a preheated 450 degree oven for 20 minutes or until hot and bubbly. Cut half loaf into 8 pieces.

Note:
Prepared loaf may be refrigerated overnight or loaf may be frozen.

Golden West Honey Wheat Bread

(This is a good sandwich bread with a delicate texture.)

Yield: 2 loaves

- 1½ cups water
- 1 cup (8-ounces) cream-style cottage cheese
- ½ cup honey
- ¼ cup butter or margarine
- 5½ to 6 cups all-purpose flour or unbleached flour
- 1 cup whole wheat flour
- 2 tablespoons sugar
- 3 teaspoons salt
- 2 packages active dry yeast
- 1 egg, room temperature

In a medium saucepan, heat water, cottage cheese, honey and butter until very warm (120 to 130 degrees). In a large mixer bowl, combine warm liquids, 2 cups all-purpose flour, wheat flour, sugar, salt, yeast and egg. Beat 2 minutes at medium speed. By hand, stir in remaining flour. On a well-floured surface, knead dough until smooth and elastic, about 2 minutes. Place in a greased bowl turning to grease top. Cover; let rise in a warm place until light and doubled in size, about 45 to 60 minutes. Grease (no oil) 2 (9x5x3) or (8x4x2½-inch) loaf pans. Punch down dough; divide and shape into 2 loaves. Place in greased pans. Cover; let rise in warm place until light and doubled in size, about 45 to 60 minutes. Bake in a preheated 375 degree oven for 35 to 40 minutes or until deep golden brown and loaf sounds hollow when lightly tapped. If loaf becomes too brown, loosely cover with foil during the last 10 minutes of baking. Immediately remove from pans. If desired, brush loaf with butter.

Good 'N' Garlicky Pan Rolls

(A quick and easy bread treat) Yield: 16 rolls

1 loaf (1-pound) frozen bread dough
¼ cup butter, melted
1 large clove garlic, minced
2 tablespoons grated Parmesan cheese

Thaw dough according to package directions, and cut into 16 equal portions; shape into balls. Arrange 8 pieces in each of 2 greased 8-inch pie pans. In a small bowl, mix melted butter and garlic, and drizzle the mixture over the rolls. Sprinkle each pan with 1 tablespoon Parmesan cheese. Cover and let rise in a warm place until rolls are light and fill pan. Bake in a preheated 375 degree oven for 15 minutes or until golden brown. Serve hot.

Food Processor French Bread

Yield: 2 loaves

7 cups unbleached flour
1 tablespoon kosher salt
1 package active dry yeast
2½ cups warm water (110 to 115 degrees)
Egg glaze: 1 egg mixed with 1 teaspoon water (optional)

Fit the processor with steel blade. Put flour and salt into work bowl; pulse twice to mix. Dissolve yeast in water and allow to stand until frothy. Turn on the processor and pour the liquid slowly through the feed tube, taking care only to pour as quickly as flour will absorb the liquid. Machine knead until dough forms a mass on one side of the bowl, about 60 seconds. Dough may be a bit tacky, but not overly sticky. If it is, add a little more flour. Remove dough from the machine and shape into a ball. Place in an oiled bowl and turn over to oil the top. Cover the bowl and let rise until doubled, about 1 hour. Punch down the dough and divide into 3 or 4 pieces. Shape each piece into long thin loaves or into rounds. Place on 2 ungreased baking sheets, cover and let rise for about 30 minutes. Brush loaves with egg glaze if desired. Make 4 or 5 slashes on the top of each loaf with a sharp knife, or use the metal blade of the food processor. (If not using the egg glaze, spray the loaves with a mist of water.) Preheat the oven to 400 degrees, place the bread in the oven and lower the heat to 350 degrees. Bake for 45 minutes to 1 hour, or until loaves are golden brown and sound hollow when tapped.

Quick and Easy Food Processor Bread

Yield: 1 loaf

2 cups unbleached white flour
½ cup cake flour
2 tablespoons sugar
1 teaspoon salt
1 package active dry yeast
2 tablespoons butter, cold and cut into 4 pieces
½ cup milk
¼ cup water

Fit processor with metal blade. Combine flours, sugar, salt and yeast in work bowl; process 5 seconds. Add butter and process 15 seconds. Warm the milk and water to 110 degrees and, with processor running, gradually add through the feed tube to the dry ingredients, processing until a ball forms. Process (knead) for an additional 30 to 40 seconds. Place dough in greased bowl, turning to grease top. Cover, and let rise in a warm place until doubled. Shape into loaf and put on a greased cookie sheet. Slash the top of the loaf with a knife or steel processor blade, and let rise again. Bake in a preheated 425 degree oven for 30 minutes, or until loaf tests done.

Note:
Can add grated orange peel and use as a breakfast treat with jam.

Whole Wheat Baguettes

Food Processor Yield: 2 baguettes
(This hearty French bread is a nice accompaniment to a simple meal)

1 package active dry yeast
2 tablespoons brown sugar
1 cup + 2 tablespoons warm water (100 to 105 degrees)
1½ cups unbleached white flour (bread flour is best)
1½ cups whole wheat flour
2 tablespoons instant dry milk, powder or crystals
Cornmeal

In a small bowl, combine yeast, brown sugar and water; stir to dissolve yeast, and allow to stand until frothy and doubled. Put flours, dry milk and salt into work bowl of food processor with metal blade in place. With machine running, add yeast mixture slowly through feed tube. When dough cleans side of bowl, process 40 seconds more. (If dough forms a knot, separate and finish processing.) Dough will be soft and fairly sticky. You can add a bit of flour if it is not manageable. Transfer dough to an oiled bowl and turn to coat all sides of dough. Cover and let dough rise until double in size, about 1 hour. Lightly oil a 17x14-inch baking sheet. Sprinkle with cornmeal; set aside. Punch down dough and transfer to lightly floured board. Divide dough in half and roll each portion into a 12x15-inch rectangle. Roll each rectangle up from a long side into a cylinder, pinching seam ends closed. Place rolls on prepared pan, seam side down. Make 4 to 5 slashes ¼-inch deep, with metal food processor blade, in every baguette. Cover with oiled plastic wrap, and let rise until doubled in bulk, about 45 minutes. Lightly sprinkle loaves with whole wheat flour before baking. Bake in center of a preheated 400 degree oven for 20 to 30 minutes, or until bread tests done (sounds hollow when tapped). Cool completely on rack.

Grissini—Italian Breadsticks

(A nice accompaniment to hot-weather salads)

Yield: 24 breadsticks

1 package active dry yeast
¼ cup warm water (110 degrees)
1 teaspoon sugar
3 cups all-purpose flour
1 teaspoon salt
1 tablespoon + 1 teaspoon olive oil
1 cup lukewarm water
Egg glaze: 1 egg mixed with 1 tablespoon water
Sesame, poppy or caraway seeds

Dissolve yeast in ¼ cup lukewarm water; once yeast is dissolved, add 1 teaspoon sugar and allow to sit for 5 minutes, or until double. Place 3 cups flour and 1 teaspoon salt in a large bowl. Add 1 tablespoon + 1 teaspoon olive oil to the yeast mixture and add this to the dry ingredients. Add one cup lukewarm water to the dry ingredients to make a dough that is soft but not sticky. 1 or 2 more tablespoons of water may be needed. Turn dough out onto a lightly floured board and knead vigorously for 10 minutes or until elastic. Place dough in slightly oiled bowl, turning once to grease top; cover and set bowl in a warm, draft-free place and let dough rise until it has doubled, about 1¼ to 1½ hours. Punch dough down and divide into 24 equal parts. Roll each part, on slightly floured board, with the palms of your hands to a thickness of ¼-inch. Arrange sticks on a lightly greased baking sheet about 1-inch apart and let them rise for 15 to 20 minutes (do not cover). Brush the sticks with the egg glaze and sprinkle lightly with sesame, poppy or caraway seeds or coarse salt. With a knife make a shallow indentation midway across each breadstick (this is the breaking point). Bake in a preheated 425 degree oven for 15 minutes, or until golden.

Variations:

1. Combine ⅓ cup grated Parmesan cheese with flour before adding liquid.
2. Brush the sticks with oil, flavored with a little garlic or garlic powder.

Pumpkin Pan Rolls

Yield: 32 rolls

1 package active dry yeast
1 cup warm water (110 degrees)
½ cup sugar
3 tablespoons butter or margarine, melted
1 teaspoon salt
½ cup powdered instant non-fat dry milk
1 cup canned pumpkin
1½ teaspoons ground cinnamon
¾ teaspoon ground cloves
¾ teaspoon ground nutmeg
¾ teaspoon ground ginger
4½ to 5 cups all-purpose flour

In a large bowl, dissolve yeast in water. Add sugar, butter, salt, dry milk, pumpkin, cinnamon, cloves, nutmeg and ginger. Beat well to blend; then gradually beat in about 4 cups of the flour to make a stiff dough. Turn dough out onto a floured board; knead until smooth—8 to 10 minutes, adding flour as needed to prevent sticking. Grease a large bowl. Put dough in and turn to grease top. Cover and let rise until doubled (1½ to 2 hours). Punch dough down; knead briefly on a lightly floured board to release air. Divide dough into 32 equal pieces. Shape each piece into a smooth ball; place balls into 2 greased 9-inch round baking pans. Cover and let rise until almost doubled (about 1 hour). Bake in a preheated 375 degree oven for 25 minutes, or until browned. Cool on racks.

Salad Rolls

(Just the right thing to serve with a main-dish salad)

Yield: 12 rolls

¼ cup warm water (110 degrees)
1 package active dry yeast
1 teaspoon sugar
¾ cup lukewarm tomato juice
1 teaspoon salt
1 teaspoon instant minced onion
1 teaspoon celery seeds
1 tablespoon minced fresh parsley
¼ cup vegetable oil
1 egg
¼ cup wheat germ
2 to 2½ cups unbleached all-purpose flour
Melted butter

In a medium mixing bowl, combine the warm water and sugar. Sprinkle the yeast over the water and let stand for 5 minutes or until frothy. Add the salt, instant minced onion, celery seeds, parsley, vegetable oil, egg and wheat germ. Mix thoroughly with spoon or mixer. Gradually add the flour to make a soft but workable dough. Knead on a slightly floured board until smooth and elastic, adding small amounts of flour as necessary to prevent sticking. Place kneaded dough in a lightly oiled bowl, turning once to grease top. Cover and let rise until double. Roll into a 12-inch circle. Brush with melted butter. Cut into 12 wedge-shaped pieces. Starting at wide end, roll toward tip. Place on a greased baking sheet, curving roll into a crescent shape. Cover, and let rise until double. Bake in a preheated 400 degree oven for 12 minutes.

Banana Bread

(An early 1900's recipe from Missouri) Yield: 2 loaves

⅔ cup shortening
2½ cups sifted flour
1⅔ cups sugar
1¼ teaspoons baking powder
1 teaspoon salt
1 teaspoon baking soda
1¼ cups mashed ripe bananas
⅔ cup buttermilk
2 eggs
⅔ cup chopped walnuts or pecans

In a medium mixing bowl, add shortening and stir to soften. Sift flour, sugar, baking powder, baking soda and salt together and add to shortening; mix until blended. Add bananas and ½ of the buttermilk and mix until all of the flour mixture is moistened, then beat vigorously for 2 minutes. Add remaining buttermilk and eggs, and beat for 2 minutes more. Fold nuts into batter. Pour mixture into 2 (8x4x2½-inch) greased pans, and bake in a preheated 350 degree oven for 35 minutes or until loaf tests done. Cool in pan for 10 minutes, and then remove to wire cooling rack.

Note:
This bread freezes well.

Cranberry Bread

(A good breakfast bread for fall!) Yield: 2 loaves

1 cup sugar
3 tablespoons butter or margarine
½ cup orange juice
Grated rind of one large orange
2 cups all-purpose flour
1 tablespoon baking powder
½ teaspoon salt
1 cup fresh cranberries, coarsely chopped
¾ cup chopped pecans
1 to 2 tablespoons melted butter or margarine

In a small saucepan, combine sugar, butter, orange juice and orange rind; bring to a boil. Pour mixture into liquid measuring cup and add enough hot water to make ¾ cup, set aside. In a large mixing bowl, combine flour, baking powder and salt. Stir in cranberries and pecans, and toss to coat. Add hot juice mixture and stir. Pour into 2 greased and floured 8x4x2½-inch loaf pans. Bake in a preheated 350 degree oven for 40 to 45 minutes. When loaves test done, remove from oven and brush the tops with melted butter while still hot. Cool 10 minutes in pans before removing loaf to cooling racks.

Persimmon Nut Bread

Yield: 1 loaf

1 cup persimmon pulp
1 teaspoon baking soda
1 cup brown sugar, firmly packed
1 egg, well beaten
2 tablespoons vegetable oil
1 teaspoon vanilla extract
½ cup California raisins or dates
2¼ cups all-purpose flour
1 teaspoon baking powder
1 teaspoon salt
1 cup chopped nuts
⅓ cup candied orange peel (optional)

In a large bowl, combine persimmon pulp and baking soda and allow to stand for 5 minutes. Add brown sugar, beaten egg, oil and vanilla extract and beat well. In a separate bowl, dust raisins with a little of the flour, and set aside. Sift the remaining flour, baking powder and salt together and add to the persimmon pulp mixture; blend just until moistened. Stir in nuts and optional candied orange peel after liquid and dry ingredients have been partially mixed together. Bake in a greased 9x5x3-inch loaf pan in a preheated 350 degree oven for 45 to 60 minutes. May be served with butter or cream cheese-sugar spread if desired.

Variation:

A combination of almonds and walnuts is especially good for the chopped nuts.

Kahlua Fruit Nut Bread

Yield: 1 loaf

1 cup pitted dates, chopped
½ cup Kahlua or coffee-flavored liqueur
½ cup warm water
1 teaspoon grated orange peel
⅔ cup brown sugar, packed
2 tablespoons shortening
1 large egg
2 cups all-purpose flour, sifted
1 teaspoon baking soda
1 teaspoon salt
⅔ cup chopped walnuts or pecans
Cheese spread (recipe follows)

In a small bowl, combine dates, Kahlua, water and orange peel and allow to stand while preparing remaining batter. In a large mixing bowl, beat sugar, shortening and egg together until fluffy. Sift flour with soda and salt and add to creamed mixture alternately with date mixture. Stir in nuts. Turn batter into a greased 10½x3½-inch loaf pan. Let stand for 5 minutes, then bake in the lower one-third of a preheated 350 degree oven for 60 to 70 minutes, or until loaf tests done. Remove loaf from pan and cool completely on wire rack. May be served with Cheese spread if desired.

Cheese Spread:

Yield: 1¼ cups spread

1 (8-ounce) package cream cheese, softened
¼ cup butter, softened
1 tablespoon Kahlua or coffee-flavored liqueur
2 teaspoons toasted sesame seeds

In a small bowl, beat cream cheese and butter together until smooth. Stir in Kahlua and sesame seeds.

Turn of the Century Date Orange Loaf

Yield: 1 loaf

2½ cups all-purpose flour, sifted
1 teaspoon salt
2 teaspoons baking powder
1 cup brown sugar, firmly packed
½ cup chopped dates
1 egg, well beaten
2 tablespoons vegetable oil
1 tablespoon grated orange peel
¾ cup fresh orange juice
1 tablespoon vanilla extract
½ teaspoon rum extract
Powdered sugar (optional)

In a large mixing bowl, stir together flour, salt, baking powder and brown sugar. Add chopped dates and toss with dry ingredients to coat. In a separate bowl, beat egg well; add oil, orange peel, orange juice, vanilla extract and rum extract and combine well. Add liquid ingredients to dry ingredients, stirring just to moisten. Pour into a greased and lightly floured 8x4x3-inch loaf pan. Bake in a preheated 350 degree oven for 30 to 40 minutes or until loaf tests done. Cool in pan 10 minutes; remove and cool completely before slicing. Loaf may be lightly dusted with powdered sugar if desired.

Prune Nut Bread

Yield: 1 loaf

1 cup pitted dried prunes
2 teaspoons grated orange peel
1 cup orange juice
2 cups all-purpose flour
¾ cup sugar
2 teaspoons baking powder
½ teaspoon salt
½ teaspoon cinnamon
2 eggs, beaten
2 tablespoons vegetable oil
½ cup chopped walnuts

Snip prunes into small pieces and place in a large bowl; add orange peel and orange juice and let stand for ½ hour. In another bowl, sift together flour, sugar, baking powder, salt and cinnamon. Add the dry ingredients to eggs, oil and walnuts. Add to liquid mixture; beat well with a fork until blended, about 2 minutes. Pour mixture into a 9x5x3-inch greased pan. Bake in a preheated 350 degree oven for 50 to 55 minutes. Remove loaf from oven and allow to stand in pan for 10 minutes before removing to wire cooling rack.

Variations:

May substitute 1 cup dried snipped apricots for dried prunes to give loaf a more tart taste.

For a sweeter-flavored loaf, substitute 1 cup snipped pitted dates for dried prunes.

Best Ever Basic Muffins with Variations

Yield: 12 muffins

2 cups flour
¼ cup sugar
1 tablespoon baking powder
½ teaspoon salt
1 egg
1 cup milk
⅓ cup vegetable oil

In a large mixing bowl, combine flour, sugar, baking powder and salt. In a small bowl, beat egg; add milk and oil, mixing well. Blend the liquid mixture into dry ingredients just to moisten. Spoon batter into greased muffin tins and bake in a preheated 400 degree oven for 20 minutes.

Variations:

Blueberry:

Add ¾ cup well-drained canned blueberries. Stir into batter after liquid and dry ingredients have been partially mixed together.

Cinnamon-Sugar:

Mix 1 teaspoon ground cinnamon with ¼ cup sugar. Sprinkle over tops of muffin batter before baking.

Orange-Raisin:

Add 1 tablespoon grated orange peel and ½ cup California raisins. Stir into batter after liquid and dry ingredients have been partially mixed together.

Orange-Nut:

Add 2 tablespoons orange peel and ⅓ cup toasted, chopped walnuts. Stir into batter after liquid and dry ingredients have been partially mixed together. Cinnamon-Sugar mixture may be sprinkled over tops of muffin batter before baking.

Bacon:

In basic recipe, reduce oil to ¼ cup and reduce salt to ¼ teaspoon. Add ½ cup crisply cooked, crumbled bacon to dry ingredients and toss together to coat.

Graham Muffins

Yield: 18 muffins

1½ cups all-purpose flour
1½ cups graham flour
1 teaspoon salt
1 teaspoon baking powder
1 egg
½ cup sugar
½ cup molasses
2 tablespoons vegetable oil
1 cup buttermilk
½ cup California raisins (optional)

Stir together all-purpose flour, graham flour, salt, baking soda and baking powder. Set aside. In a large bowl, beat egg and sugar together. Add molasses, oil and buttermilk; mix. Add the dry ingredients and mix just until moistened. Fold in raisins. Divide batter among 18 greased and floured muffin tins and bake in a preheated 350 degree oven for 20 minutes.

Fudgy Brownie Muffins

Yield: 36 muffins

2 cups unsalted butter
8 ounces sweet baking chocolate
3½ cups sugar
2 cups all-purpose flour, sifted
Pinch of salt
8 eggs
2 teaspoons vanilla extract
4 cups coarsely chopped walnuts or pecans
36 nut halves (optional)

Preheat oven to 300 degrees. Line muffin pans with paper muffin liner cups. Melt butter with chocolate in top of a double boiler, set over simmering water. In a large bowl, combine sugar, flour and salt; stir in chocolate mixture. Add eggs and vanilla and mix just until ingredients are evenly moistened; do not overmix. Fold in nuts and spoon batter into muffin cups, filling ⅔ full. Top each muffin with one pecan or walnut half, if desired. Bake muffins about 40 minutes or until tester inserted in center comes out clean. Cool on racks.

Blueberry Muffins

Yield: 12 muffins

1¾ cups all-purpose flour, sifted
2½ teaspoons baking powder
¾ teaspoon salt
¼ cup sugar
1 egg
⅓ cup vegetable oil
¾ cup milk
1 cup fresh blueberries
2 tablespoons sugar
1 teaspoon grated lemon peel

In a large bowl, combine flour, baking powder, salt and sugar. In a small bowl, beat egg; add oil and milk, mixing well. Blend the liquid mixture into dry ingredients only to moisten. In another small bowl, combine blueberries, 2 tablespoons sugar and lemon peel. Fold fruit mixture into muffin batter and spoon into well-greased muffin tins. Bake in the upper third of a preheated 400 degree oven for 25 minutes.

<u>Do not use muffin tin liners.</u>

Skyline Apple Muffins

(These are beautifully moist brunch muffins.) Yield: 15 muffins

⅓ cup sugar
1 tablespoon butter, room temperature
1½ cups brown sugar, firmly packed
⅔ cup vegetable oil
1 egg
1 cup buttermilk
1 teaspoon baking soda
1 teaspoon salt
1 teaspoon vanilla extract
2½ cups all-purpose flour, sifted
1½ cups peeled apple, cut into ¼-inch die
½ cup chopped pecans, toasted

Preheat oven to 325 degrees. Grease and lightly flour four muffin pans. In a small bowl, combine sugar and butter and mix until crumbly, reserve. In a large bowl, combine brown sugar, oil and egg. In another bowl, combine buttermilk, soda, salt and vanilla extract. Blend flour into brown sugar mixture alternately with buttermilk mixture, stirring just until combined; do not overmix. Fold in apple and pecans. Divide batter among muffin pans and sprinkle with all of the reserved sugar/butter mixture. Bake in oven for about 30 minutes, or until toothpick inserted comes out clean.

French Coffee Cake

Yield: Serves 8

3 cups all-purpose flour
2 teaspoons baking powder
1 teaspoon baking soda
½ cup butter
½ cup vegetable shortening
1½ cups sugar
5 eggs
½ teaspoon vanilla extract
1 cup dairy sour cream
2 squares (2-ounces) unsweetened chocolate, grated
½ cup sugar
1 tablespoon cinnamon

Sift the flour, baking powder and soda together 3 times. Set aside. In a large mixing bowl, cream together the butter, shortening and sugar until fluffy. Add the eggs and vanilla and mix well. Next, add the flour mixture alternating with the sour cream. In a separate bowl, mix the chocolate, sugar and cinnamon. Grease a 10-inch tube or 10-cup bundt pan, and alternate the batter with the chocolate mixture, cutting the chocolate mixture through the batter to make a ribbon effect. Bake in a preheated 350 degree oven for 1 hour or until cake tests done. Cool.

Orange Date Coffee Cake

Yield: Serves 6 to 8

2 cups all-purpose flour
½ cup sugar
1 tablespoon baking powder
½ teaspoon salt
1 egg, slightly beaten
½ cup milk
½ cup vegetable oil
½ cup chopped dates
2 teaspoons grated orange peel
½ cup orange juice

Topping:

2 tablespoons butter
½ cup brown sugar
1 teaspoon cinnamon
½ cup chopped walnuts

Sift the flour, sugar, baking powder and salt together into a large mixing bowl. In another bowl, combine egg, milk and oil. Add all at once to the dry ingredients; stir just until blended. Combine dates, orange peel and orange juice and stir into batter until just blended. Spread batter evenly in a greased 7x11-inch pan. With a pastry blender or fork, cut the butter, brown sugar, cinnamon and walnuts together until crumbly. Sprinkle mixture over batter. Bake in a preheated 375 degree oven for 25 to 30 minutes. Serve warm.

Variation:

¼ cup pecans and ¼ cup California raisins may be substituted for the dates.

Tropical Coffee Cake

Yield: Serves 6 to 8

1½ cups all-purpose flour
1 cup sugar
2 teaspoons baking powder
½ teaspoon salt
½ cup vegetable oil
2 eggs
1 (8-ounce) carton plain or fruit flavored yogurt or dairy sour cream (about 1 cup)

Place flour, sugar, baking powder, salt, oil, eggs and yogurt or sour cream in a large mixing bowl; stir 70 to 80 strokes until well blended. Pour batter into a greased 10-cup bundt pan or a 9x11-inch baking pan. Set aside while topping is prepared.

Topping:

1 cup shredded coconut
¾ cup crushed or chunk-style pineapple (fruit cocktail or canned mandarin oranges)
⅓ cup sugar
1 teaspoon cinnamon

Spoon fruit over the batter. Sprinkle the coconut over the fruit. Combine sugar and cinnamon and sprinkle over top of cake. Bake in a preheated 350 degree oven for 45 to 55 minutes or until toothpick comes out clean.

Quick and Easy Kuchen

Yield: 1 Kuchen

1 (16-ounce) package hot roll mix
1 egg
1 cup fruit—suggestions: California grapes, boysenberries, sliced peaches, apricots, plums—can be fresh, frozen or canned

Follow package directions for making hot roll mix. Spread dough in the bottom of a greased 9x13-inch pan. Push fruit pieces slightly into dough.

Custard Topping:

1 egg, beaten
½ cup sugar
2 tablespoons flour
½ cup dairy sour cream

Mix egg, sugar, flour and sour cream together and spread over fruit in the pan. Cover, and let dough rise about 45 minutes.

Crumb Topping:

¼ cup melted butter
1 cup flour
½ cup sugar

Combine butter, flour and sugar to make crumb topping. Sprinkle crumbs over custard topped dough and bake in a preheated 350 degree oven for 30 minutes. Cool.

Sour Cream Coffee Cake with Cinnamon-Walnut Topping

Yield: 2 (9-inch) coffee cakes

1 package active dry yeast
¼ cup warm water (110 to 115 degrees)
1 tablespoon sugar
½ cup boiling water
¼ cup butter
¼ cup sugar
¼ cup half and half
1 egg, lightly beaten
⅓ cup dairy sour cream
1 teaspoon salt
4 cups all-purpose flour, sifted

Topping:

½ cup brown sugar
2 teaspoons cinnamon
5 tablespoons butter, softened
3 tablespoons flour
⅓ cup chopped walnuts

Dissolve yeast in ¼ cup warm water and add the 1 tablespoon sugar; allow to proof and set aside. In a large bowl, combine boiling water, butter and the ¼ cup sugar; allow to cool to lukewarm. Add half and half, egg and sour cream and blend well. Stir in proofed yeast mixture. Add salt and enough of the flour to make a workable soft dough. Turn dough onto a floured board and knead for 5 minutes, adding additional flour if needed. Shape dough into a ball. Place in a greased bowl; turn ball over to grease top. Cover bowl and place in a warm spot; allow to rise for 1½ hours or until doubled. Mix brown sugar and cinnamon together from Topping recipe; set aside. Divide dough into two equal balls. Roll first ball into a 12-inch circle and sprinkle with 2 tablespoons of the reserved sugar-cinnamon mixture. Reform dough into a ball and roll out again into a 9-inch circle. Place in a greased 9-inch cake pan. Repeat process with the other half of dough, placing dough in a second greased cake pan. Add 2 tablespoons soft butter, 3 tablespoons flour and nuts to the remaining sugar-cinnamon mixture and work with fingers until crumbly. Spread dough circles lightly with the remaining 2 tablespoons softened butter and sprinkle liberally with sugar-cinnamon crumb mixture. Cover with plastic wrap and allow to rise for 1 to 1½ hours or until doubled. Bake in a preheated 350 degree oven for 25 to 30 minutes or until cakes test done.

M.C.'s Famous Moist Cornbread

Yield: 9 servings

1 cup flour
1 cup yellow corn meal
⅔ cup sugar
½ teaspoon salt
1 tablespoon baking powder
½ teaspoon baking soda
½ cup shortening
1 cup buttermilk
2 eggs

In a large mixer bowl, stir together the flour, corn meal, sugar, salt, baking powder and baking soda. Add shortening and ½ cup of the buttermilk and beat vigorously by hand using 150 strokes or for 2 minutes at medium setting if using mixer. Beat eggs with remaining buttermilk and add to batter, beating in the same manner. Pour batter into a greased and wax-paper lined 8-inch square pan. Bake in a pre-heated 350 degree oven for 30 to 40 minutes or until lightly golden. Allow to cool in pan for 10 minutes before cutting into serving pieces.

To see if the dough has risen enough, press two fingers into the dough. If the dough is not ready, the depression made by the fingers will fill quickly. If the holes remain, it has risen enough.

Vegetables

Artichokes Florentine

(May be used as a brunch dish or a vegetarian entree)

Yield: Serves 6 to 8

6 to 8 cooked artichoke bottoms (use either drained, canned or thawed, frozen bottoms)

Creamed spinach:

2 pounds spinach, well washed, drained, with stems removed

Bechamel sauce:

2 tablespoons butter or margarine
2 tablespoons all-purpose flour
½ cup chicken broth
½ cup half and half or light cream
Freshly grated nutmeg

Mornay sauce:

2 tablespoons butter or margarine
2 tablespoons all-purpose flour
½ cup chicken broth
½ cup half and half or light cream
2 tablespoons shredded Gruyere or Swiss cheese
2 tablespoons grated Parmesan cheese
Salt to taste
Cayenne pepper to taste
½ cup shredded Gruyere or Parmesan cheese

To Make Creamed Spinach:

Place tender, washed and drained spinach leaves into a large pan. Cover and cook over low heat in a small amount of water until leaves are just wilted, stirring once or twice. Drain well and chop. There should be about 2 cups (or use 2 cups frozen, thawed, drained spinach). Blend spinach with one recipe of the Bechamel Sauce and heat through, stirring well.

To Make Bechamel Sauce:
Melt 2 tablespoons butter in a small pan over medium heat. Mix in 2 tablespoons all-purpose flour and cook, stirring, until flour is light golden color. Remove from heat and blend in ½ cup chicken broth and ½ cup half and half. Return to heat and bring to a full, rolling boil, stirring. Season to taste with salt and pepper and freshly grated nutmeg.

To Make Mornay Sauce:
Prepare Bechamel Sauce according to above recipe but omit the nutmeg. Stir into the simmering sauce 2 tablespoons shredded Gruyere cheese and 2 tablespoons Parmesan cheese. Remove from heat and add salt and cayenne pepper to taste.

To Assemble:
Arrange artichoke bottoms side by side in a shallow 1½-quart casserole. Cover artichokes with one recipe of Creamed Spinach; then spoon one recipe of Mornay Sauce over spinach. Sprinkle with ½ cup shredded Gruyere or Parmesan cheese. (At this point, the casserole may be covered and refrigerated until the next day.) Bake, uncovered, in a preheated 375 degree oven for 30 minutes or until bubbly.

Note:
For refrigerated casserole, add 10 to 15 minutes to baking time.

Sesame Broccoli

Yield: Serves 6 to 8

2 pounds fresh broccoli, trimmed and cut into 2-inch florets
2½ tablespoons sugar
2 tablespoons sesame seeds
2 tablespoons vegetable oil
2 tablespoons red wine vinegar
2 tablespoons soy sauce

To cook the broccoli, bring a saucepan of lightly salted water to a rolling boil, add broccoli, and cook for about 2 minutes after the water returns to a boil. Drain well. While the broccoli is cooking, combine the remaining ingredients in a small saucepan and bring to a boil over medium heat. Pour over the broccoli, turning to coat well. Serve immediately.

Asperges Neapolitaine

Yield: Serves 8 to 10

- 1 pound cleaned, fresh asparagus
- 3 tablespoons butter
- 2 tablespoons finely chopped onion
- 2 tablespoons very finely chopped celery
- 1 tablespoon freshly grated Parmesan cheese
- 1 tablespoon fresh soft bread crumbs
- 1 (14½-ounce) can Italian style tomatoes
- Salt
- Pepper
- Fresh or dried thyme
- Sugar
- Fresh or dried oregano

In ovenproof dish, melt the butter. Lay the asparagus evenly in rows in the bottom of the dish. Sprinkle the spears with onion, celery, Parmesan cheese and bread crumbs. Remove tomatoes from purée in the can and chop them. Mix with purée and season with salt, pepper, sugar, thyme and oregano to taste. Pour the mixture over the top of the dish and bake in preheated 375 degree oven for 35 to 40 minutes.

Green Beans in Dill Sauce

Food Processor
(A great summer dish)

Yield: Serves 8

- 1½ pounds fresh green beans
- 2 tablespoons sugar
- ⅓ cup cider vinegar
- ⅔ cup olive oil
- ¾ cup thinly sliced green onions, tops too
- 3 tablespoons parsley
- 3 tablespoons fresh dill, minced or 1½ teaspoons dried dill weed
- ½ cup coarsely chopped walnuts

Cook the green beans à la the Paul Meyer's method by placing 2 tablespoons of sugar into a medium saucepan. At the same time bring 2 cups of water to boil in another saucepan. Turn the heat onto high in the pan with the sugar. Watch the sugar carefully and when the sugar just begins to melt and bubble, place the vegetables into the pan, then immediately pour the boiling water over the vegetables. Cover pan and cook until tender (about 3-5 minutes). Drain and run cool water over the vegetables to stop the cooking process. Drain again thoroughly. Blend the vinegar and oil into an emulsion by pouring vinegar into a food processor or blender, then add oil in a slow thin stream. Whirl emulsion for one minute, and add scallions, parsley, dill and walnuts. Toss the emulsion mixture with the beans while they are still warm; season with salt and freshly ground pepper to taste. Chill for a few hours. Bring beans to room temperature and garnish with sprigs of fresh dill before serving.

Cheddar Cabbage Wedges

Yield: Serves 8

1 medium head cabbage, cut into 8 wedges
½ cup finely chopped onions
¼ cup butter or margarine
¼ cup flour
½ teaspoon salt
⅛ teaspoon pepper
2 cups milk
¾ cup shredded Cheddar cheese
½ cup mayonnaise
3 tablespoons chili sauce

Cook cabbage in small amount of salted water until tender, about 12 minutes. Drain well and place in 9x13x2-inch baking dish. Cook onion in butter or margarine until limp. Blend in flour, salt, pepper; add milk all at once. Cook and stir mixture until thick. Pour sauce over cabbage. Bake uncovered in a preheated 375 degree oven for 20 minutes. Combine cheese, mayonnaise and chili sauce in a small bowl. Spoon on cabbage wedges and bake 5 minutes more.

Glazed Honeyed Carrots

Yield: Serves 4

1 pound carrots, peeled and cut into 1-inch pieces
⅓ cup fresh orange juice
⅓ cup water
¼ cup honey
3 tablespoons unsalted butter
1 teaspoon grated orange peel
¼ teaspoon ground ginger
Salt to taste

In a stainless steel or enameled saucepan, combine the carrots, orange juice, water, honey, butter, orange peel, ginger and salt to taste; bring the liquid to a boil, and simmer the mixture, covered, for 6 to 8 minutes, or until the carrots are just tender. Cook the mixture, uncovered, over moderately high heat until the cooking liquid is reduced to about ¼ cup. Cook the mixture, shaking the pan, until the liquid is almost completely reduced and the carrots are glazed evenly and transfer the honey carrots to a heated serving dish.

Golden Carrot Bake

Yield: Serves 8

3 cups shredded peeled carrots (about 1 pound)
⅔ cup long grain rice
½ teaspoon salt
1½ cups water
2 cups shredded Cheddar cheese
1 cup milk
2 eggs, beaten
2 tablespoons instant minced onions
¼ teaspoon white pepper

In a medium saucepan combine shredded carrots, rice, salt and water. Bring to a boil; reduce heat and simmer, covered, for 25 minutes. Do not drain. Stir in 1½ cups of the shredded cheese, milk, eggs, onion and pepper. Turn mixture into a 1½-quart casserole. Bake, uncovered, in a preheated 350 degree oven for about 1 hour. Top with remaining shredded cheese (½ cup). Return to oven to melt cheese.

New Year's Blackeye Peas

(Terrific! Served for good luck in Creole country)

Yield: Serves 8

1 pound blackeye peas
½ pound bacon
1 cup onion, chopped
1 cup green pepper, chopped
1 cup celery, chopped
2 tablespoons chili pepper
3 cloves garlic, minced
2 cups canned tomatoes, chopped
2 teaspoons salt, or to taste
½ teaspoon pepper
¾ teaspoon dried oregano
½ teaspoon dried thyme

Rinse peas in cold water. Place peas in a large pan, cover with hot water, allow peas to soak overnight. Drain. Bring 5 cups of water to a boil. Add peas and simmer for ½ hour. Cut bacon into 1-inch pieces. Cook until crisp. Drain and set aside. In bacon drippings, cook onions, green pepper, celery, chili pepper, garlic, tomatoes and seasonings for 20 minutes over low heat. Add the mixture to the soaked peas; bring to a boil. Reduce heat and simmer until peas test done.

Springtime Peas

Yield: Serves 4

2 pounds fresh peas, unshelled
3 to 6 lettuce leaves
⅓ cup sliced green onion
1 teaspoon sugar
½ teaspoon salt
Dash pepper
Dash dried thyme, crushed
3 tablespoons butter or margarine

Shell peas. Cover bottom of skillet with lettuce; top with peas and onion. Sprinkle on sugar, salt, pepper and thyme; add butter. Cover tightly and cook over low heat 10 to 15 minutes or till peas are done.

Eggplant Moussaka

Yield: Serves 6 to 8

Step 1:

2 tablespoons butter or margarine
2 cups chopped onion
1½ pounds ground meat (can use ½ lamb and ½ beef, or ½ bulk pork sausage and ½ beef)
1 clove garlic, crushed
1 teaspoon crushed basil
½ teaspoon cinnamon
½ teaspoon crushed oregano
Salt and pepper to taste
2 (8-ounce) cans tomato sauce

In a large saucepan, melt butter and sauté onion, add the meat and brown well. Drain off excess fat. Add garlic, basil, cinnamon, oregano, salt, pepper and tomato sauce to the meat mixture. Simmer a few minutes to blend flavors. Set aside.

Step 2:

2 large eggplants
Salt
½ cup butter or margarine

Next, take 2 large eggplants; peel and slice and lightly sprinkle with salt. Broil until brown, brushing with melted butter. (You may not need all of the butter, depending on how much eggplant you have.)

Step 3:

2 tablespoons butter, melted
3 tablespoons all-purpose flour
2 eggs, well beaten
½ teaspoon salt
½ teaspoon pepper
2 cups milk

In a saucepan, mix butter and flour into a smooth paste. Stir in eggs, salt and pepper, and cook, stirring constantly, until mixture just comes to a boil and thickens.

Step 4:

½ cup Parmesan cheese
1 cup Cheddar cheese

When assembling, layer the eggplant in the bottom of a 1½-quart casserole. Top with the meat mixture, ½ cup Parmesan cheese, ½ cup of the Cheddar cheese, the white sauce and top with another ½ cup of Cheddar cheese. Bake, uncovered, in a preheated 350 degree oven for 30 minutes, or until hot and bubbly.

Eggplant Cairo

Yield: Serves 8 to 10

⅔ cup olive oil
3 cloves garlic, minced
1 large onion, coarsely chopped
1 green pepper, coarsely diced
1 teaspoon powdered coriander
1 teaspoon tumeric
¼ teaspoon cayenne
1 teaspoon fresh ginger root, finely minced
½ teaspoon powdered ginger
2 bay leaves (discard later)
1 medium eggplant, cut into ¾-inch cubes with peel intact
1 (1-pound, 12-ounce) can tomatoes, cut up
1 beef or vegetable bouillon cube
1 tablespoon brown sugar

In a large pan, put oil, garlic, onion, green pepper, coriander, tumeric, cayenne, ginger root, ginger and bay leaves. Sauté until the onion is transparent. Add the eggplant, tomatoes, crumbled bouillon cube and brown sugar. Stir well. Bake in a 3-quart casserole in a preheated 325 degree oven for 60 minutes, stirring once about halfway through baking time. If possible leave in oven for 1 more hour at 275 degrees so that flavors are absorbed. Remove bay leaves and serve with rice and a dollop of plain yogurt.

Cottage Cheese and Leek Pie

(A traditional Albanian dish) Yield: Serves 6

1 bunch fresh leeks, thinly sliced (including greens)
2 tablespoons butter or margarine
¼ cup milk
2 eggs, beaten
1 pint cottage cheese
½ teaspoon salt
Pinch of pepper
Pastry for 2-crust pie
Milk or buttermilk (optional)

Thoroughly clean leeks. In a large skillet, sauté the leeks in butter or margarine until soft, but not brown. Add milk; simmer for 5 minutes. Cool until lukewarm; add beaten eggs, cottage cheese and salt and pepper. Line 9-inch pie pan with half of pastry; fill with leek mixture. Cover with top crust; flute edges and cut steam vents. Brush top crust with milk or buttermilk if desired. Bake in a preheated 375 degree oven for 40 minutes or until done.

Note:
This dish may be served hot or cold.

Mushroom-Onion-Cheese Casserole

Yield: Serves 6 to 8

1 pound medium-size mushrooms
6 tablespoons butter or margarine
1 (1-pound) can small whole onions, drained
1½ tablespoons flour
1 cup milk
1 cup shredded Cheddar cheese
½ teaspoon dried oregano leaves, crumbled
2 tablespoons parsley, chopped
1 cup seasoned croutons

Melt 4 tablespoons of the butter or margarine in a large skillet. Sauté mushrooms over medium heat until almost all of the juices evaporate, about 10 minutes. Cut any large onions in half, then combine them with the mushrooms in a shallow 1½ to 2-quart casserole. In the same skillet, slowly add the flour to the mushroom juices and cook, stirring, until bubbly. Blend in milk and cook, stirring constantly until thickened. Remove from heat. Add the cheese, oregano and parsley; stir until the cheese melts. Pour over the mushrooms and onions and mix gently. Casserole can be made to this point and held in the refrigerator. When ready to serve, melt the remaining 2 tablespoons of butter and toss with the slightly crumbled croutons; sprinkle mixture over the top. Bake uncovered in a preheated 350 degree oven for 25 to 35 minutes.

Curried Apples, Onions & Raisins

(A good accompaniment to pork or chicken)

Yield: Serves 6

¼ cup bacon drippings
1 teaspoon curry powder
4 yellow onions, peeled and quartered
4 red apples, unpeeled, cored and cut into eighths
⅓ cup California raisins

Heat bacon drippings in a 12-inch skillet; add curry powder and cook, stirring for one minute. Add onions and apples and sauté 5 minutes. Cover and cook 5 minutes longer. Add raisins and simmer slowly, uncovered, until onions and apples are tender but still hold their shape.

Creamed Onion Casserole

(Very good with Thanksgiving dinner) Yield: Serves 6 to 8

1½ to 2 pounds small white boiling onions
5 ounces canned evaporated milk
3 tablespoons flour
3 tablespoons butter or margarine
¾ to 1 teaspoon Worcestershire sauce
1 chicken bouillon cube
Salt to taste
White pepper to taste
½ cup slivered almonds
½ cup chopped parsley

If onions are larger than the size of walnuts, split them horizontally almost halfway through to hasten cooking and assure more even doneness. Cover onions with water and bring to a quick boil. Drain; repeat once again. Cover with water again (this is the third time) and salt lightly; cook until tender. (At this point onions can be held up to 24 hours, covered, in the refrigerator.) Reserve the final cooking water. Mix the evaporated milk with enough water (stored onion water) to make two cups liquid. In a heavy skillet, melt the butter; add flour, stir, and cook until bubbly and lightly golden. Quickly stir the 2 cups of onion liquid into the butter-flour mixture, stirring constantly. Cook until smooth, bubbly and thick. Be careful not to scorch! Add the Worcestershire sauce and bouillon cube and mix well. Salt and pepper to taste. Place onions in a 1 to 1½-quart casserole dish and sprinkle with half of the almonds. Cover with the sauce. Sprinkle the remaining nuts and the chopped parsley on top. Casserole may be held in the refrigerator at this time. Bake in a preheated 350 degree oven for 30 minutes or until sauce is bubbly and browned on top.

Roasted Sweet Peppers

(This is a great side dish to serve with eggs or roasted meats.)

Yield: Serves 10 to 12

2 sweet green peppers
2 sweet red peppers
Salt
½ cup olive oil

Wash and dry peppers; place them on a baking sheet and bake in a preheated 400 degree oven for 20 to 30 minutes, or until they begin to darken and the skins can be peeled off. Remove peppers from oven; cut each in half lengthwise, and allow to drain; cool slightly. Strip off the blistered skin while still fairly warm. Cut peppers into strips. Place in a bowl and sprinkle lightly with salt. Add olive oil and let stand at room temperature for 5 hours, or refrigerate overnight. If chilled, remove from refrigerator ½ hour before serving.

California Sweet Potato Bake

(Nice at Thanksgiving instead of candied yams)

Yield: Serves 6 to 8

4 medium sweet potatoes
4 cooking apples
Salt to taste
½ cup brown sugar, firmly packed
1½ tablespoons cornstarch
¼ teaspoon salt
1 cup orange juice
¼ cup butter
3 tablespoons California dry sherry
2 tablespoons chopped walnuts
½ teaspoon grated orange peel

Cook sweet potatoes in boiling salted water until tender; drain, peel and cut in half lengthwise or slice. Peel apples and slice. Layer sweet potatoes and apples in a 2-quart baking dish. Sprinkle lightly with salt. In a medium saucepan mix brown sugar, cornstarch and salt; blend in orange juice. Cook over high heat, stirring constantly, until mixture comes to a boil. Add butter, sherry, walnuts and orange peel; pour over potatoes and apples. Bake uncovered in a preheated 350 degree oven for 20 to 30 minutes or until well glazed.

Gin's Easy Potato Cheese Casserole

(Can be made in a microwave) Yield: Serves 8

2 pounds frozen hash brown potatoes, partially or fully thawed
½ cup butter or margarine, softened
1 teaspoon salt, or to taste
¼ teaspoon pepper, or to taste
½ cup minced onion
1 (10-ounce) can cream of chicken or cream of mushroom soup
2 cups grated Cheddar cheese
16 ounces dairy sour cream

Topping:

⅓ cup butter or margarine
2 cups crushed corn flakes

Lightly butter an 8½x11-inch baking dish. In a large mixing bowl mix the potatoes, butter or margarine, salt, pepper, onion, cream soup, cheese and sour cream. Turn mixture into the buttered dish. In a small pan, melt ⅓ cup butter or margarine and combine with the crushed corn flakes. Sprinkle topping on casserole. Bake in a preheated 350 degree oven for 45 minutes or microwave for 20 minutes on High, turning dish 2 to 3 times.

Make-Ahead Mashed Potatoes

(This is a great recipe for the busy homemaker since it will hold up to two weeks. Good with or without gravy.) Yield: Serves 10 to 12

5 pounds potatoes, peeled
½ cup butter or margarine
2 (3-ounce) packages cream cheese, softened
1 cup dairy sour cream
4 ounces shredded sharp Cheddar cheese
½ cup grated Parmesan cheese
4 green onions, chopped
1 tablespoon salt
1 teaspoon white pepper

Boil potatoes until tender. Mash or rice while hot. Add butter, cream cheese, sour cream, Cheddar cheese, Parmesan cheese, onions, salt and pepper and beat well. Turn into a 3-quart casserole. Cover and store in refrigerator up to 2 weeks. On party day, remove casserole from refrigerator 1 hour before baking. If desired, fluff up potatoes with a little milk. Bake uncovered in a preheated 350 degree oven for 45 minutes or until heated through.

Pommes De Terre Suisse

Yield: Serves 6 to 8

3 pounds russet potatoes, sliced ¼-inch thick
Softened butter
1 clove garlic, crushed
4 to 6 ounces grated Gruyere or Swiss cheese
Salt and pepper to taste
Freshly ground nutmeg
1½ cups chicken stock, heated to a boil

Wash and peel potatoes and slice ¼-inch thick. Generously butter the bottom and sides of a 9x13-inch casserole dish and rub with garlic. Arrange half of the potatoes in the dish, sprinkle with half the cheese, dot with half of the butter, and sprinkle with salt, pepper and nutmeg according to taste. Repeat with remaining potatoes, cheese, butter, salt, pepper and nutmeg. Pour heated stock over the top. Bake in a preheated 325 degree oven for about 1½ hours. Casserole should be crispy on top and all of the liquid should be absorbed.

Spinach Custard

Yield: Serves 8 to 10

- 2 medium yellow onions, chopped
- 1 clove garlic, minced
- 4 tablespoons vegetable oil
- 2 (10-ounce) packages frozen spinach
- 6 eggs, beaten
- 1 teaspoon salt
- ¼ teaspoon pepper
- 2 cups shredded Monterey Jack cheese
- 1 cup shredded sharp Cheddar cheese
- ¼ cup cottage cheese

Sauté onions and garlic in oil until soft. Cook spinach in medium saucepan over low heat until thawed, breaking blocks apart. Drain well and add to onion mixture. In large bowl beat eggs until foamy and season with salt and pepper. Stir in the cheeses and then combine with spinach mixture. Pour into a 2-quart casserole and bake in a preheated 400 degree oven for 40 minutes or until soft set. Stir 2 or 3 times while it bakes to insure even cooking.

Spaghetti Squash

Microwave

Yield: Serves 4 to 6

- 1 (4 to 5-pound) spaghetti squash
- ½ cup butter or margarine, softened
- ½ teaspoon Italian seasoning
- 3 tablespoons parsley, finely chopped
- ¼ teaspoon garlic powder
- ½ cup grated Parmesan cheese
- Dash of white pepper

Prick squash with a fork all over, including ends. Microwave for 5 to 6 minutes per pound on HIGH. (When squash is ready it yields to pressure and liquid bubbles from the fork slits.) Remove the squash from microwave with hot pads. Let stand, covered, for 10 minutes on a bread-board. To remove seeds slice down the middle and remove them with a fork from both halves. While the squash is cooling mix the softened butter, Italian seasoning, parsley, garlic powder, Parmesan cheese and pepper in a large bowl. Scoop out the spaghetti squash with a fork and add to the mixture in the bowl. Mix well. Warm for one minute in the microwave and serve. The shell of the squash may be used as a serving container if desired. Once the seeds are removed, fluff up the strains of squash with the tines of a fork. Within each half-shell, toss squash with the seasonings, warm for 1 to 2 minutes on HIGH if needed and serve.

Stufn' Squash Casserole

Yield: Serves 6 to 8

7 cups crookneck or zucchini squash, sliced
½ cup onion, chopped
1 (10¾-ounce) can condensed cream of chicken soup
1 cup dairy sour cream
1 cup shredded raw carrot
3 cups herb seasoned stuffing mix
1 cup butter or margarine, melted

Cook squash and onion, uncovered, in boiling salted water for 5 minutes, drain well. Combine soup, sour cream and carrot and blend with squash-onion mixture. Sprinkle two-thirds of the stuffing mixture in a 12-inch quiche dish or a 12x7½x2-inch baking dish. Spoon vegetable mixture on top. Sprinkle remaining stuffing around edges of the dish. Bake, uncovered, in preheated 350 degree oven for 20 to 25 minutes for quiche dish or 30 to 35 minutes for baking dish.

For economy of time and energy, when planning a menu around a casserole dish, choose accompanying dishes which require the same baking temperature.

Italian Zucchini Crescent Pie

Yield: Serves 6

4 cups thinly sliced unpeeled zucchini
1 cup coarsely chopped onion
½ cup butter or margarine
½ cup chopped parsley
½ teaspoon salt
½ teaspoon pepper
¼ teaspoon garlic powder
¼ teaspoon dried sweet basil leaves
¼ teaspoon dried oregano leaves
2 eggs, well beaten
2 cups (8-ounces) shredded Muenster or mozzarella cheese
1 (8-ounce) can refrigerated crescent dinner rolls
2 teaspoons Dijon or prepared mustard

Heat oven to 375 degrees. In 10-inch skillet, cook zucchini and onion in butter or margarine until tender, about 10 minutes. Cool mixture. Stir in parsley, salt, pepper, garlic powder, basil and oregano. In large bowl, blend eggs and cheese. Stir in vegetable mixture. Separate crescent dough into 8 triangles. Place in ungreased 11-inch quiche pan; press over bottom and up sides to form crust. Spread crust with mustard. Pour vegetable mixture evenly into crust. Bake at 375 degrees for 18-20 minutes or until knife inserted near center comes out clean; if crust becomes too brown, cover with foil during last 10 minutes of baking. Let stand 10 minutes before serving. Cut into wedges to serve. Serve hot.

Zucchini Provencale

Food Processor Yield: Serves 6
(A good summer vegetable with grilled meat-very colorful)

3 medium tomatoes, sliced
2 medium zucchini, sliced
¼ cup olive or vegetable oil
½ cup chopped parsley
2 teaspoons chopped shallots or green onions
1 clove garlic, minced
¼ teaspoon basil, crushed
¼ teaspoon thyme, crushed
¼ teaspoon salt
⅛ teaspoon pepper

Arrange tomatoes and zucchini in a 9x13-inch baking dish. In small bowl, combine oil, parsley, shallots, garlic, basil, thyme, salt and pepper. Pour over vegetables. Bake in a preheated 375 degree oven for 30 minutes, basting vegetables occasionally with liquids in pan.

Garlic Tomatoes

Yield: Serves 8 to 10

8 to 10 medium-sized tomatoes
Salt
2 tablespoons olive oil
2 tablespoons garlic, finely chopped
2 tablespoons parsley, minced
2 tablespoons fine bread crumbs
1 teaspoon salt
Pinch pepper

Core the tomatoes and cut in half horizontally. Squeeze the halves to remove juice and seeds. Sprinkle the bottom of a 9x13-inch baking dish with salt. Place tomatoes, cut side up, in the dish. Drizzle with the olive oil. Bake uncovered in a preheated 400 degree oven for 10 minutes. Combine the garlic, parsley, bread crumbs, salt and pepper. Sprinkle this mixture over the tomatoes and continue baking uncovered for 15 minutes longer or until tomatoes are soft throughout. Serve hot.

Vera Cruz Tomatoes

Yield: Serves 4

4 medium tomatoes
3 strips bacon
½ cup chopped yellow onion
8 ounces fresh spinach, snipped
½ cup dairy sour cream
Dash of hot pepper sauce
½ cup (2-ounces) shredded mozzarella cheese

Cut tops from tomatoes; remove the centers, leaving the shells. Lightly salt the shells. Invert shells on paper toweling and drain well. Meanwhile, cook bacon until crisp, reserving 2 tablespoons of the drippings. Crumble bacon and set aside. Cook onion in reserved bacon drippings until tender. Stir in spinach; cook, covered, until tender (about 3 to 5 minutes). Remove from heat and drain well. Combine sour cream, pepper sauce and bacon with spinach. Fill drained tomatoes with the spinach mixture and place in an 8-inch square casserole. Bake in a preheated 375 degree oven for 20 to 25 minutes. Top with shredded mozzarella and bake until cheese melts.

Captain Spaulding's Vegetables

Yield: Serves 10

7 to 9 carrots
2 bunches fresh broccoli
4 tablespoons butter or margarine
¼ cup cornstarch
3 cups milk
2½ cups shredded Cheddar cheese
1 (6-ounce) jar marinated artichoke hearts
Cayenne, salt, pepper, oregano, thyme and basil
½ to ¾ cup slivered, blanched almonds

Peel and halve carrots; cut into ½-inch julienne sticks. Cut broccoli tops into 1½ to 2-inch florets. Peel stalks and slice into ½-inch pieces. Steam carrots and broccoli separately until almost tender. Do not overcook. While vegetables steam, prepare sauce. Melt butter or margarine in pan. Combine cornstarch with milk and add to the melted butter. Stir over medium heat until thick. Blend in 1 cup of the grated cheese to the sauce. Place steamed carrots in buttered casserole dish. Drain artichokes and reserve marinade. Cut artichokes into bite-sized pieces and layer over carrots. Season lightly with cayenne, salt, pepper, oregano, thyme and basil. Add the broccoli, repeat the seasonings and sprinkle the artichoke marinade over the vegetables. Pour the cheese sauce over the vegetables and sprinkle with the remaining cheese and almonds. Bake in preheated 375 degree oven for 30 to 40 minutes or until bubbly.

Mixed Summer Vegetables

Yield: Serves 8

½ cup chopped onion
1 clove garlic, minced
2 tablespoons butter or margarine
2 cups coarsely chopped unpeeled zucchini
2 cups fresh corn kernels
2 cups peeled, seeded, and chopped tomato
2 to 3 tablespoons fresh snipped basil or 2 to 3 teaspoons dried basil, crushed

In a 10-inch skillet, cook the onion and garlic in the butter or margarine until tender but not brown. Add the zucchini; cook and stir over medium heat about 3 minutes. Stir in the corn; cook and stir 2 to 3 minutes more or until vegetables are tender-crisp. Stir in the tomato and basil. Cook 1 minute more or until vegetables are heated through but tomatoes are still firm. Season to taste with salt and pepper.

Ratatouille with Sausage

(Great light supper with a green salad and French bread)

Yield: Serves 6

1 large eggplant, peeled and cut into strips
4 medium zucchini, cut in ½-inch slices
Flour
Olive oil
3 large onions, sliced
3 cloves garlic, minced
3 green peppers, diced
4 tomatoes, peeled, seeded and cut into strips
½ cup parsley, chopped
1 teaspoon oregano
1 teaspoon thyme
1 teaspoon basil
Salt and pepper to taste
6 sweet or mild Italian sausages
Chopped parsley for garnish

Dredge eggplant and zucchini in flour. Heat oil in a large heavy skillet. Briefly sauté eggplant and zucchini in batches, over medium heat, for about 5 minutes. Remove and drain on paper toweling, reserve. Sauté onion, garlic and green pepper in same oil until soft. Add more oil if needed. Save pan to sauté sausages. Preheat oven to 350 degrees. Layer sautéed vegetables, tomatoes, parsley, oregano, thyme, basil, salt and pepper in a 3-quart casserole. Stir gently to mix. Cover, and bake for 35 minutes. Meanwhile, sauté sausages in reserved pan until browned. Remove sausages; drain on paper toweling and cool. Cut sausages into slices ¼-inch thick and return to pan. Sauté slices an additional 2 to 3 minutes on each side. Add more oil to pan if needed. Add sausages to baked vegetables, pushing slices down into the mixture, but reserving some for the top of the casserole. Return to the oven and bake, uncovered, for 20 minutes. Garnish with fresh parsley.

Note:
Flavor improves by making casserole 24 hours ahead and refrigerating. Bring to room temperature before reheating.

Stacked Vegetable Bake

(Use fresh grated cheese. Wonderful with lamb or beef)

Yield: Serves 12 to 16

2 medium eggplants, peeled and sliced crosswise into circles ½-inch thick
Salt
3 tablespoons vegetable oil
2 large zucchini, sliced
½ pound mushrooms, sliced
1 large green pepper, seeded and diced
2 large tomatoes, sliced
1 bunch fresh spinach, well washed and stems removed
2 cups grated asiago or Parmesan cheese
3 large tomatoes, chopped
Oregano
Salt and freshly ground pepper

Sprinkle eggplant generously with salt, place in colander and allow to stand at least 30 minutes. Rinse well and pat dry. Heat about 3 tablespoons oil in large skillet. Sauté eggplant in batches until lightly browned, adding oil as necessary; additional oil may be needed. Preheat oven to 375 degrees. Layer half the eggplant, zucchini, mushrooms, green pepper, sliced tomatoes, spinach, cheese and chopped tomatoes in greased 5 to 6-quart casserole or 2 (3-quart) casseroles. Sprinkle generously with oregano, salt and pepper. Repeat layering with remaining ingredients. Bake uncovered 30 to 40 minutes until vegetables are tender.

When baking more than one dish at the same time, stagger the containers on the oven racks so that one dish is never directly above another. Dishes should not touch each other or the sides of the oven.

Quick Blender Hollandaise

(Takes only a few minutes to prepare. This is great for Eggs Benedict or over asparagus.)

Yield: 1 cup

3 egg yolks
2 teaspoons fresh lemon juice
¼ teaspoon salt
Dash of cayenne
½ cup melted hot butter

Combine egg yolks, lemon juice, salt and cayenne in blender jar. Turn machine on and off several times to blend. With motor running, add hot melted butter in a slow steady stream to blender ingredients. Keep sauce warm until serving time by placing it in a small covered bowl which is placed in a shallow pan of very warm water or by holding it in a pre-warmed, wide-mouthed thermos bottle.

Notes

Rice & Pasta

Emerald Rice

Yield: Serves 8

- 2 bunches (1½ to 2-pounds) spinach, washed, stems removed, chopped to make about 10 cups
- 2 cloves garlic, minced
- ¼ cup butter or margarine
- 1½ cups (6-ounces) shredded Cheddar cheese
- ½ cup small curd cottage cheese
- ½ teaspoon salt
- ¼ teaspoon pepper
- 1½ cups (6-ounces) shredded mozzarella cheese
- 3 cups cooked rice

In a covered saucepan, cook spinach in the water that clings to the leaves. Cook only until spinach leaves are limp but still bright green. Drain well. In a small pan, sauté garlic in 1 tablespoon of the butter until light brown; add remaining 3 tablespoons butter, stirring over low heat until melted. Pour garlic butter over drained, cooked spinach. Stir in Cheddar and cottage cheese, salt and pepper. Spoon cooked rice into a buttered 1½-quart shallow baking pan; top with spinach mixture. Bake in a preheated 350 degree oven until cheeses are melted and blended, about 15 minutes. Top spinach layer with the mozzarella cheese. Broil until cheese is melted and light brown.

Pistachio Pilaf

Yield: Serves 2 to 4

- ¾ cup shelled pistachios
- 3 tablespoons butter
- 1 small onion, finely chopped
- 1 cup long-grained rice
- 2 cups chicken stock or broth
- ¾ cup California raisins
- Salt and pepper to taste

Blanch pistachios in boiling water for one minute; remove skins and halve them. Melt 2 tablespoons of the butter in a skillet; add onion and sauté until golden brown. Stir in the rice and cook, stirring all the while until the rice appears transparent and begins to brown. Add the stock and raisins and bring to a boil. Cover and let simmer 20 minutes until rice is tender. Let the rice stand covered for another 10 minutes. Stir in the pistachios and the remaining butter with a fork. Salt and pepper to taste.

Saffron Rice

Yield: Serves 6 to 8

4 cups chicken stock or consommé
½ teaspoon saffron
1 bay leaf
1 yellow onion, chopped
1 green pepper, finely diced
1 red pepper, finely diced
1 clove garlic, chopped
1 tablespoon safflower oil
2 cups long grain brown rice

Simmer the stock with the saffron and bay leaf for about 20 minutes. In a large frying pan sauté the onion, peppers and garlic in the oil until the onions turn translucent. Add the rice and cook, stirring, until the rice turns opaque. (Cooking the rice like this prevents it from becoming gummy when the liquid is added.) Strain the saffron and bay leaf from the chicken stock and add the stock to the rice. Cover frying pan and cook over very low heat until rice has absorbed all the liquid, approximately 50 minutes. Well cooked rice should still be slightly crunchy and be able to be separated into individual grains.

Nonee's Rice Torta

(This rice torta can also be served at room temperature as an appetizer.)

Yield: Serves 4 to 6

4½ cups water
2 teaspoons salt
1 tablespoon butter
2 cups rice
1 medium onion, chopped
2 tablespoons olive oil
½ cup (¼-pound) butter or margarine
6 eggs
1 cup grated Parmesan cheese
2¼ cups milk
⅛ teaspoon nutmeg
½ teaspoon basil
Salt to taste
1 teaspoon onion salt
½ teaspoon pepper
1 teaspoon garlic powder
½ pound fresh parsley, chopped
¼ cup dry bread crumbs

Topping:

1 egg
2 tablespoons melted butter
¼ cup Parmesan cheese

Bring water, salt and 1 tablespoon butter to a boil in a large pan. Add rice, stir to even out; lower temperature and simmer, covered, for 15 to 20 minutes. Meanwhile, in a small skillet, sauté onions in olive oil and ¼ pound butter or margarine. When rice is cooked, stir in sautéed onion-butter mixture and mix well to coat rice thoroughly. In a separate bowl, beat eggs; add Parmesan, milk, nutmeg, basil, salt, onion salt, pepper and garlic powder and blend together. Combine this mixture with rice and mix well. Add fresh parsley and toss to blend. Butter a 9x13-inch casserole; cover bottom and sides with bread crumbs. Pour in rice mixture and bake in a preheated 350 degree oven for 25 to 30 minutes. Remove from oven. Combine egg, melted butter and Parmesan together from the topping ingredients. Beat well and spoon over the rice mixture. Return casserole to oven and bake an additional 10 to 15 minutes or until topping mixture is lightly golden.

Green Fettucine with Scallops and Parsley Sauce

Food Processor

Yield: Serves 6

¼ cup fresh minced parsley
1 shallot, minced
4 tablespoons butter
½ cup California dry white wine
1 pound sea scallops, cut horizontally into ¼-inch slices
1 cup half and half or light cream
½ cup whipping cream or heavy cream
1 cup freshly grated Parmesan cheese, plus additional cheese for serving
⅓ cup + 2 tablespoons fresh parsley, minced
Freshly grated nutmeg
Salt and freshly ground pepper to taste
1 pound green fettucine
2 tablespoons unsalted butter, softened

In a skillet (other than cast iron) sauté the parsley and shallot in 2 tablespoons butter for 5 minutes. Add wine to the pan and reduce over high heat to about 6 tablespoons liquid. Add the scallops and cook, stirring, for 1 minute. Then add the light and heavy creams; simmer for 2 minutes. Remove from heat and add 1 cup Parmesan cheese, ⅓ cup parsley, nutmeg, salt and pepper to taste. Keep warm. Cook pasta in boiling salted water until al dente. Drain well and toss with unsalted butter, and then with completed sauce. Serve immediately.

Put butter in the water when cooking spaghetti, rice, etc., to prevent boiling over.

Fettucini Alla Romana

Yield: Serves 4 to 6

1 pound sweet or spicy Italian sausage
3 cups fresh mushrooms, sliced
1 large green pepper, cut into 1-inch squares
1 cup green onion, chopped
1 cup parsley, chopped
2 cloves garlic, minced
1 teaspoon dried basil
½ teaspoon dried rosemary
½ teaspoon dried oregano
½ cup olive oil
½ cup butter
1 pound fettucini, hot and cooked al dente
Grated Parmesan cheese

Remove casing from sausage. Crumble sausage and brown; drain off all excess fat. Set aside and keep warm. Sauté mushrooms, green pepper, green onion, parsley, garlic, basil, rosemary and oregano in olive oil-butter combination until green pepper is soft. Remove from heat. Stir in cooked sausage. Toss mixture with hot fettucini. Serve with Parmesan cheese.

Linguine with Clam and Shrimp Sauce

Yield: Serves 4 to 6

(This recipe goes quickly if all the ingredients are chopped and measured. Make the sauce while the linguine is cooking.)

8 tablespoons butter
3 cloves garlic, chopped
1 medium onion, chopped
¼ pound fresh mushrooms, sliced
1 tablespoon California dry sherry
2 tablespoons clam juice
1½ cups half and half or light cream
1 (4½-ounce) can clams
1 (4½-ounce) can shrimp
Parmesan cheese
2 dozen fresh clams
12 ounces linguine noodles
2 medium tomatoes, chopped
3 tablespoons fresh parsley, chopped
Parmesan cheese

Melt 6 tablespoons of the butter in a heavy saucepan. Add garlic and onion and sauté for 2 minutes. Meanwhile, in another pan, sauté the sliced mushrooms in 1 tablespoon of the butter and dry sherry. Add sautéed mushrooms to the onions and garlic along with the clam juice, half and half, canned clams, canned shrimp, and Parmesan. Stir until thickened. Steam fresh clams. Pluck meat from one dozen and add to sauce. Cook linguine noodles according to package directions. Drain linguine and return to pan with 1 tablespoon butter; toss. Add sauce, clams in shell, fresh tomatoes and parsley. Gently toss and serve immediately with additional Parmesan cheese.

Pasta with Marinated Artichoke Hearts

(A great meatless entree)

Yield: Serves 4

1 (6-ounce) jar marinated artichoke hearts
1 tablespoon olive oil
1 tablespoon butter or margarine
1 to 2 cloves garlic, finely minced
1 cup sliced onions
1 teaspoon dried basil
½ cup dairy sour cream
½ cup cottage cheese
Salt, pepper, cayenne and grated Parmesan cheese to taste
1 pound pasta of your choice

Drain liquid from marinated artichokes into skillet. Slice the drained artichoke hearts into bite size pieces and set aside. Add olive oil and butter or margarine to the marinade in the skillet. Heat mixture; add garlic and onions; sauté until soft (5 to 8 minutes). Add artichoke hearts and basil; sauté 3 to 5 minutes. Remove from heat; stir in sour cream, cottage cheese, salt, pepper, cayenne and Parmesan cheese. Keep sauce warm in a double boiler or on lowest heat setting. Cook and drain pasta according to directions on package. Toss immediately with warm sauce.

Pasta Primavera

(Hearty, colorful and fantastic) Yield: Serves 4 to 6

½ cup unsalted butter
1 medium onion, chopped
1 clove garlic, minced
1 pound asparagus, ends trimmed and sliced diagonally
10 large mushrooms, sliced
6 ounces cauliflower, broken into florets
1 medium zucchini, cut into ¼-inch slices
1 small carrot, halved lengthwise, cut into ½-inch diagonal slices
1 cup heavy or whipping cream
½ cup chicken broth
2 tablespoons fresh basil, chopped or 2 teaspoons dried basil
1 cup frozen small peas, thawed
2 ounces prosciutto or ham, chopped
5 green onions, chopped
Salt and pepper to taste
1 pound fettucini or linguini, cooked al dente and thoroughly drained
1 cup Parmesan cheese, freshly grated
Parmesan cheese

In a large skillet or wok, over medium heat, melt butter; add onion and garlic, sauté until soft—about 2 minutes. Add asparagus, mushrooms, cauliflower, zucchini and carrots and stir fry for 4 minutes. Remove vegetables; set aside and keep warm. Increase heat to high; add cream, broth and basil; boil until liquid is reduced and somewhat thickened—about 3 minutes. Stir in peas, ham, and green onion and cook 1 minute more. Season to taste with salt and pepper. Add pasta and Parmesan cheese, tossing until thoroughly combined. Turn onto large, heated platter and garnish with reserved vegetables. Pass additional Parmesan cheese.

Spaghetti—Coal Venders' Style

Yield: Serves 3 to 4

- 4 cloves garlic, slightly crushed
- 2 tablespoons olive oil
- ⅓ to ½ pound pancetta or bacon, chopped
- ¼ to ⅓ cup California dry white wine
- 3 large whole eggs, slightly beaten
- ½ cup or more Parmesan and/or Romano cheese, freshly grated
- Freshly ground black pepper, to taste
- Salt to taste
- 2 tablespoons parsley, finely chopped
- 1 pound spaghetti or spaghettini

Sauté garlic in olive oil until garlic is golden. Discard garlic. Add pancetta or bacon and sauté until edges curl slightly. Do not overcook. Add wine and let boil for 3 to 4 minutes. Remove from heat and set aside. In large bowl from which you will serve the pasta, place beaten eggs, grated cheese, black pepper, salt, and parsley; beat together, blending well. Place in warm, but not hot, spot. (Too hot a spot, like an oven, will cook the eggs. The eggs should not cook; they will help coat the pasta and make a delicious sauce.) Cook the pasta in salted boiling water (3 tablespoons salt to 5-quarts of water). Reheat pancetta mixture. Drain pasta; place drained pasta in bowl with egg mixture; mix vigorously to coat pasta. Pour very hot pancetta mixture over the pasta and mix again. Serve immediately with more freshly grated Parmesan or Romano cheese.

Spaghetti Asparagus Francaise

(A marvelous springtime dish when asparagus is at its peak.)

Yield: Serves 4

¼ cup butter or margarine
1½ tablespoons olive oil
½ onion, thinly sliced
1 slice Parma ham, chopped (Italian-type ham)
½ pound asparagus, washed and cut into very thin, diagonal slices
½ cup water
1 chicken bouillon cube
½ pound thin spaghetti or vermicelli
½ cup half and half or light cream
¼ cup grated Parmesan cheese
Freshly ground pepper

Heat butter and oil in 1-quart saucepan over medium-high heat. Add onion and sauté until golden (do not brown). Add ham and sauté briefly. Add asparagus, water and bouillon cube. Reduce heat and simmer 15 minutes. Add spaghetti to large pot of rapidly boiling salted water and cook al dente, about 5 to 6 minutes. Drain well. Return spaghetti to pot. Add asparagus mixture and half and half and cook over medium-low heat until warmed through. Top with Parmesan and pepper before serving.

Spaghetti Pie

(Children are fascinated by the idea of a spaghetti crust.)

Yield: Serves 4 to 6

6 ounces thin spaghetti (spaghettini)
2 tablespoons butter or margarine
⅓ cup Parmesan cheese
2 eggs, well beaten
1 pound ground beef or Italian bulk sausage
½ cup onion, chopped
¼ cup green pepper, chopped
1 (8-ounce) can tomatoes, cut up
1 (6-ounce) can tomato paste
1 teaspoon sugar
1 teaspoon oregano
½ teaspoon garlic salt
1 cup ricotta or small curd cottage cheese
½ cup grated mozzarella cheese

Cook and drain spaghetti according to package directions. Toss with butter, Parmesan cheese, and eggs. Form into crust in a buttered 10-inch pie plate. Cook ground meat or sausage, onion and green pepper until meat is browned. Drain off excess fat. Stir in undrained tomatoes, tomato paste, sugar, oregano and garlic salt; simmer 2 to 3 minutes. Spread ricotta or cottage cheese over crust. Top with ground meat mixture. Bake, uncovered, in a preheated 350 degree oven for 20 minutes. Sprinkle with mozzarella cheese. Return to oven and bake until cheese melts. Cut in wedges to serve.

Company Lasagna

Yield: Serves 8 to 10

2 pounds lean ground beef
1 clove garlic, minced
1 tablespoon parsley, minced
1 tablespoon basil, minced
1½ teaspoons salt
1 (1-pound) can tomatoes, cut up with liquid
2 (6-ounce) cans tomato paste
1 cup sliced ripe olives, drained
1 (10-ounce) package lasagna noodles
2 eggs, beaten
3 cups cottage cheese
1½ teaspoons salt
½ teaspoon pepper
½ cup Parmesan cheese, grated
16 ounces mozzarella cheese, grated

Brown meat; drain off fat. Add garlic, parsley, basil, salt, tomatoes, tomato paste and olives. Simmer uncovered for 30 minutes. Cook noodles according to package directions; drain and rinse in cold water. Combine eggs, cottage cheese, salt, pepper and Parmesan cheese. In a 9x13-inch dish, layer ½ noodles, ½ cottage cheese mixture, ½ mozzarella cheese, ½ meat sauce. Repeat layers, reversing meat sauce and mozzarella cheese. Bake in a preheated 375 degree oven for 30 minutes or until hot and bubbly throughout. Allow casserole to stand for 10 to 15 minutes before cutting into serving portions.

Stuffed Jumbo Pasta Shells

Yield: Serves 6 to 8

Sauce:

1½ pounds ground beef
½ pound pork sausage
2 tablespoons oil
1 large onion, chopped
2 cloves garlic, minced
1 teaspoon dried basil
½ teaspoon dried rosemary, crushed
1 bay leaf
2 teaspoons salt
½ teaspoon pepper
3 (8-ounce) cans tomato sauce
2 (15-ounce) cans tomato puree
3 cups water
1 teaspoon dried oregano

Cook ground beef and sausage until brown and crumbly. Drain off excess fat. Set aside. In large saucepan, sauté onions and garlic in the oil. Add meats, basil, rosemary, bay leaf, salt, pepper, tomato sauce, tomato puree, water and oregano. Bring to a boil; reduce heat and simmer for 2½ hours, stirring occasionally.

Shell Stuffing:

1 pound ground round
1 small yellow onion, finely chopped
1 clove garlic, minced
3 tablespoons butter or margarine
1 (10-ounce) package frozen chopped spinach, thawed and well drained
1 pound ricotta cheese
1 cup grated mozzarella cheese
½ cup Parmesan cheese
2 eggs beaten
½ teaspoon salt
½ teaspoon pepper
¼ cup chopped parsley
1 (12-ounce) package jumbo pasta shells

In a wide skillet cook meat until brown. Drain excess fat. Set aside. Sauté onion and garlic in butter or margarine. Add spinach and cook five minutes. Drain off any liquid and set aside to cool. In a large bowl combine ricotta cheese, ½ cup of the mozzarella cheese, the Parmesan cheese, eggs, salt, pepper and parsley. Add the meat mixture and mix until well blended. Set aside. Cook pasta shells according to package directions. Drain and place shells in cold water. Drain again. Stuff shells with cheese and meat mixture. Spoon enough sauce into the bottom of a 9x13-inch baking dish to cover. Arrange shells in a single layer. Pour over more sauce to cover shells. Sprinkle the remaining ½ cup grated mozzarella cheese over top of shells. Bake in a preheated 350 degree oven for about 20 minutes or until hot and bubbly.

Malfatti

(Malfatti is like the inside of a ravioli. If overcooked they fall apart.)

Yield: Serves 6 to 8

2 cups diced sweet French bread
½ cup water
½ cup milk
2 (10-ounce) packages frozen chopped spinach
1 medium yellow onion, diced
1 clove garlic, minced
½ cup chopped parsley
3 tablespoons butter or margarine
3 tablespoons vegetable oil
2 eggs, well beaten
⅔ cup grated Parmesan cheese
Salt and pepper to taste
All-purpose flour
Tomato sauce or cream sauce (your own favorite)

Soak bread in ½ cup water and ½ cup milk until soft. Drain and squeeze dry. Parboil spinach, drain and squeeze dry. In a medium skillet, sauté spinach, bread, onion, garlic and parsley in butter and oil. Cool completely. Add beaten eggs to mixture and mix together in a large bowl. Add cheese and salt and pepper and mix well. Dust bread board with flour and roll a tablespoon of above mixture into a cylinder shape about the size of a small sausage. Continue until all mixture is shaped. (The malfatti may be dusted with flour at this point and layered in a container and frozen for later use. They can be removed directly from freezer to be cooked as indicated below.) Drop the malfatti into a large kettle of boiling salt water. When the malfatti rise to the surface of the water, they are done. Remove with a slotted spoon and drain well. Serve as you would ravioli, with your favorite tomato sauce or white cream sauce.

Marinara Sauce
(Fish of the Sea Sauce)

Yield: Serves 6 to 8

1 onion, finely chopped
3 cloves garlic, minced
3 carrots, finely chopped
3 to 4 stalks celery, chopped
½ cup parsley, minced
3 to 4 tablespoons olive oil
2 tablespoons butter
2 (28-ounce) cans tomatoes
1 teaspoon dried oregano, crumbled
2 teaspoons dried basil, crumbled
1 to 2 teaspoons sugar
1 teaspoon baking soda
1 (2-ounce) can anchovies
1½ pounds of tuna, whole baby clams, shrimp, or combination of all three

In a large stock pot, sauté onion and garlic in olive oil and butter until golden. Add carrots, celery and parsley and cook until soft. Add tomatoes, oregano, basil, sugar, baking soda and anchovies. Simmer 40 minutes. Add fish and cook for an additional 20 minutes longer adjusting seasonings if needed. Serve over linguine or other types of pasta.

Pesto Sauce

Food Processor

Yield: 4 to 6 cups

2 cups (packed) fresh basil leaves
3 cloves garlic
2 to 4 tablespoons pine nuts
1 teaspoon salt
¾ cup light olive oil
½ cup freshly grated Parmesan cheese
¼ cup freshly grated romano cheese

In a food processor or a blender, combine the basil, garlic, pine nuts and salt. Process until smooth. With the motor running, add the oil through the feed tube and process until well blended. Pour the basil mixture into a bowl and mix in the cheeses. Toss sauce with hot pasta of your choice. This sauce freezes well and is nice to serve with a salad for summer supper.

Pistachio Sauce for Pasta

Yield: about 1 cup

¼ cup fresh basil
2 tablespoons chopped parsley
3 cloves garlic
4 fresh spinach leaves, washed and dried
6 tablespoons shelled pistachios
6 tablespoons olive oil
¼ cup grated Parmesan cheese
2 tablespoons butter
Salt and pepper to taste
Hot pasta

Place basil, parsley, garlic, spinach, pistachios and olive oil in a blender jar or processor work bowl and puree. Add Parmesan cheese and process for a few more seconds. Toss hot pasta with the 2 tablespoons butter; then with pistachio sauce. Add salt and pepper to taste. Top with additional Parmesan if desired.

"A PINT'S A POUND THE WORLD AROUND"

1 wineglass	= ¼ cup
1 gill	= ½ cup
1 teacup	= a scant ¾ cup
1 coffee cup	= 1 scant cup
1 tumbler	= 1 cup
1 pint	= 2 cups
1 quart	= 4 cups
1 peck	= 2 dry gallons
1 pinch	= what can be picked up between thumb and first two fingers
½ pinch	= what can be picked up between thumb and one finger
1 saltspoon	= ¼ teaspoon
1 teaspoon	= 1 teaspoon or 1 kitchen teaspoon
1 dessertspoon	= 2 teaspoons or 1 soupspoon
1 spoonful	= 1 tablespoon, more or less

Foothills
Auberry

Auberry Road runs from the city of Clovis, up through the foothills toward the high Sierra and the John Muir Wilderness Area. As the road winds through the little hills and valleys, the magnificent California White Oaks dot the landscape offering shade to a variety of mountain animals. In the spring the green grass is ablaze with wildflowers; the golden-orange of the California Poppy, the purple-blue of mountain Lupin, the dusty-rose of Indian Paintbrush. Each flower a delight to the spirit and a treasure to the state.

During the "gold rush" days, the foothills were alive with little mining camp towns. Names like Drunken Gulch, Dogtown, Poverty Flat, Poison Springs, Break-neck and Tarantula Flat were legend among the miners. The most infamous of all, however, was Hornitos. Founded in 1850, by Mexican miners, gamblers and dance-hall women who had been invited to leave Quartzburgh by a well-armed "law and order committee", the town soon became one of the most important travel stops between Los Angeles and the port of Stockton.

Hornitos "Little Ovens", was named after Los Hornitos, Durango, Mexico, which would indicate that the "founding fathers" were from that region. A wide-open town, Hornitos was the "hideout" of early-day bandidos. The most famous bandido of them all was Joaquín Murrieta. He is a well-loved and romantic felon, called "El Famoso" by the Mexicans, and the true story of his life is lost in legend. As the story goes, Joaquín came up from Sonora, Mexico with his young wife and his brother, to work the land. Some time later, he was attacked by five "gringo" miners, his brother hanged and his wife assaulted. It was then that he started his life of crime and vengence. He soon dispatched all five "gringos" and began to run with a gang that included Manuel Duarté, the famous "Three-fingered Jack". Together, they managed to terrorize the area. It is said that he had a secret tunnel under the main street of Hornitos for use in escaping from a saloon to the stable.

In 1853, the authorities believed that they had ended his life in a "shoot-out" at Cantúa, but the Mexicans believed that he died in his bed, two days later, and was quietly buried by a sister. No one knows for sure; but what they do know, is that on warm spring and summer nights, his ghost can be seen riding through the foothills.

Fish

Halibut Provencal

Yield: Serves 4

3 tablespoons olive oil
1 medium onion, cut in half and thinly sliced
2 cloves fresh garlic, minced
1 large green bell pepper, diced or cut in julienne strips
4 anchovy fillets, chopped
12 black pitted olives, sliced
1½ teaspoons fennel seeds
Salt and pepper to taste
4 halibut steaks
½ cup tomato puree
1 tomato, thinly sliced
1 tablespoon chopped parsley
½ cup California red wine

In a skillet heat oil; add onion, garlic, green pepper and cook until the onion is soft but not browned. Add the anchovy, olives and fennel. Place the fish in a greased skillet and spread with the mixture and top each piece of fish with a tomato slice. Brush with oil and salt and pepper. Mix the wine and the purée together and pour over the fish. Cook in either the oven or the broiler until done, about 7 minutes. Sprinkle with the chopped parsley.

Note:
This recipe may be used with fish fillets, cooking 1 minutes less.

Dilled Salmon Steaks

Yield: Serves 4

4 fresh or frozen salmon steaks or fillets
2 tablespoons fresh lemon juice
2 teaspoons minced onion
Salt and white pepper
¼ cup dairy sour cream
½ teaspoon dried dillweed
1 teaspoon grated lemon peel

Place fresh or thawed steaks in a lightly greased baking dish. Combine lemon juice and onion; sprinkle over fish. Season with salt and white pepper. Bake, uncovered, in a preheated 350 degree oven until fish flakes easily when tested with a fork, about 20 minutes. Remove from oven and spread mixed sour cream and dill over salmon, and sprinkle with lemon peel. Bake 3 minutes longer; serve with lemon wedges if desired.

Salmon with Leeks and Caviar

Yield: 4 servings

1½ to 2 pounds fresh salmon fillet
Salt and pepper
1½ cups dry California white wine
1 cup heavy or whipping cream
2 leeks, white part only, julienned
Juice of 1 lemon
1 tomato, chopped
½ cup (1-stick) unsalted butter
Fresh herbs (Herbs de Provence)
Fresh caviar

Cut the salmon fillet into 4 equal portions. Season with salt and pepper and slowly poach it in the white wine for 5 to 8 minutes. Carefully remove the salmon and keep warm. Reduce the wine in the poaching pan to ½ cup. Add the cream and the leeks, bring to a boil until slightly thickened. Stir in the lemon juice, chopped tomato and swirl in the sweet butter. Taste for salt and pepper. Add the fresh herbs. Spoon sauce over the cooked fillets and garnish with fresh caviar.

Sole with Shrimp Sauce

(The beauty of this dish is that it calls for no last-minute preparation)

Yield: Serves 8

6 to 8-ounces fish trimmings
½ cup water
½ cup California dry white wine
½ medium onion, sliced
½ carrot, sliced
1 small celery stalk with leaves
1 tablespoon fresh lemon juice
¼ teaspoon sugar
Salt and freshly ground pepper

8 small sole fillets (use a firm sole such as Petrale)
3 tablespoons butter
2 tablespoons all-purpose flour
⅓ cup heavy or whipping cream
Salt and freshly ground white pepper
1 pound small or medium cooked shrimp

In a medium saucepan, combine fish trimmings, water, wine, onion, carrot, celery, lemon juice and sugar, with salt and pepper to taste. Place over high heat and bring to a boil; reduce heat and simmer about 30 minutes. Strain and set aside. Preheat oven to 400 degrees. Fold fish fillets crosswise in thirds, as if folding a letter, and place in baking dish large enough to hold them in a single layer. Sprinkle lightly with salt and pour reserved stock over. Cover and bake 10 minutes. Transfer fish to individual ovenproof gratin dishes, reserving cooking liquid. Cover and refrigerate. Melt butter in skillet over medium heat. Stir in flour. Remove from heat and gradually stir in 1 cup reserved cooking liquid. Return to heat and cook until thickened. Add cream and season to taste with salt and pepper. Remove from heat and stir in shrimp. Spoon sauce over fish, cover and return to refrigerator. When ready to serve, preheat oven to 400 degrees. Bake fish uncovered for 10 to 15 minutes, or until sauce bubbles and fish is completely heated through.

Sole Florentine

Yield: Serves 4 to 6

3 (10-ounce) packages frozen chopped spinach
2 cups dairy sour cream
3 tablespoons flour
½ cup green onions, finely chopped, including some tops
Juice of 1 lemon
1 to 2 teaspoons salt
2 tablespoons butter
1½ to 2 pounds thin fillets of sole
Paprika

Cook spinach according to package directions; blot dry completely. Blend sour cream with flour, onion, lemon juice and salt and combine ½ of this mixture with the spinach. Spread spinach mixture evenly over the bottom of a large shallow baking dish about 10x15-inches. (Select one suitable for serving). Arrange sole fillets on top of spinach, overlapping as needed. Dot with butter. Spread remaining sour cream mixture evenly over fish, leaving a border to show spinach. Dust lightly with paprika. (At this point you can refrigerate dish until ready to cook.) Bake in a preheated 375 degree oven for 25 minutes, or until fish flakes when broken with a fork.

Merry Old Sole

Yield: 1 to 2 servings

2 small fillets of sole
5 to 6 medium scallops
¼ cup Dungeness crab
¼ cup small salad shrimp
¼ cup shredded mozzarella or Monterey Jack cheese
¾ cup hollandaise sauce (use your favorite recipe)
Paprika and minced parsley for garnish

Preheat oven to 450 degrees. Lightly butter a small or individual-size casserole. Place 1 sole fillet on bottom and layer with scallops, crab, shrimp and cheese. Top with second fillet and cover with hollandaise. Bake until fish flakes and sauce is bubbly, 10 to 15 minutes. Sprinkle with paprika and parsley.

Hot Crab Sandwiches

(Good for luncheon or a light dinner) Yield: 6 sandwiches

3 small loaves French bread
2 (7½-ounce) cans crabmeat
½ cup mayonnaise
2 tablespoons fresh lemon juice
2 tablespoons green onion, finely chopped
2 tablespoons water chestnuts, minced
1 teaspoon salt
¼ teaspoon pepper
6 slices Swiss cheese
Sesame seeds

Slice loaves in half, lengthwise, set aside. In a medium bowl, combine crabmeat, mayonnaise, lemon juice, green onions, water chestnuts, salt and pepper. Just before serving time, spread an equal amount of filling on each bread half. Top with cheese and sprinkle with sesame seeds. Place sandwich halves under broiler until cheese melts.

Lobster Newburg

Yield: Serves 4 to 6

6 tablespoons butter or margarine
4 tablespoons flour
3 cups cooked or canned lobster meat
⅛ teaspoon nutmeg
Paprika
1 teaspoon salt
3 tablespoons California dry sherry
3 egg yolks
2 cups light cream
Toast points

Melt butter or margarine in double-boiler, over low heat. Stir in flour, lobster, nutmeg, paprika, salt and sherry. Beat yolks slightly; add cream and mix well. Slowly stir yolk mixture into lobster; cook over hot water, stirring until just thickened. Serve at once on toast points or in patty shells.

Note:
May substitute 3 cups scallops or 3 cups shrimp for lobster.

Coquilles St. Jacques À La Provencale

Yield: Serves 4 to 6

1 clove garlic, minced
⅓ cup minced onion
1 tablespoon butter
1½ teaspoons green onion, minced

Sauté onions and garlic in butter until translucent, but not browned. Set aside.

1½ pounds raw scallops, rinsed well
Salt and pepper to taste
1 cup all-purpose flour, sifted
2 tablespoons butter
1 tablespoon olive oil

Dry scallops well and slice ¼-inch thick. Sprinkle with salt and pepper, and roll in flour, shake off excess and sauté in butter and olive oil mixture until lightly golden.

⅔ cup California dry white wine
½ bay leaf, crumbled
⅛ teaspoon thyme
¼ cup grated Swiss cheese

Pour wine into skillet with scallops. Add bay leaf, thyme, and sautéed onion mixture. Cover and simmer 5 minutes. Uncover, and cook for 1 minute more or until slightly thickened. Adjust seasoning to taste. Spoon scallops into individual buttered, oven-proof dishes; sprinkle with cheese and broil until bubbly and lightly golden, just before serving.

Note:
May also use as a hot appetizer.

Scallop and Vegetable Pesto

Yield: Serves 2

Pesto Sauce:

1 tablespoon grated Parmesan cheese
2 tablespoons dried basil
4 tablespoons fresh parsley
1 tablespoon vegetable oil

In a small bowl, blend Parmesan, basil, parsley flakes and oil together. Reserve.

Scallops and Vegetables:

⅓ to ¾ pound scallops
3 tablespoons butter or margarine
1 carrot, sliced in ¼-inch thick pieces
1 small onion, cut into 1-inch squares
1 small zucchini, sliced into ¼-inch thick pieces
8 to 10 small mushrooms, halved
½ small green pepper, cut into 1-inch squares
Pesto sauce or 2 tablespoons thawed frozen pesto mix prepared according to package directions
Grated Parmesan cheese

Rinse the scallops well; drain, then pat dry with paper toweling. Cut scallops into slices about ¼-inch thick, cover and set aside. In a large frying pan, melt 1 tablespoon of the butter or margarine over medium-high heat. Add the carrot slices and onion and sauté, stirring, for 2 minutes. Add another tablespoon of the butter or margarine along with the zucchini, mushrooms and green pepper; cook, stirring, for about 2 more minutes or until vegetables are tender-crisp. Turn the vegetables out of the pan and keep warm. Add the remaining 1 tablespoon butter or margarine to the pan. Stir in the pesto sauce. Add the scallops and cook, stirring, until scallops are firm and just opaque throughout, about 4 minutes. Return vegetables to pan and heat, stirring, for several minutes. Turn the mixture into a shallow serving dish or 2 individual ramekins (about 2-cup size). Sprinkle with grated Parmesan cheese and serve with hot cooked rice.

Scallop-Shrimp Curry

Yield: Serves 6

6 tablespoons butter or margarine
6 tablespoons flour
2 teaspoons curry powder
1 teaspoon salt
¼ teaspoon pepper
½ teaspoon Beau Monde seasoning
2 teaspoons onion juice
Juice of 2 lemons
10½ ounces condensed bouillon
1 cup milk
1 to 1½ cups low-fat milk (depending on desired thickness of sauce)
1 pound small raw scallops
1 pound small cooked shrimp

Melt butter or margarine and stir in flour until smooth. Blend in curry powder, salt, pepper, Beau Monde seasoning, onion juice and lemon juice. Add the bouillon and milk gradually and cook over low heat, stirring constantly until thickened. Add 1 pound scallops to sauce and simmer for 6 minutes. Do not overcook scallops. Add 1 pound small shrimp. Heat and serve over hot rice.

Honey Broiled Scallops

Yield: Serves 4

1 pound fresh scallops
3 tablespoons fresh lime juice
2 tablespoons vegetable oil
1 tablespoon honey
1 tablespoon soy sauce
¼ teaspoon ground ginger
¼ teaspoon sesame seeds, toasted

Rinse scallops. In a 2-quart mixing bowl, combine lime juice, oil, honey, soy sauce and ginger. Add scallops and toss until well coated. Cover and chill 3 to 6 hours, stirring frequently. Remove scallops from marinade, reserving marinade. Thread scallops evenly on 4 skewers. Broil 4-inches from source of heat for 3 to 5 minutes, or until scallops are opaque, turning occasionally and basting with reserved marinade. If desired, place sesame seeds on waxed paper and roll each broiled skewer over the seeds to evenly coat scallops. Serve immediately.

Note:
When using wooden skewers, soak skewers in water for at least 1 hour before threading. This prevents the skewers from burning during the broiling step.

Scampi A La Créme

Yield: Serves 2 to 4

2 tablespoons olive oil
4 tablespoons butter
¼ cup chopped onion
1 clove garlic, minced
¼ teaspoon salt
⅛ teaspoon pepper
1 pound raw jumbo shrimp, shelled, deveined and rinsed
⅔ cup California dry white wine
2 egg yolks
⅓ cup heavy or whipping cream
½ cup California brandy

Heat oil and butter in chafing dish or frying pan, and sauté onion and garlic for 3 minutes. Season with salt and pepper and stir in shrimp. Cook about 8 to 10 minutes, or until shrimp are done and pink. Spoon out shrimp to a heated platter, leaving pan juices. Pour wine into juices and cook over high heat until wine is reduced by one-third. Beat egg yolks and cream together and add to sauce. Reduce heat and cook until sauce starts to thicken, stirring constantly. Do not boil. Pour warmed brandy over shrimp and ignite. As soon as flames die, pour sauce over and serve immediately.

Shrimp Supper Pie

(Nice for a ladies' luncheon, or light supper)

Yield: Serves 4 to 6

- 1 (9-inch) unbaked pieshell
- 1 cup (4-ounces) shredded sharp Cheddar cheese
- 1 (4½-ounce) can small shrimp, drained and well rinsed
- ¼ cup sliced green onions, including tops
- 3 eggs, beaten
- 1 (6½-ounce) can evaporated milk, undiluted
- ½ teaspoon salt
- ¼ teaspoon dry mustard
- 1 tablespoon fresh lemon juice

Sprinkle cheese evenly over the bottom of unbaked pastry shell. Place well-drained shrimp over cheese and top with green onions. Combine eggs, evaporated milk, salt, dry mustard and lemon juice, and pour over mixture in shell. (If made ahead, place in refrigerator until ready to bake.) Bake in a preheated 325 degree oven for about 40 minutes or until filling is set. Remove from oven and let stand 10 minutes before cutting.

Fireworks Shrimp

Wok

Yield: Serves 4

1 pound raw medium shrimp, shelled and deveined
3 garlic cloves, finely minced
⅓ to ½ teaspoon finely minced fresh ginger
1 tablespoon Chinese chili paste with garlic
3 tablespoons tomato sauce or purée
2 tablespoons California dry sherry
1 tablespoon Chinese oyster sauce
1 tablespoon light soy sauce
1 teaspoon red wine vinegar
1 teaspoon sesame oil
½ teaspoon sugar
2 tablespoons peanut oil
¼ pound snow peas, trimmed
4 bok choy (Chinese cabbage) stalks, cut diagonally into 1½-inch pieces
3 green onions, cut diagonally in 3-inch pieces
2 tablespoons cornstarch mixed with 3 tablespoons cold water

Cut shrimp in half lengthwise and set aside. Combine minced garlic, ginger and chili paste in small bowl and set aside. Blend tomato sauce, sherry, oyster sauce, soy sauce, vinegar, sesame oil and sugar in another bowl and set aside. Heat wok to very hot over high heat. Add 1 tablespoon peanut oil and roll around sides of wok. When oil just begins to smoke, add shrimp and stir-fry only until translucent. Tip shrimp out onto a plate and cover with wok top. Immediately return wok to high heat. Add remaining 1 tablespoon peanut oil and roll around sides of wok. Add garlic mixture, snow peas, bok choy and green onion pieces and stir-fry until snow peas turn bright green. Pour tomato sauce mixture around sides of wok. Return shrimp to wok. Stir in small amount of cornstarch solution to thicken. Taste and adjust seasoning. Serve immediately.

Shrimp Etouffé

Yield: Serves 2 to 4

½ cup (1-stick) butter
½ cup prepared chili sauce
¼ cup chopped onion
¼ cup chopped celery
2 pounds raw shrimp, shelled, deveined and seasoned with salt, pepper and cayenne
¼ cup California dry white wine
¼ cup chopped parsley
2 tablespoons shallots, minced
Hot cooked rice

In a large skillet, melt butter over medium heat. Add chili sauce, onion and celery and sauté until vegetables are tender. Add shrimp and wine and sauté until shrimp turns pink, about 5 minutes. Stir in parsley and shallots. Serve immediately over rice.

Sweet and Sour Sauce

(Great for fried won tons, fish or chicken)

Yield: 2 cups

3 tablespoons corn starch
1 cup sugar
1 (20-ounce) can pineapple chunks
½ cup cider vinegar
1 cup water
¼ cup catsup
½ green pepper, diced
Red food coloring (optional)

Combine corn starch and sugar together in a saucepan. Drain pineapple chunks and set aside. Add the drained juice, vinegar, water and catsup to the saucepan; heat, stirring constantly, until mixture thickens. Stir in drained pineapple chunks and green pepper and cook until heated through. Optional red food coloring may be added to achieve desired sauce color.

Oven-Barbecued Shrimp

(*A simple and delicious Creole recipe*) Yield: Serves 2 to 4

2 pounds large shrimp; peeled, slit down back and cleaned
½ cup unsalted butter
3 tablespoons olive oil
2 tablespoons prepared chili sauce
1 tablespoon Worcestershire sauce
1 tablespoon fresh lemon juice
½ lemon, thinly sliced
2 cloves garlic, minced
1 teaspoon minced fresh parsley
¾ teaspoon cayenne pepper
¾ teaspoon Liquid Smoke
½ teaspoon paprika
½ teaspoon oregano
¼ teaspoon Tabasco sauce

Clean shrimp; pat dry and spread in shallow baking pan. Combine unsalted butter, olive oil, chili sauce, Worcestershire sauce, lemon juice, lemon slices, garlic, parsley, cayenne, Liquid Smoke, paprika, oregano and Tabasco sauce in a small saucepan and simmer 10 minutes. Pour over shrimp and mix thoroughly. Cover and refrigerate 2 to 3 hours, stirring every 30 minutes. Preheat oven to 300 degrees. Bake shrimp, turning frequently, until they just turn pink, about 15 to 20 minutes. Do not overbake. Adjust seasonings to taste with salt and pepper. Serve in soup bowls with lots of French bread to soak up sauce.

Do not overcook fish. It is ready to serve when the flesh is easily "flaked" with a fork.

Poultry

Chicken Sautéed with Roasted Garlic and Candied Lemon Peel

Yield: Serves 2 to 4

2 whole chickens
1 head garlic
3 tablespoons vegetable oil
Salt and pepper
¼ cup California white wine
1 shallot, chopped
1 cup chicken stock
1 cup whipping cream or heavy cream
Juice of 1 lemon
2 tablespoons butter, softened
1 tablespoon chives

Bone the chickens, reserving the bones for stock. Peel garlic and separate into cloves. Place in a foil-lined pan and sprinkle with a little oil, salt and pepper. Roast in a preheated 375 degree oven for 45 minutes. In a sauté pan, heat 3 tablespoons of oil until very hot; add the chicken (skin side down) and sauté until brown, about 8 minutes. Turn the chicken over and sauté for another 2 minutes. Remove the chicken and keep warm. In the same pan, deglaze with the white wine and add the shallot and the roasted garlic; reduce until the liquid evaporates. Add the chicken stock and reduce by half. Discard garlic. Add the heavy cream and bring to a boil until it thickens. Add the lemon juice, salt and pepper to taste. Stir in the soft butter and add the fresh chives. To serve, pour the sauce over the chicken and garnish with the candied lemon peel.

Candied Lemon Peel:

Peel of 1 lemon
¼ cup sugar
¼ cup water

To candy the lemon peel, boil the peel in equal parts of sugar and water until water evaporates.

FIRST UNITED
METHODIST
CHURCH
PASTOR
FIRST UNITED
METHODIST
CHURCH
CHURCH SCHOOL
FAMILY WORSHIP

First United Methodist Church
Selma

The First United Methodist Church of Selma, California was organized in 1881. The present church building, of English-Normandy style, was designed by the well-known architect Roger K. Nisson. Following its completion in 1939, it became known as "The Beautiful Church In The Valley".

In the Mariposa Gazette, August 3, 1867, the following appeared. "A California gold-digger, having become rich, desired a friend to procure for him a library of books. The friend obeyed and received a letter of thanks, thus worded: 'I am obliged to you for the pains of your selection. I particularly admire a grand religious poem about Paradise by a Mr. Milton, and a set of plays, quite delightful, by a Mr. Shakespeare. If these gentlemen should write and publish anything more, be sure and send me their new works.' "

In his search for a better life, the miner knew that education was important, even if his letter was a few hundred years off, and the early settlers were no exception. In 1872, the first secondary school in Fresno County was established in the town of Academy. The school had fifty students, the children of local farmers and miners, and a library of fifty-six volumes.

Today, in Fresno, there are 56 elementary schools, 13 middle schools, 7 high schools, 9 Parochial schools, 1 junior college, 5 colleges, 1 University (the home of the "Battling Bulldogs" and the famous "Red Wave") and a variety of vocational schools.

Chicken Alberghetti

(This recipe was given to a Junior League member while interviewing actress Anna Maria Alberghetti, well known for her cooking skills.)

Yield: Serves 6

3 whole chicken breasts, boned and skinned
2 eggs, well beaten
Seasoned bread crumbs
Salt and pepper to taste
Butter and olive oil—equal amounts
1 (10¼-ounce) can marinara sauce
1 marinara sauce can milk + 2 tablespoons water
1 teaspoon dried oregano
Mozzarella and Swiss cheeses, thinly sliced
Freshly grated Parmesan cheese

Cut chicken breasts in half, then slice each half horizontally through the middle so that the finished product is the thickness of a veal cutlet. Dip chicken pieces in beaten egg and salt and pepper to taste. Roll in seasoned bread crumbs. Sauté chicken pieces in a combination of equal parts butter and oil. Drain on paper toweling for a few minutes. Meanwhile, mix marinara sauce with milk and water. Cover the bottom of a 9x13-inch baking dish with about ⅓ of the mixture. Place chicken on top of the sauce. Crumble oregano and sprinkle on top. Pour remaining marinara sauce over chicken. Layer on slices of mozzarella and Swiss cheese, then sprinkle on the Parmesan. (At this point the dish may be refrigerated overnight or for several hours.) Just before baking, dot each chicken piece with butter. Bake in a preheated 300 degree oven for 45 minutes or until tender.

Breast of Chicken A L'Archiduc

Yield: Serves 8

8 (7 to 8-ounce) chicken breast halves, skinned and boned
2 tablespoons butter
½ pound mushrooms, sliced
⅔ cup (about 3-ounces) shredded boiled ham
1 tablespoon California dry sherry
1 teaspoon fresh tarragon or ½ teaspoon dried tarragon
1 small garlic clove, minced
2 cups (about 8-ounces) grated Swiss cheese
Salt and freshly ground pepper to taste
Flour
4 tablespoons butter
2 tablespoons Cognac or brandy
1 teaspoon tomato paste
1 teaspoon Dijon mustard
3 tablespoons flour
1¼ cups chicken broth, preferably homemade
1 cup whipping cream or heavy cream
2 tablespoons California dry white wine
1 tablespoon California dry sherry
½ teaspoon white pepper
4 tablespoons butter
8 large mushroom caps, fluted, if desired
8 artichoke bottoms
½ cup grated Gruyere cheese
Cherry tomatoes for garnish
Parsley sprigs for garnish

Carefully insert sharp-pointed knife into thickest part of side of each chicken breast. Make as long and deep an opening as possible without cutting through. (On some boned breasts it may be difficult to cut a uniform horizontal line; instead, use opening left where bone was removed.) Melt 2 tablespoons butter in large skillet over medium-high heat. Add mushrooms and sauté 3 to 4 minutes. Stir in ham, sherry, lemon juice, tarragon and garlic and cook a few minutes more. Remove from heat and mix in cheese. Season to taste with salt and pepper. Stuff a heaping tablespoon of mixture into each chicken breast. Place chicken on large baking sheet and cover with waxed paper. Place another baking sheet over chicken and put books or cans on top to weight chicken down. Refrigerate for a few hours or overnight. When ready to cook breasts, coat each lightly with flour, shaking off excess. Grease a 9x13-inch baking dish. Melt 4 tablespoons butter in a 12 to 14-inch skillet over medium-high heat and sauté chicken until deep golden brown on both sides and almost cooked through. Warm brandy carefully and flame chicken. Transfer chicken to baking dish and set aside. Reserve skillet with pan juices. Preheat oven to 350 degrees. Stir tomato paste and mustard into pan juices. Mix flour with small amount of chicken broth and blend until smooth. Stir in remaining broth, then add to skillet. Place over medium heat and simmer 5 minutes, stirring constantly with whisk until slightly thickened. Gradually add cream, stirring to blend well, then add wine, sherry and white pepper. Pour over chicken and bake 15 minutes. Melt 4 tablespoons butter in large skillet over medium-high heat. Add mushroom caps and artichoke bottoms and sauté briefly. Place one artichoke bottom, cup side up, on each breast and sprinkle with cheese. Bake 4 to 5 minutes, or until cheese is melted. Transfer chicken to heated platter. Place mushroom caps, fluted side up, atop artichokes. Garnish with cherry tomatoes and parsley sprigs. Serve immediately.

When baking poultry and game, you will have juicier meat and less shrinkage if you use a constant low temperature.

Oriental Chicken Marinade

(Good on chicken, turkey, pork or beef; also good heated and served at table)

Yield: About 4 cups

1½ cups vegetable oil
¾ cup soy sauce
½ cup red wine vinegar
⅓ cup fresh lemon juice
¼ cup Worcestershire sauce
1 tablespoon pepper
2¼ teaspoons salt
2 cloves garlic, minced
1½ teaspoons chopped parsley
2 tablespoons dry mustard

Put all ingredients in blender and thoroughly process. Enough marinade for 8 to 10 chicken breasts or a large roast.

Chicken Elizabeth
(Coronation Chicken)

(This dish was created by the Cordon Bleu Cooking School in Wakefield, England for the coronation of Queen Elizabeth II.)

Yield: Serves ??

4 to 5 pounds chicken breasts
1 large onion, chopped
1 large carrot, diced
2 stalks celery, chopped
1 teaspoon minced parsley
1 large bay leaf
½ teaspoon thyme
6 black peppercorns
1 cup chicken stock, preferably homemade
½ teaspoon salt

Place whole or boneless chicken breasts in roasting pan with the remaining above ingredients. Mix together with a spoon; cover and cook for 30 minutes in a preheated 375 degree oven or on the top of the range in a pot or skillet with a tight fitting lid. Cook until very well done, basting every few minutes. Let chicken stand and cool in its own juices; then refrigerate.

Sauce Base:

2 egg yolks
½ teaspoon salt
1 cup olive or vegetable oil
½ teaspoon prepared mustard
½ teaspoon lemon juice
1½ tablespoons cider vinegar

Beat egg yolks until very thick and pale in color. Add salt; keep beating until very creamy and thick. Add oil in a thin stream or ½ teaspoon at a time to eggs, beating constantly (use your electric mixer here). After ½ the quantity of oil has been added and the mixture has thickened, oil may be added in larger quantities, 1 teaspoon at a time. When the mixture is quite thick, add the mustard, lemon juice and cider vinegar. Refrigerate at once until needed.

Elizabeth Sauce:

1 onion, chopped
1 tablespoon vegetable oil
2 teaspoons curry powder
½ cup red wine
½ cup tomato juice
3 tablespoons apricot jam
Salt to taste

Sauté the onion in the oil for 2 minutes until soft but not brown. Add the curry and cook for 2 more minutes; add the red wine and tomato juice. Cook to reduce liquid by one-half to two-thirds. Add the apricot jam and mix well. Let cool and strain into sauce base mixture. Mix well; sauce should be very smooth and coat the back of a spoon with an even coat. Salt to taste. Refrigerate until ready to serve.

To Serve:

Cut the chilled chicken into ½-inch slices and arrange on a serving plate. Pour the sauce over the sliced chicken in a ribbon effect to coat, but not saturate. Serve cold.

Imperial Chicken

(An all-family favorite)

Yield: Serves 4 to 6

1 cup grated Parmesan cheese
1 cup seasoned or fresh bread crumbs
½ cup fresh chopped parsley
1 teaspoon salt
1 teaspoon pepper
8 halved or 4 whole chicken breasts, boned and skinned if desired
¾ cup (1½-sticks) butter, melted
1 to 2 cloves garlic, crushed

Mix Parmesan cheese, bread crumbs, parsley, salt and pepper in a medium mixing bowl. Melt butter and add garlic. Dip chicken breasts in garlic butter; roll in bread crumb mixture. Place in a 9x13-inch glass baking dish. Bake uncovered in a preheated 350 degree oven for 50 minutes or until golden.

Chicken Monterey

Yield: Serves 6 to 8

2/3 cup all-purpose flour
1 (1 1/4-ounce) package taco seasoning mix
8 large chicken breasts, halved
3/4 cup melted butter
3 cups crushed tortilla chips

Combine flour and taco seasoning mix in a heavy plastic bag. Add pieces of chicken and shake to coat. Melt butter in a foil-lined (shiny side up) 11x13-inch pan. Place chicken in pan, turning once to coat with butter. Roll in crushed tortilla chips and return to baking pan. Bake in a preheated 375 degree oven for 45 to 50 minutes or until well browned and tender.

3 tablespoons chopped onions
3 tablespoons butter
3 tablespoons flour
1/4 teaspoon garlic powder
1/2 teaspoon celery salt
1 1/2 cups milk or half and half
1 1/2 teaspoons chicken stock base
1/4 to 1/2 teaspoon Tabasco sauce
1 1/2 cups grated Jack cheese
1/2 cup grated Cheddar cheese
1/4 cup sliced olives, drained
Yellow food coloring (optional)
Garnishes: additional grated Cheddar cheese, lettuce, ripe olives, avocado slices, tortilla chips, tomato wedges

Sauté chopped onion in butter until limp but not brown. Cool. In a small bowl, blend the flour, garlic powder and celery salt together; add to the cooled sautéed onions and stir into a paste. (Sauce may be held at this point until chicken is almost done.) When ready to complete sauce, add milk or cream, chicken stock base and hot sauce; cook and stir until mixture thickens. DO NOT ALLOW TO BOIL. Add grated cheeses, ripe olives and optional food coloring, and stir until cheeses melt. To serve, line a large serving dish with lettuce leaves. Top with a mound of shredded lettuce and the baked chicken. Spoon some of the cheese sauce over the chicken and sprinkle with additional sliced ripe olives and grated Cheddar cheese. Add a few whole tortilla chips. Attractive additional garnishes would include avocado slices and tomato wedges. Pass the remaining cheese sauce in a separate bowl.

Far East Chicken and Rice

Wok

Yield: Serves 4

¾ to 1 pound chicken breast
1 (11-ounce) can mandarin orange slices, drain and reserve liquid
2 tablespoons cornstarch
3 tablespoons soy sauce (low-salt soy sauce may be used)
1 chicken bouillon cube, crumbled
2 tablespoons white distilled vinegar
1 tablespoon sugar
1 to 2 tablespoons peanut oil
½ to ¾ cup blanched almonds, whole or coarsely chopped
1 (10-ounce) package French-cut frozen green beans
4 servings hot cooked rice, white or brown

Bone, skin and slice chicken into thin, short strips. Drain orange slices and reserve juice. Mix reserved juice with cornstarch, soy sauce, bouillon cube, vinegar and sugar. Add chicken and marinate 15 to 30 minutes, at room temperature. Heat oil in frying pan or wok until it sizzles. Add almonds and stir-fry until golden. Remove nuts with slotted spoon onto paper toweling. Remove chicken from sauce with slotted spoon and stir-fry in hot oil until cooked through. Add slightly thawed beans and stir-fry until hot. Stir in well mixed cornstarch mixture and reduce heat to low. Stir gently until sauce is thickened. Add drained oranges and toasted almonds; heat through. Serve immediately over hot rice.

Note:
Pork or beef may be substituted for the chicken in this recipe.

Oriental Walnut Chicken Stir-Fry

Wok Yield: Serves 6

6 large half-chicken breasts
2 (16-ounce) cans cling peach slices, packed in juice or extra light syrup
2 large tomatoes
3 large stalks celery
2 cups fresh broccoli florets
1 cup diagonally sliced green onions
¼ cup soy sauce
¼ cup California dry sherry
2 cloves garlic, minced
2 tablespoons cornstarch
⅓ cup light oil (preferably peanut oil)
1 tablespoon minced fresh ginger, or 1½ teaspoons powdered ginger, stirred into the soy mixture
½ cup chopped toasted walnuts

Remove skin from chicken breasts. Cut into thin strips ½-inch wide by approximately 1½-inches long. Drain peaches well, reserving liquid for another use. Cut tomatoes into wedges and celery into ¼-inch diagonal slices. Set vegetables aside with broccoli and onions. Combine soy sauce, sherry, garlic and cornstarch in a small bowl. Heat oil in wok; stir in ginger and chicken, tossing until chicken has completely turned opaque. Add broccoli and stir-fry until it turns bright green. Add celery and onions and stir until coated with oil. Add peach slices and tomatoes to wok, and pour soy mixture over all, stirring until thickened. Add walnuts, toss lightly and serve.

Pollo Carolína

Yield: Serves 6 to 8

6 to 8 half chicken breasts
Flour
½ cup butter or margarine
2 to 3 cloves garlic, pressed
½ pound sliced fresh mushrooms
1 cup California dry white wine
1 (14-ounce) can artichoke hearts, drained and quartered
3 to 4 tablespoons fresh lemon juice
Salt and white pepper
2 teaspoons chopped fresh flat-leafed parsley

Bone and skin chicken. Cut chicken into ½-inch wide strips. Dip a few chicken strips at a time in the flour, making sure the strips remain separated. Shake off excess flour. Melt butter in a large skillet. Sauté ½ of the strips at a time, until golden brown. Remove chicken to a warm platter. (The sautéing process will go very quickly!) Add garlic, mushrooms, white wine, artichoke hearts, lemon juice, salt and white pepper to pan; mix thoroughly and simmer for 5 to 10 minutes, or until liquid is reduced as much as desired. Add browned chicken strips to the skillet, toss to glaze well, and heat only long enough to heat chicken through. Taste and adjust seasonings. Remove skillet from heat and add parsley. Serve from a warmed platter or dish.

Terrific Chicken

Yield: Serves 4

6 chicken breasts, halved, or 8 chicken thighs
Seasoned salt
Garlic powder
Bisquick

Season chicken pieces with salt and garlic powder then dip in Bisquick. Place in a 8x8-inch baking dish. Bake in a preheated 350 degree oven for 30 minutes.

Sauce:

¼ cup vegetable oil
½ cup California dry white wine
¼ teaspoon pepper
¼ teaspoon paprika
¼ teaspoon thyme
½ teaspoon dried oregano
¼ teaspoon dried rosemary
½ teaspoon salt
1 onion, chopped
1 clove garlic, minced
½ pound mushrooms, chopped

In a medium saucepan combine oil, wine, pepper, paprika, thyme, oregano, rosemary, salt, onion, garlic and mushrooms and bring to a boil. Boil for 5 minutes, and pour over chicken. Cover and bake in a preheated 350 degree oven for 1 hour.

Auntie Beau's Chicken Dish

Yield: Serves 6 to 8

1 whole (3 to 4-pound) chicken plus 2 whole breasts
1 onion, peeled and quartered
1 bay leaf
2 stalks celery, cut into 2-inch pieces
½ teaspoon peppercorns
1 pound fresh mushrooms, sliced
2 tablespoons butter or margarine
1 (10¾-ounce) can cream of mushroom soup
½ soup can evaporated milk or light cream
½ soup can California dry white wine
1 (8-ounce) package Herb Seasoned Stuffing or Corn Bread Stuffing

Remove skin and excess fat from chicken. In a large stockpot cover chicken with water; add onion, bay leaf, celery and peppercorns. Simmer chicken until tender. Drain chicken well and reserve stock. Remove cooled chicken from bones - leave in fairly large pieces. Place chicken pieces in a 9x13-inch casserole. Sauté mushrooms in butter and sprinkle on top of chicken. Mix together mushroom soup, evaporated milk or cream and wine, and pour over chicken and mushrooms. Prepare stuffing mix according to package directions, substituting chicken broth for the water. Spread stuffing over chicken mixture in a ½-inch thick layer. Bake in a preheated 350 degree oven for 30 minutes.

Baked Chicken with Orange Soy Sauce

Yield: Serves 4

1 (3-pound) broiler/fryer, cut up or 3 pounds of chicken parts
2 tablespoons soy sauce
½ teaspoon salt
½ teaspoon celery seed
¼ teaspoon ground ginger
¼ teaspoon hot pepper sauce
½ cup orange juice
1 tablespoon butter or margarine

Place chicken in single layer in a shallow 9x13-inch baking pan; sprinkle with soy sauce, salt, celery seed, ginger and hot pepper sauce. Pour orange juice over all and dot with butter. Bake in upper third of a preheated 425 degree oven for 45 minutes or until fork tender, turning chicken pieces three times during cooking period and glazing with pan drippings.

Chicken Romano

Yield: Serves 6

1 pound Italian sausage
2 tablespoons butter
2 tablespoons vegetable oil
2 fryer chickens (about 3-pounds each), cut into pieces
1 (1-pound) can tomato puree
1 (6-ounce) can sliced mushrooms, reserve liquid
1 (8-ounce) can pitted olives, reserve liquid
¼ cup sweet pepper flakes
1 tablespoon parsley
2 teaspoons minced celery
1½ teaspoons Italian seasoning
1 teaspoon dehydrated minced onion
½ teaspoon salt
¼ teaspoon garlic powder
½ cup mushroom liquid
¼ cup olive juice
1 bay leaf

Crumble and brown Italian sausage, drain well and set aside. In a large frying pan, sauté chicken parts in 2 tablespoons each of butter and oil. Remove chicken from pan and pour off excess fat. Add tomato purée, sliced mushrooms, drained olives, sweet pepper flakes, parsley, celery, Italian seasoning, onion, salt, garlic powder, mushroom liquid, olive juice and bay leaf to pan. Return chicken and sausage to sauce, cover and simmer 30 to 40 minutes, or until chicken tests tender.

Chicken Curry

Yield: Serves 5

1 (3-pound) chicken, cut into pieces, or 8 half chicken breasts
2 tablespoons butter or margarine
1 medium tart apple, peeled and sliced
1 small onion, chopped
1½ teaspoons curry powder
1½ teaspoons salt
1 (10¾-ounce) can cream of mushroom soup
1 cup light cream or milk
1½ teaspoons paprika

Cut up chicken and skin. Place in a 9x13-inch casserole. Sauté apple and onion in butter until tender. Combine the curry, salt, soup and cream or milk; pour mixture over chicken and sprinkle with the paprika. Bake in a preheated 350 degree oven for 1½ hours or until fork tender.

Golden Harvest Casserole

Yield: Serves 6 to 8

2½ to 3 pounds chicken parts
½ cup all-purpose flour
1 tablespoon salt
1 teaspoon pepper
½ cup vegetable oil
2 cloves garlic, minced
1 cup diced onion
1 cup sliced celery
1 small green pepper, cut into strips
½ pound mushrooms, sliced
1 teaspoon dried thyme
¼ teaspoon cayenne
1 bay leaf
1 (16-ounce) can plum tomatoes, undrained
1 cup California dry white wine
2 tablespoons tomato paste (optional)
½ pound raw shrimp (optional)
Chopped parsley for garnish

Shake chicken in flour mixed with 1½ teaspoons of the salt and the pepper. Reserve flour mixture. Brown well in hot oil. Remove to a 10-cup casserole or Dutch oven. Discard all but 2 tablespoons of the oil in the frying pan and brown garlic and onion until tender. Add celery, peppers and mushrooms and sauté until tender-crisp. Add remaining 1½ teaspoons salt, 2 tablespoons of the reserved flour, thyme, cayenne and bay leaf. Toss to coat vegetables. Add tomatoes, undrained, wine and tomato paste. Stir and bring to a boil. Pour over chicken and cover. Bake in a preheated 350 degree oven for 25 minutes. Add optional shrimp and bake an additional 20 minutes. Garnish with chopped parsley.

Oven Barbecued Cranberry Chicken

Yield: Serves 4 to 6

1 (2 to 4-pound) chicken, cut up (or 8 to 10 half-breasts)
1 (8-ounce) can whole cranberry sauce
1 (8-ounce) bottle French-style salad dressing
1 (1¼-ounce) package dry onion soup mix

Place chicken in a 9x13-inch baking pan. Mix cranberry sauce, salad dressing and soup mix together and pour over chicken, turning to coat all sides. Cover baking pan tightly with foil. Bake in a preheated 350 degree oven for 1½ hours or until tender.

Note:
Jellied cranberry sauce may be substituted for whole cranberry sauce, if you prefer.

Hong Kong Chicken with Cashews

Wok

Yield: Serves 4

1 tablespoon light soy sauce
1 tablespoon California dry sherry
1 tablespoon cornstarch
½ teaspoon salt
½ teaspoon pepper
2 cups chicken pieces, cut into ½-inch thick slices

In a medium bowl, combine 1 tablespoon soy sauce, sherry, 1 tablespoon cornstarch, salt and pepper. Add chicken pieces and toss. Marinate chicken pieces for 30 minutes at room temperature. Refrigerate, if marinating for a longer time. While chicken marinates, prepare and organize other ingredients.

Peanut oil
¾ cup diced celery
¾ cup diced onion
Sugar and salt to taste
¾ cup diced red bell pepper
1 cup fresh or frozen peas
1 garlic clove, crushed
1 piece fresh ginger (about the size of a quarter), crushed
1 (4-ounce) can button mushrooms, drain and reserve liquid
½ to 1 cup cashew nuts
½ cup reserved mushroom liquid (add water if necessary to make ½ cup)
2 tablespoons cornstarch
1 teaspoon light soy sauce

Assemble oil, celery, onion, seasoning, bell pepper, peas, garlic, ginger, mushrooms and cashews near the cooking area. Combine the reserved mushroom liquid, 2 tablespoons cornstarch and 1 teaspoon soy sauce to form a sauce; set aside. To cook, heat wok and add 1 tablespoon oil. Stir-fry celery and onion for 1 to 2 minutes. Season lightly with sugar and salt; remove from wok and set aside. Add 1 tablespoon oil to wok and heat. Add red pepper and stir-fry for 2 minutes; add peas and stir-fry for 1 minute. Remove from wok and set aside. Heat 2 tablespoons oil in wok; add garlic and ginger and stir-fry until golden, to just flavor the cooking oil; remove and discard. Add chicken and marinade to the wok and stir-fry until opaque. Add the reserved sauce ingredients to the chicken and cook until mixture thickens. Add reserved vegetables, drained mushrooms and cashews to wok; stir mixture together to heat through completely. Serve immediately.

Spanish Style Chicken Paella

(Super served with salad and lots of French bread)

Yield: Serves 4

4 ounces Mexican chorizo or Italian sausage, sliced
4 chicken legs
4 chicken wings
Salt and pepper
½ cup chopped onions
1 small sweet red or green pepper, cut into chunks
1 clove garlic, minced
¾ cup long grain rice, uncooked
1½ teaspoons instant chicken bouillon granules
¼ teaspoon ground turmeric
3 cups hot water
4 baby carrots or 3-inch carrot chunks
1 (10-ounce) package frozen peas
1 (10-ounce) package frozen artichoke hearts (optional)
¼ cup pitted ripe olives
6 cherry tomatoes, halved or ½ cup tomato wedges

In a 12-inch skillet or 4-quart Dutch oven, brown sausage over medium heat about 10 minutes. Drain, reserving drippings in pan; set sausage aside. Season chicken with salt and pepper to taste. Brown chicken in reserved drippings; remove chicken, reserving 1 tablespoon drippings in pan. Add onion, pepper and garlic to pan; sauté until onion is tender. Stir in uncooked rice, bouillon granules, turmeric and water; bring to a boil. Add sausage and carrots, and arrange chicken on top. Reduce heat, cover and simmer 20 minutes. Meanwhile, rinse frozen peas and artichoke hearts under hot tap water to separate. Arrange peas, artichokes and olives on top of the chicken. Cover and cook an additional 15 to 20 minutes or until rice and chicken tests tender. Just before serving, add tomatoes and heat through. To serve, toss mixture gently together or arrange attractively on a preheated platter.

Mexican Chicken Lasagne

Yield: Serves 8 to 10

- 2 tablespoons vegetable oil
- 1 large onion, chopped
- 2 cloves garlic, minced
- 1 green pepper, seeded and chopped
- 2 (10¾-ounce) cans condensed tomato soup
- 1 (10-ounce) can enchilada sauce
- 1½ teaspoons salt
- ½ teaspoon pepper
- 2 tablespoons chili powder
- 1 teaspoon ground cumin
- 1 (10-ounce) package lasagne noodles, cooked according to package directions
- 2 cups (1 pint) small curd cottage cheese
- 2 eggs, well beaten
- ⅓ cup chopped parsley
- 2 to 4 tablespoons diced green chiles
- 4 cups cooked chicken, torn into large pieces
- 6 ounces sliced Cheddar cheese
- 6 ounces sliced Monterey Jack cheese

In a large frying pan, heat oil; add onion, garlic and bell pepper. Cook, stirring frequently, over medium heat until onion is transparent. Add both cans of soup, enchilada sauce, salt, pepper, chili powder and cumin. Simmer, uncovered, for 10 minutes or until thickened, stirring often. Meanwhile, combine cottage cheese, eggs, parsley and diced chiles in a medium bowl for the cheese filling; reserve. Cover bottom of a 9x13-inch casserole with one-half of the noodles. Spread one-half the cheese filling over the noodles, then top with one-half the sauce, arrange one-half of the chicken over the sauce, then one-half the sliced cheese. Repeat layering with the remaining ingredients. Casserole may be covered and refrigerated overnight if desired. Bake, covered, in a preheated 375 degree oven for 35 to 45 minutes or until bubbly. Add an additional 10 minutes baking time if casserole has been chilled. Let stand uncovered for 10 minutes before serving.

Tule Fog In Winter
Fresno

Pronounced "Too-lee", these fogs rise out of the marshes and rivers during the winter months, covering the Valley in a low, thick blanket.

Until the Central Pacific line had been built through the Valley, steamers landed freight at the head of Fresno Slough. From there, the only means of transportation was the stagecoach and the wagon train. The good of the early railroad system was the construction of towns and jobs along the line, the bad was that the railroad dominated the land in the Valley.

On May 11, 1880, the Mussel Slough "war" was fought in a wheat field outside of Hanford. The settlers on one side and the Southern Pacific railway on the other. Eight good and honest men died that day, and though the casualties were small, as wars go, the battle changed the politics of the state and the control that the railroad had over the common citizen.

The railroad had laid claim to the land around the area, but had neglected to use it, and exact ownership was uncertain. In 1869, settlers began to file homestead claims on the same land. On November 20, 1869, the Secretary of the Interior, decided against granting the disputed land to the railroad. The railroad took the matter to Court and won. The settlers appealed, and while they were waiting for a decision, the railroad began a series of depositions. The settlers maintained that the lands were legally forfeited and that they had invested heavily in irrigation systems. The railroad then charged the settlers for their own improvements. The President of the railroad was also the Governor of the state, the Legislature was dominated by the railroad, and very few had confidence in the appointed Courts or of ever seeing an objective decision.

The settlers had appealed to the United States Supreme Court and were waiting for a decision when the railroad sent a Marshal to evict the settlers in 1880. The settlers were waiting when the Marshal broke down the locked gate of the Braden ranch. Words were exchanged, guns were drawn and eight men died. The survivors were sentenced to eight months for resisting a Marshal.

All of the settlers involved in the land fight eventually lost their land, and the end of the fight came in 1910, when Hiram Johnson, a noted foe of the railroad, was elected Governor. Nevermore would the freedoms of the citizens be circumvented by a few powerful men.

Compliments of An Anonymous Friend

Crockpot Chicken Tortillas

Yield: Serves 4 to 6

3 to 4½ cups cooked boned chicken
1 (10¾-ounce) can cream of chicken soup
1 cup Mexican-style stewed tomatoes, or regular stewed tomatoes with mild green chili salsa added to taste to make 1 cup
2 tablespoons quick-cooking tapioca
6 to 8 fresh corn tortillas, torn into pieces
1 medium onion, chopped
2 cups grated sharp Cheddar cheese

Cut chicken into bite-sized pieces; mix with soup, Mexican-style stewed tomatoes and tapioca. Line bottom of crockpot with torn tortilla pieces. Add ⅓ of chicken mixture; sprinkle with ⅓ of the onions and ⅓ of the cheese. Repeat layering twice more, ending with onions and cheese. Cover and cook in crockpot on Low for 6 to 8 hours, or on High for 3 hours.

Savory Crescent Chicken Squares

Yield: 4 sandwiches

1 (3-ounce) package cream cheese, softened
3 tablespoons butter, melted
2 cups cooked, cubed chicken
½ teaspoon salt
¼ teaspoon pepper
2 tablespoons milk
1 tablespoon chopped chives, or green onions
1 tablespoon minced dehydrated onion
1 tablespoon chopped pimiento (optional)
1 (8-ounce) can refrigerated crescent dinner rolls
¾ cup crushed, seasoned croutons

In a medium bowl, blend cream cheese and 2 tablespoons butter (reserve 1 tablespoon) until smooth. Add the chicken, salt, pepper, milk, chives, onion and optional pimiento; mix well. Separate crescent roll dough into 4 rectangles; firmly press perforations to seal. Spoon ½ cup meat mixture onto center of each rectangle. Pull 4 corners of dough to top center of chicken mixture, twist slightly and seal edges. Brush tops with reserved 1 tablespoon butter and dip into crouton crumbs. Place on an ungreased cookie sheet. Bake in a preheated 350 degree oven for 20 to 25 minutes or until golden brown.

California Game Hens

Yield: Serves 4

4 Rock Cornish game hens
1⅓ cups Minute rice
1 cup water
¾ cup California rosé wine
½ teaspoon salt
Few grains pepper
⅛ teaspoon nutmeg
⅛ teaspoon ground allspice
1 teaspoon sugar
¼ cup California golden raisins
¼ cup butter or margarine
¼ cup slivered, blanched almonds

Wash hens in cold water and pat dry. Combine rice and water in saucepan, mix to moisten. Bring quickly to a boil, fluffing rice with a fork once or twice. Add wine, salt, pepper, nutmeg, allspice, sugar and raisins. Melt butter in small skillet over low heat; add almonds, stir frequently until lightly browned. Add to the rice mixture and stuff, lightly, into hens. Tie legs close to body and tuck wings behind back.

Basting Sauce:

¼ cup California rosé wine
2 tablespoons butter or margarine, melted
2 teaspoons fresh lemon juice

Combine wine, butter and lemon juice and brush over hens. Arrange birds on rack in a shallow baking pan. Roast in a preheated 450 degree oven for 15 minutes. Lower heat to 350 degrees and continue to roast for another 30 minutes, basting once or twice. Reserve the pan drippings.

Gravy:

1 tablespoon butter or margarine
½ cup currant jelly
1 tablespoon fresh lemon juice
3 cloves
Few grains cayenne pepper
½ cup water
½ cup California rosé wine
Pan juices from hens
Cornstarch

Combine butter, currant jelly, lemon juice, cloves, cayenne and water, in a saucepan. Simmer for 5 minutes. Strain; add the rosé wine and pan juices. Thicken with cornstarch if desired.

Rock Cornish Hens with Black Cherry Sauce

Yield: Serves 4

4 Rock Cornish game hens
Salt and pepper
¼ cup butter, melted
⅔ of an 8-ounce jar of currant jelly
½ cup California dry sherry
1 teaspoon grated orange peel
2 tablespoons fresh orange juice
1 to 2 teaspoons cornstarch, dissolved in cold water
1 (16-ounce) can black pitted cherries, drained

Lightly salt and pepper hens and arrange in a shallow baking pan. Rub generously with melted butter. Roast in a preheated 350 degree oven for 30 minutes. To prepare sauce, melt currant jelly; add sherry, orange peel and orange juice. Gradually stir in dissolved cornstarch and boil until mixture thickens, stirring constantly. Add drained cherries. Pour ½ of the sauce over hens and roast, uncovered, for an additional 30 minutes, basting once or twice. Serve remaining sauce hot to accompany baked hens.

Note:
Serve with wild rice and a green salad.

Braised Valley Dove

Yield: Serves 4 to 5

10 to 12 doves
Salt, pepper and flour
¼ cup vegetable oil
3 cloves garlic, minced
2 onions, chopped
1 teaspoon dry Italian seasonings
½ pound fresh mushrooms, sliced
1 cup California dry sherry
Water
Cornstarch to thicken (amount depends on consistency desired)

Salt and pepper prepared doves. Dip in flour; shake off excess flour and brown on both sides in a large skillet, in the oil. Add garlic, onions, Italian seasonings, mushrooms and sherry. Add enough water to just cover the birds. Cover and simmer for 1½ hours, checking periodically to see if more water needs to be added. Add cornstarch to thicken gravy, if desired.

San Joaquin Dove

Yield: Serves 4 to 6

12 to 16 doves
Flour or Bisquick
Vegetable oil
1 (10¾-ounce) can chicken consommé
1 cup California dry red wine
Juice of 2 oranges
1 cup chopped celery
½ pound fresh mushrooms, sliced
Salt and pepper to taste

Roll prepared dove in flour or Bisquick. In a large skillet, brown birds, in about ¼ cup oil. Arrange browned doves in a 9x13-inch casserole. Combine consommé, wine, orange juice, celery, mushrooms, salt and pepper and pour over doves. Bake, covered, in a preheated 300 degree oven for 2 hours.

Duck with Sauce Constance

Yield: Serves 4

1 or 2 (¾ to 1-pound) small wild duck per person
Garlic powder
Beau Monde seasoning
Lemon pepper

Rinse ducks well and pat dry. Season inside and out with garlic powder, Beau Monde and lemon pepper. Place ducks in a shallow roasting pan, do not crowd ducks in pan. Bake in a preheated 400 to 450 degree oven for 45 minutes or until skin is crispy. Serve with Sauce Constance.

Sauce:

Yield: 2 cups

1 cup cranberry-orange relish, canned or homemade
1 cup currant jelly
½ cup California dry red wine (a little more if needed to blend relish and jelly into a thin consistency)
1 large clove garlic, crushed
1 teaspoon rosemary leaves, crushed
¼ teaspoon summer savory
½ teaspoon lemon pepper

In a saucepan, combine relish, jelly, wine, garlic, rosemary, summer savory and lemon pepper and bring to a boil, stirring frequently. Reduce heat to simmer and cook to reduce sauce to a medium consistency, about 45 minutes to 1 hour. Serve hot at the table to spoon over baked duck.

Note:
This sauce can be made ahead and reheated at serving time. Sauce also freezes well.

Duck with Plum Sauce

Yield: Serves 4 to 6

2 (3-pound) ducks, cut in half with backbone removed, reserving carasses for duck stock

Arrange duck halves on a rack in a shallow roasting pan. Roast in a preheated 425 degree oven until tender, turning once, about 35 minutes for breasts and 40 minutes for legs. Transfer to preheated serving platter and keep warm.

Sauce:

1 cup + 2 tablespoons California plum wine
2 tablespoons butter or margarine
1 tablespoon powdered sugar
4 firm fresh plums, halved and pitted
2 fresh nectarines or firm fresh peaches, peeled and quartered
1½ cups duck stock (recipe follows or you may substitute chicken stock)
2 tablespoons red wine vinegar
3 tablespoons orange flavored liqueur
1½ teaspoons cornstarch
Watercress sprigs for garnish

In a medium frying pan, cook ½ cup of the plum wine over medium-high heat until reduced to 3 tablespoons. Set aside. Melt butter in a large heavy skillet over medium-high heat; stir in powdered sugar. Add fruit and sauté until glazed but still firm, about 4 minutes. Spoon glazed fruit around the duck; keep warm. Degrease the roasting pan. Place pan over medium-high heat and add ½ cup plum wine and stir, scraping up any browned bits to deglaze the pan. Add to reduced wine in skillet. Stir in the 1½ cups duck or chicken stock and the vinegar. Place frying pan over medium-high heat and bring mixture to a boil. Cook sauce, stirring constantly, until reduced to 1 cup. Blend remaining 2 tablespoons of plum wine with liqueur and cornstarch. Stir cornstarch mixture into sauce. Cook until thickened, about 3 minutes. Pour hot sauce over ducks. Garnish with watercress and serve immediately.

Duck Stock:

1 to 2 duck carcasses, halved, with wings and all giblets except liver included
2 carrots, quartered
1 onion, quartered
1 celery stalk, quartered
½ teaspoon dried thyme, crumbled

Combine all ingredients in a large stockpot with enough water to cover. Place over high heat and bring to a boil. Reduce heat, cover and simmer for 2½ hours. Skim surface frequently. Strain into container. Before using, discard fat from surface.

Note:
Can be prepared ahead and stored in refrigerator up to 1 week, or frozen for up to 3 months.

Rob's Wild Duck

Yield: Serves 4 to 6

1 oven-baking bag, floured inside
2 or 3 wild ducks, dressed and cleaned
1 (6-ounce) can frozen concentrated orange juice, thawed
4 ounces plum or peach jam or jelly
¼ cup brown sugar
¼ cup California dry white wine
1 bay leaf, crumbled
2 tablespoons soy sauce
4 tablespoons butter or margarine
Garlic salt, seasoned salt and pepper to taste

Flour inside of baking bag and place duck inside. Place bag in roasting pan. Combine orange juice concentrate, jam or jelly, brown sugar, wine, bay leaf, soy sauce, butter, garlic salt, seasoned salt and pepper in sauce pan. Heat until ingredients are well blended. Pour sauce over ducks and tie bag securely. Turn several times to coat ducks with sauce. Place back in baking pan. Cut 6 small slits in top of bag. Bake in a preheated 350 degree oven for about 2 hours, depending on size of ducks. Serve with degreased pan juices.

Duck Stuffed with Raw Fruit

(Duck cooked with raw fruit is invariably moist, succulent, and devoid of fat. Recommended as being the easiest and one of the best duck recipes)

Yield: 1 duck

Season the duck, inside and out, with salt and pepper. Peel, core and quarter tart apples. Fill the inside of the duck with the apples and uncooked dried prunes. Do not pack in the fruit; just fill the cavity. Place the duck on a rack and pierce with a sharp fork or skewer to aid the fat in dripping out. Place the rack in a roasting pan and roast at 350 degrees allowing 25 minutes per pound. You will find that the fruit gives the duck a delicious flavor and absorbs all the fat. Throw away the apples but eat the prunes or use around the duck as a garnish. A suggestion is serve red cabbage with the duck and thin pancakes rolled around spicy apple-raisin filling. Or, how about serving with wild rice and asparagus accompanied with a hollandaise. Top the duck with an orange sauce. Want to dazzle your guest, try this: Grate orange rind over the duck; sprinkle with brandy or Grand Marnier and set aflame as you serve.

Remember: Cook it with care, serve it with love and add a drop or two of your imagination.

Chandler Pheasant

(Marvelous served with wild rice)

Yield: Serves 4

1 (2 to 3-pound) pheasant, cut up for frying
Salt, pepper and flour
¼ cup butter or margarine
1 cup dairy sour cream
2 (4-ounce) cans sliced mushrooms, drained, or ½ pound fresh mushrooms sliced and sautéed
¼ to ½ cup California dry white wine

Cut up pheasant for frying. Salt, pepper and flour pieces. Melt butter in a large skillet and brown meat on both sides, turning occasionally. Place pheasant in a 9x13-inch casserole. Scrape pan drippings on top. Combine sour cream, mushrooms and wine and pour over pheasant to cover. Cover, and place in a preheated 300 degree oven. Bake for 1½ hours.

Lapin Au Moutarde

Yield: Serves 2 to 3

¼ cup all-purpose flour
¼ teaspoon ground nutmeg
Dash of pepper
1½ to 2 pounds ready to cook rabbit, cut up
2 slices bacon
8 to 12 whole boiling onions
1 cup beer
1 large bay leaf, crumbled
1 teaspoon instant chicken bouillon granules
¼ teaspoon dried crushed thyme
½ cup half and half or light cream
2 egg yolks
1 tablespoon prepared mustard
¼ teaspoon salt
Dash of white pepper
2 tablespoons snipped parsley

Combine flour, nutmeg and a dash of pepper; coat rabbit with mixture. In a 10-inch skillet, fry bacon until crisp; drain and reserve drippings in pan. Crumble bacon; set aside. Brown rabbit in reserved drippings for about 5 minutes on each side, or until lightly golden. Add onions, beer, bay leaf, bouillon granules, thyme and crumbled bacon. Cover and simmer 50 to 60 minutes or until meat is tender. Remove rabbit, onions and bacon to platter; keep warm. Strain pan juices, add water if necessary so that juices equal ½ cup liquid. Pour juices into a small saucepan. Beat cream with egg yolks, mustard, salt and a dash of pepper; stir into pan juices. Cook and stir constantly until thickened, but DO NOT BOIL. Pour sauce over meat. Garnish with a sprinkling of fresh snipped parsley.

Barbecue Chicken Marinade

Yield: ½ cup

2 teaspoons fresh lime juice
¼ cup vegetable oil
2 tablespoons red wine vinegar
1 tablespoon Worcestershire sauce
⅛ teaspoon Tabasco sauce
1 teaspoon sugar
1 teaspoon salt
½ teaspoon garlic salt
½ teaspoon paprika

Mix lime juice, oil, vinegar, Worcestershire sauce, Tabasco sauce, sugar, salt, garlic salt and paprika. Marinate chicken in the refrigerator at least 2 hours.

Barbecue Sauce

(Great on barbecued chicken, hamburgers and other meats)

Yield: 1 quart

1 cup brown sugar
1 cup strong coffee
2 tablespoons Worcestershire sauce
1 tablespoon dry mustard
1 (14-ounce) bottle catsup
3 tablespoons cider vinegar
2 tablespoons liquid smoke
1 tablespoon instant minced onions

In a saucepan, bring brown sugar, coffee, Worcestershire sauce, dry mustard, catsup, vinegar, liquid smoke and onions to a boil; reduce heat and simmer for 30 to 40 minutes. Store sauce in the refrigerator.

Meats

Steak with Mustard Sauce

Yield: Serves 4 to 6
depending on size of steak

1 rib, loin or flank steak
1 tablespoon butter or margarine
1 tablespoon olive oil or vegetable oil

Basic Steak Sauté:

In a wide frying pan, over medium-high heat, melt 1 tablespoon butter with 1 tablespoon oil. Add meat and cook, uncovered, until well browned on each side. Allow 3 to 5 minutes per side for rare, or cook to desired doneness.

Mustard Sauce:

3 to 4 tablespoons butter or margarine
1 tablespoon Dijon-style mustard
2 tablespoons dry vermouth
¼ teaspoon Worcestershire sauce

In a small pan, melt butter, blend in mustard, vermouth and Worcestershire sauce. Stir briskly.

Method:

Pour sauce over steak. Slice meat and swirl through juices. Place on warm platter and serve.

To tenderize meat: add 1 teaspoon of vinegar while cooking. It won't change the taste.

Chinese Pepper Steak

(Deliciouso!)

Yield: Serves 6 to 8

1½ pounds sirloin steak, or any left-over roast or steak
¼ cup vegetable oil
3 cloves garlic, crushed
1 teaspoon salt
1 teaspoon ground ginger or 2 teaspoons freshly grated ginger
½ teaspoon pepper
12 large, fresh mushrooms
½ pound beansprouts
3 large green peppers, sliced
2 large onions, thinly sliced
3 or 4 stalks celery, sliced
¼ cup soy sauce
½ teaspoon sugar
½ cup beef broth
1 (6-ounce) can water chestnuts, drained and sliced
1 tablespoon cornstarch, or more if needed
4 green onions, cut into 1-inch long pieces

Freeze steak for 1 hour so that it will be easier to slice. When ready to cook, cut meat into ⅛-inch thick slices. Heat oil in skillet or wok, and add garlic, salt, ginger and pepper. Sauté mixture until golden brown, remove garlic and discard. Add steak slices and brown lightly. Remove meat from pan and reserve. Add mushrooms, bean sprouts, green peppers, onions and celery; stir-fry about 3 minutes. Return beef to pan. Add soy sauce, sugar, broth, water chestnuts, green onions and cornstarch dissolved in a small amount of water. Stir-fry for 3 or 4 minutes over moderate-low heat or until sauce thickens. Serve over hot rice or chow mein noodles.

Note:
The trick to successful Chinese cooking is to have all ingredients prepared and organized before starting the stir-fry procedure.

AWARD WINNER

Beef Round Steak Roll

(A winner in the California Beef Cookoff. Also took National honors)

Yield: Serves 6

2 pounds round steak, ½-inch thick
¼ cup red wine vinegar
3 cloves garlic, minced
½ teaspoon leaf thyme
½ teaspoon ground pepper
2 small bay leaves

In a large glass bowl, combine the red wine vinegar, garlic, thyme, ground pepper and bay leaves, to form a marinade. Place round steak in the mixture and marinate for 1 hour in the refrigerator.

Filling:

¼ cup butter, cut into very thin slices
1½ cups soft bread crumbs, softened in one beaten egg
2 cups fresh spinach leaves
¾ cup thinly sliced onion
6 carrots about 8-inches long, left whole or quartered lengthwise
⅓ cup chopped parsley
1 (14½-ounce) can beef broth

Remove meat from marinade, and reserve marinade. Arrange layers of butter, bread crumbs, spinach, onions and carrots on the meat. Sprinkle with parsley. Roll up steak, starting at one of the long sides. Tie roll securely in several places. Brown well, in hot shortening, in large frying pan, over moderate heat. Place roll in shallow 1½-quart baking dish. Pour pan drippings, reserved marinade and broth over meat. Cover with foil, crimping edges to rim of dish. Bake in a preheated 350 degree oven for about 2 hours, or until meat is tender. Remove meat from pan, keeping warm. Pour drippings into a large measuring cup. Spoon off excess fat. Add water to make 1½ cups of liquid. Mix ¼ cup water and flour until free of lumps. Combine mixture into drippings and cook until thickened, stirring constantly. Pour thickened sauce over the sliced beef roll. Garnish with parsley and pimiento.

Immigrant Flank Steak

Yield: Serves 4

¼ cup soy sauce
3 tablespoons honey
2 tablespoons cider vinegar
1½ teaspoons garlic powder
1½ teaspoons ground ginger, or 1 tablespoon minced fresh ginger
¾ cup vegetable oil
1 green onion, finely chopped
1 flank steak (approximately 1½-pounds)

Mix soy sauce, honey and vinegar together; blend in garlic powder and ginger. Add oil and chopped onion. Pour marinade over meat and let marinate at least 4 hours or longer in the refrigerator, turning meat occasionally. Barbecue or broil meat to desired doneness, basting during cooking. Slice on the diagonal to serve.

An Energy-Efficient Way To Cook A Roast:

Start cooking 3 to 5 hours before you plan to serve the roast. Preheat oven to 375 degrees. Have meat at room temperature. Place roast fat-side up in a shallow pan. Place in the oven and cook for exactly 1 hour. DO NOT OPEN OVEN DOOR AT ANY TIME! When time is up, turn oven off, and forget about the roast until 1¼ hours before it is to be carved. At this time, turn the oven on to 300 degrees and let the roast stay in the oven for exactly 45 minutes more. REMEMBER, DO NOT OPEN THE OVEN DOOR. At the end of the 45 minutes, take the roast out and carve it.

If you have followed the directions, then you will have a truly wonderful roast.

Oriental Beef-Vegetable Sauté

(Have all ingredients ready, at your fingertips, before starting the cooking process.)

Yield: Serves 6

2 pounds round steak, cut into thin strips
2 tablespoons lemon juice
6 tablespoons soy sauce
6 tablespoons California dry sherry
6 tablespoons vegetable oil
4 tablespoons cornstarch
4 tablespoons chopped fresh ginger
3 cloves garlic, chopped fine
Dash of black pepper

Place meat strips in a glass bowl. Combine lemon juice, soy sauce, dry sherry, oil, cornstarch, ginger, garlic and pepper and pour over meat. Marinate meat for 1 hour, at room temperature, or overnight in the refrigerator.

2 cups sliced water chestnuts
2 cups snow peas or Chinese pea pods
2 cups fresh asparagus, cut into 1-inch lengths
¼ teaspoon salt, or more, to taste
9 tablespoons vegetable oil (for frying)

Heat 6 tablespoons of the oil in a frying pan, electric skillet or wok, to just below the smoking point. Add water chestnuts, pea pods and asparagus; sprinkle on salt. Sauté for 4 minutes, stirring often. Remove to a platter. Heat remaining 3 tablespoons oil in the same pan and sauté meat mixture until medium rare, 3 to 4 minutes. Put vegetable mixture back in with the meat.

Glaze:

2 tablespoons cornstarch
3 teaspoons soy sauce, or to taste
1 cup water

In a small bowl, combine cornstarch, soy sauce and water. Pour over hot beef and vegetable mixture in pan; stirring constantly until thickened.

Note:
This recipe may be prepared at the table. Use any combination of vegetables in season, especially mushrooms and green onions in the winter months.

Flank Steak with Herb Butter Sauce

Yield: Serves about 4
depending on size of steak

1 flank steak
Vegetable oil
1 clove garlic
½ cup butter or margarine, melted
1 small onion, minced
1 clove garlic, minced
2 teaspoons Worcestershire sauce
½ teaspoon salt
4 tablespoons chopped parsley
¼ teaspoon rosemary
¼ teaspoon summer savory
Dash cayenne pepper

Rub flank steak with oil and 1 clove of garlic. Set aside. To the melted butter, add onion, garlic, Worcestershire sauce, salt, parsley, rosemary, summer savory and cayenne pepper. Heat until bubbly. Broil flank steak for 3 minutes on each side. Slice against grain and place on warm platter. Serve warm sauce in separate bowl to be spooned over steak slices.

Vintner's Casserole

Yield: Serves 6

1 pound lean ground beef
1 tablespoon butter or margarine
1 medium onion, chopped
½ green pepper, chopped
2 stalks celery, chopped
2 (8-ounce) cans tomato sauce
½ cup California dry red wine
1 (4-ounce) can sliced mushrooms, drained
1 teaspoon oregano
Salt and pepper to taste
1 (8-ounce) package wide egg noodles
1 cup (½-pint) dairy sour cream
1 cup (½-pint) large curd cottage cheese
1 teaspoon poppy seeds
⅓ cup grated Parmesan cheese
1 cup shredded mozzarella or Cheddar cheese

In a large, heavy skillet sauté beef in butter or margarine until it is no longer red, stirring to separate it into bits. Add onion, green pepper, and celery; sauté 5 minutes longer. Drain off all excess fat. Add tomato sauce, wine, mushrooms, oregano, salt and pepper; cover and simmer 10 minutes, stirring often. Cook noodles in boiling water just until tender; drain. In a large bowl, mix together noodles, cottage cheese, sour cream, and poppy seeds. In a greased 3-quart casserole spread half the noodle mixture, then half the meat sauce; sprinkle with half the cheeses. Repeat layers finishing with cheese. Bake in a preheated 350 degree oven for 45 to 50 minutes or until hot and bubbly. Pass extra Parmesan cheese when serving.

Onion and garlic odors on hands can be eliminated by washing hands with vinegar and rubbing with celery salt.

Stuffed Flank Steak

(Great for a cold winter's night) Yield: Serves 6

- 1/4 cup vegetable oil
- 3 tablespoons butter or margarine
- 3 cups bread cubes, made from firm, homemade bread slices, cut 1/2-inch thick
- 1 pound lean ground beef
- 1 cup finely chopped onion
- 1/4 cup finely chopped celery
- 1 egg, beaten
- 2 garlic cloves, minced
- 1 tablespoon minced fresh parsley
- 1 1/2 teaspoons salt
- 1/4 teaspoon dried thyme
- Freshly ground pepper
- 1 (1 1/2 to 1 3/4 pound) trimmed, thick flank steak
- 2 tablespoons butter
- 1 tablespoon vegetable oil
- Salt and freshly ground pepper
- 2 bay leaves, crumbled
- 1 carrot, thinly sliced
- 1 onion, finely chopped
- 1 large tomato, coarsely chopped
- 1 teaspoon thyme leaves
- 1 cup California dry red wine
- 2 cups beef stock
- 2 tablespoons cornstarch, dissolved in 1/4 cup cold water

Heat oil and 3 tablespoons butter in a large skillet over medium-low heat. Add bread cubes and sauté until brown on all sides. Remove from heat. Combine ground beef, onion, celery, egg, garlic, parsley, salt and thyme with pepper to taste in a large mixing bowl and blend well. Gently stir in bread cubes. Cut pocket lengthwise in steak. Fill with stuffing, securing with string. Melt remaining butter and oil in deep casserole or Dutch oven. Sprinkle steak with salt and pepper and brown on all sides. Add bay leaves, carrot, onion, tomato and thyme and cook over medium heat, uncovered, for 5 minutes. Add wine and stock and bring to a boil. Reduce heat to low, cover and cook 1 1/4 hours. Transfer meat to heated platter and keep warm. Add dissolved cornstarch to pan juices and stir constantly over medium-high heat until thickened; remove bay leaves. Slice meat and spoon sauce over top.

Note:
This dish is also excellent served cold.

Beef and Brew Bake

Yield: Serves 6 generously

3 tablespoons butter or margarine
2½ pounds beef chuck, cubed
1½ teaspoons salt
¾ teaspoon black pepper
1 teaspoon dried marjoram
½ pound sharp Cheddar cheese, shredded
1 large onion, sliced thinly
½ pound fresh mushrooms, cooked and drained
1 large green pepper, sliced
1¼ cups cranberry juice
1 cup beer
3 drops Tabasco sauce

Heat butter or margarine in a skillet and brown beef cubes. In a small bowl, combine salt, pepper and marjoram; set aside. Grease a 4-quart casserole and arrange successive layers of browned beef, cheese, onion, mushrooms and green pepper sprinkling with salt mixture. Combine cranberry juice, beer and Tabasco sauce and pour over top of layered beef. Cover and bake in a preheated 350 degree oven for 2 hours, or until meat is tender. Remove from oven and let stand for 10 minutes before serving.

Slotstekk

(A treasured Danish recipe)

Yield: Serves 4 to 6

3 pounds beef brisket, peppered
2 tablespoons vegetable oil
2 onions, sliced
2 tablespoons flour
2 tablespoons molasses
2 cups beef broth or bouillon
6 anchovies

In a large oven-proof Dutch oven, sear beef in oil until browned. Remove meat from pan. Add onions; cook until tender. Sprinkle flour over onions and stir until smooth. Add molasses, beef broth and anchovies. Return meat to pan; cover and bake in a preheated 325 degree oven for approximately 3 hours.

Layered Company Roast

Yield: Serves 6 to 8 generously

- 3 to 4 pound boneless rump roast
- 1 cup chopped green pepper
- 1 cup sliced mushrooms
- 1 cup sliced celery
- 1 cup sliced and quartered carrots
- 1 medium onion, chopped
- ½ cup sliced almonds
- 1 pound bulk pork sausage
- ⅛ cup sliced almonds for topping
- Salt to taste
- Pepper to taste
- Garlic powder to taste

Slice roast into 3 horizontal layers, consisting of top, middle and bottom. Combine green pepper, mushrooms, celery, carrots, onion and almonds in a medium bowl. In an appropriate sized roasting pan, lay a section of aluminum foil long enough to cover the roast. Next, lay 3 or 4 lengths of heavy string, long enough to secure all the layers of meat together. Place bottom layer of meat centered on top of string. Season with garlic powder, salt and pepper. Spread a quarter of vegetables (approximately 1¼ cups) on top of meat. Take half of the sausage and make a patty about the size of the meat layer, and place it on top of the vegetables. Spread one half of vegetables on top of sausage and top with next layer of meat. Repeat this procedure, ending with top layer of meat. Season with garlic powder, salt and pepper. Tie the roast tightly with string and enclose it in the foil. Bake in a preheated 300 degree oven for 2½ to 3 hours. Remove from oven and let stand for 30 minutes before slicing. Make gravy from drippings and spoon over the top. Sprinkle with almonds to garnish.

Make two or more casseroles at a time and freeze the extras for later use. Use aluminum foil to line the dishes of those casseroles you plan to freeze. When thoroughly frozen, remove foil and food, leaving casserole dishes free for use. Later, simply place the frozen-foil package back into the same casserole dish for baking.

Saucy Spanish Pot Roast

Yield: Serves 6

3 to 3½-pound chuck roast
3 tablespoons all-purpose flour
3 tablespoons vegetable oil
2 medium onions, chopped
2 cloves garlic, minced
3 cups canned tomatoes
1 (8-ounce) can tomato sauce
½ cup parsley, chopped
1 bay leaf
5 to 6 rosemary leaves, broken
½ cup California dry red wine, Burgundy or Zinfandel
1 teaspoon salt
Pepper to taste
1 teaspoon nutmeg
1 teaspoon paprika
½ teaspoon ground cloves
¼ teaspoon allspice
Cherry tomatoes
Parsley

Coat meat with flour on both sides. In heavy skillet or Dutch oven (with tight fitting lid), brown meat on both sides in oil, over medium heat. When browned, carefully remove meat to a platter. Add onions and garlic to the pan and brown slightly. Add tomatoes, tomato sauce, parsley, bay leaf, rosemary leaves and wine. In a small bowl, combine salt, pepper, nutmeg, paprika, cloves and allspice and divide in half. Sprinkle ½ of these spices into the sauce and mix well. Return browned roast to the sauce in the pan and sprinkle the remaining ½ of the spices directly onto the meat. Spoon some of the sauce over the meat and simmer, tightly covered, for 3 hours. Occasionally spoon sauce over the meat. When tender, arrange the pot roast on a deep platter. Spoon sauce over and around the meat. Garnish with tiny cherry tomatoes and parsley.

Note:
Serve roast accompanied by cooked egg noodles if desired.

Meatloaf in a Breadbasket

Food Processor

Yield: Serves 6 to 8

1 large round loaf French bread, 9 to 10-inches in diameter
½ cup milk
1½ to 1¾ pounds ground sirloin or chuck
1 small onion, chopped
½ cup packed parsley sprigs, chopped
2 eggs, well beaten
2 cloves garlic, minced
1¼ teaspoons salt
¼ teaspoon pepper
¾ teaspoon oregano leaves
¾ teaspoon dry basil
1 cup (4-ounces) Jack or Swiss cheese, grated
2 tablespoons butter or margarine, softened

Using a long serrated knife, slice the bread in half horizontally. Pull soft bread out of both halves, leaving a ½-inch thick shell. Place the removed soft bread in processor work bowl, fitted with metal blade; process enough bread to make 1¼ cups of crumbs. Turn crumbs into large bowl and stir in milk. Let stand for 5 minutes. Trim excess fat from meat and cut into 1-inch cubes. Chop meat in food processor, 1 cup at a time, using on/off bursts, until medium fine. Add meat to bread crumbs. In processor work bowl, chop onion and parsley; add eggs, garlic, salt, pepper, oregano and basil and process 2 seconds to blend. Add to meat mixture. Add grated cheese to meat mixture, and mix well. Pack meat mixture into bottom half of bread shell; press lid in place. Rub butter over outside of loaf. Securely wrap loaf in foil and bake in a preheated 350 degree oven for 2 hours. To serve, cut loaf into wedges.

Use a light touch when shaping balls, burgers or loaves of ground meat. Too much handling will result in compacted, juiceless meat.

Crocked Meatloaf

Crockpot Yield: Serves 6 to 8

2 pounds ground beef or 1 pound ground beef and 1 pound ground pork
1 (1½-ounce) envelope Sloppy Joe seasoning mix
2 eggs, beaten
3 tablespoons catsup
1 onion, grated
1 cup instant oatmeal
1 small green pepper, diced
½ cup water chestnuts, diced (optional)
Salt and pepper to taste

Combine meat with Sloppy Joe seasoning mix, eggs, catsup, onion, oatmeal, green pepper, water chestnuts, salt and pepper. Shape meat into a loaf that will fit the bottom of your crockpot. Prepare sauce (recipe follows).

Sauce:

2 (8-ounce) cans tomato sauce
4 teaspoons sugar
⅓ cup dehydrated vegetable flakes
Few dashes of Tabasco sauce

Combine tomato sauce, sugar, vegetable flakes and Tabasco. Pour over meat loaf. Cover pot and cook on low for 4 to 5 hours.

Roasting:

Beef/rare (12 to 15 minutes per pound)
Beef/well-done (18 to 20 minutes per pound)
Veal (30 to 35 minutes per pound)
Mutton (15 to 18 minutes per pound)
Leg of lamb (18 to 20 minutes per pound)
Pork (30 to 35 minutes per pound)
Venison (12 to 15 minutes per pound)

Beef Vagabond

(Great for picnics or tailgate parties!) Yield: Serves 8

½ pound fresh mushrooms, chopped
2 green peppers, chopped
1 red pepper, chopped
2 white onions, chopped
3 cloves garlic, minced
4 tablespoons butter or margarine
3 pounds extra lean ground beef
2 tablespoons olive oil
Paprika to taste
Salt and pepper to taste
1 (6-ounce) can tomato paste
1 (8-ounce) can tomato sauce
½ cup minced parsley
8 pita pocket breads, cut in half to reveal pocket

In a large skillet, sauté mushrooms, green peppers, red pepper, onions and garlic in 2 tablespoons of butter for 3 to 4 minutes. Set aside. In the same skillet, in olive oil and remaining butter, brown meat in small batches until completely cooked. Season well with paprika, salt and pepper. Return vegetables to pan. Add tomato paste, tomato sauce and parsley; simmer 10 to 15 minutes. Add water if mixture seems too dry. Remove from heat; cover and refrigerate. Before serving, reheat mixture and serve tucked into pita bread for a portable sandwich.

Note:
Filling should be prepared ahead and may be frozen.

Serve a light salad with a hearty meal, a tart salad with fish, a hearty salad as a main course, and a fruit salad as an appetizer or dessert.

Chimichangas with Machacha Filling

(This oven-baked version is easy to prepare and lower in calories.)

Yield: Serves 12

Machacha Filling:

1 pound boneless chuck
1 cup water
6 black peppercorns
¼ medium onion, chopped
Salt
1 clove garlic, mashed
¼ teaspoon salt
½ medium onion, chopped
1 tablespoon vegetable oil
1 (7-ounce) can whole green chiles, cut in short strips
2 small tomatoes, chopped
¼ teaspoon cumin
Ground pepper

Place meat in large pan. Add water, black peppercorns, onion and salt to taste. Bring to boil; then reduce heat and simmer until tender - about 1½ hours. Cool meat in broth, then drain, reserving ½ cup broth. Shred meat using two forks and set aside. In large skillet, add garlic, ¼ teaspoon salt, and onion to oil and cook until tender. Add chile strips and chopped tomatoes to onion mixture; cook an additional 3 minutes. Add shredded meat, cumin and pepper to taste. When meat is heated through, add reserved broth and salt if needed. Set aside.

Chimichangas:

12 large, fresh, flour tortillas
¼ cup butter or margarine, melted
Dairy sour cream
Guacamole (see recipe page 299)
Salsa (see recipe page 382)

Brush both sides of the tortillas with melted butter or margarine. Place about ¼ cup filling in the center of the tortilla. Fold ends of tortilla over meat and then fold sides to center to make a packet. Secure with wooden toothpick, if needed. Continue with remaining tortillas and place on rimmed baking sheet, seam side down. Bake in a preheated 475 degree oven for 8 to 10 minutes or until golden.

Serve with sour cream, your favorite guacamole and salsa as condiments.

Note:
Chimichangas may be frozen before the baking step.

Armenian Hamburgers

(Make sure that you have lots of napkins on hand when you eat these yummy burgers)

Yield: Serves 4

Sauce:

1½ tablespoons butter or margarine
1 large onion, thinly sliced
1 large green pepper, thinly sliced
1 large tomato, chopped
1 clove garlic, minced
1 (8-ounce) can tomato sauce
1 tablespoon dried parsley flakes
1 tablespoon sweet basil
1 teaspoon seasoned salt

Sauté onion in butter or margarine until soft and lightly browned. Add green pepper, tomato, garlic, tomato sauce, parsley, basil and salt. Cook over medium-high heat until liquid is reduced and sauce is slightly thickened.

1 pound ground sirloin
½ pound ground lamb
1 tablespoon dried parsley flakes
1 teaspoon garlic salt
Pepper to taste
4 individual peda buns or hamburger buns

Combine sirloin, lamb, parsley, garlic salt and pepper. Shape into 4 patties and barbecue or broil to desired doneness. Cut buns in half. Place patty on bottom half; cover with sauce, and top with remaining half of bun.

Old Settlers' Baked Beans

Yield: Serves 12

1 pound ground beef
½ pound bacon, diced
1 large onion, chopped
⅓ cup brown sugar
¼ cup sugar
¼ cup catsup
¼ cup barbecue sauce
2 tablespoons prepared mustard
2 tablespoons molasses
1 teaspoon chili powder
½ teaspoon pepper
1 (15¼-ounce) can red kidney beans, drained
1 (16-ounce) can pork and beans
1 (15-ounce) can butter beans or lima beans, drained

In a large frying pan, brown ground beef, bacon and onion. Drain off all excess fat. Combine brown sugar, sugar, catsup, barbecue sauce, mustard, molasses, chili powder, pepper, kidney beans, pork and beans and butter beans, and add to meat mixture. Pour into large baking dish and bake in a preheated 350 degree oven for 25 to 35 minutes or until bubbly.

Note:
Best if made a day ahead. A larger amount can be made by adding an extra can or two of any of the beans.

Chili and Beans

(A well tested family favorite)

Yield: 1 gallon

2 pounds ground chuck
3 medium yellow onions, chopped fine
3 cloves garlic, chopped fine
2 (28-ounce) cans peeled plum tomatoes with basil (Progresso)
3 (20-ounce) cans kidney beans (Progresso)
4 tablespoons chili powder
Salt and pepper to taste
Cumin to taste

Brown meat slowly in large skillet. Remove meat and add onions and garlic. Sauté slowly until transparent. Place browned meat, onions, garlic, plum tomatoes, kidney beans, chili powder, salt, pepper, and cumin in large pot. Cook slowly over low heat for at least 2 hours. Best if cooked several days ahead. Serve with assorted condiments of your choice such as chopped onions, salsa, grated sharp Cheddar cheese, chopped olives, etc.

Spicy Valley Chili

Yield: Serves 4 to 6

2 cups dry pinto beans
1½ pounds lean chuck, cut into small cubes
2 tablespoons vegetable oil
1 onion, chopped
2 cloves garlic, minced
2 tablespoons all-purpose flour
2 tablespoons chili powder
1 teaspoon cumin
1 teaspoon cayenne
1 to 2 teaspoons salt
1 teaspoon coarse ground pepper
Dash sugar
¼ cup water

Sort beans and soak overnight in water. Drain. Place beans in large stock pot, and add enough water to cover; simmer for 1 hour. Meanwhile, in a large pot, sauté beef cubes in oil until brown. Remove meat and reserve. Add onion and garlic and sauté. In a small bowl, combine flour, chili powder, cumin, cayenne, salt, pepper, sugar and water to make a pasty gravy. Put meat back in pot with onion and garlic. Add gravy mixture and toss together. Simmer for 5 minutes. Add beans with water and simmer until beans are tender but not mushy, about 2 to 2½ hours. Taste and adjust seasonings.

Pinquito Beans

Yield: Serves 4 or more

2 pounds Pinquito beans
6 tablespoons chili powder
1 tablespoon cumin
2 fresh jalapeño peppers
1 tablespoon beef stock base
2 smoked pork hocks or 10 ounces chopped ham
1 tablespoon oregano
1 tablespoon chopped cilantro
3 cloves garlic, minced
4 tablespoons Kitchen Bouquet
3 slices thick bacon, chopped
1 level tablespoon black pepper

Sort through beans and rinse well. Drain and place in at least an 8-quart pot. Cover with boiling water. Cover pot and soak for 1 hour. Add chili powder, cumin, jalapeño peppers, beef stock base, pork hocks or ham, oregano, cilantro, garlic, Kitchen Bouquet, bacon, black pepper and more water to cover. Bring mixture to a rolling boil. Reduce heat, cover and simmer about 3 to 4 hours or until beans are tender. Add water as necessary, stirring occasionally. Remove pork hocks from beans and shred meat. Discard all fat and bones, and stir meat back into beans.

Note:
These beans freeze well, covered tightly. They also taste better if made a day in advance. When re-heating, add water and heat slowly.

Frontier Chili Beans

Yield: Multitudes (4-gallons)

5 pounds ground beef
4 cups chopped onion
8 garlic cloves, minced
Olive oil
2 tablespoons oregano
3 tablespoons red pepper flakes
1 tablespoon beef bouillon
2 tablespoons chili powder
1 (16-ounce) can tomato paste
1 tablespoon cumin
2 gallons canned pinto beans
2 (18-ounce) cans whole tomatoes
2 teaspoons sugar
2 (7-ounce) cans chopped green chiles
Salt and pepper

In a large frypan, brown ground beef, onion and garlic in olive oil. When meat is browned, drain and remove mixture to a large stockpot. Add oregano, red pepper, bouillon, chili powder, tomato paste, cumin, beans, whole tomatoes, sugar and green chiles, and bring to a boil. Reduce heat and simmer for 1 hour, stirring occasionally. Add salt and pepper to taste.

Veal Oscar

Yield: Serves 4

4 thin veal cutlets (5-ounces each)
6 tablespoons butter or margarine
16 hot cooked asparagus spears
8 crab legs, sautéed in butter
Bernaise sauce

Sauté veal cutlets in butter until golden brown on both sides and tender. Place cutlets on a warm platter. Arrange asparagus and crab legs on veal so that equal portions can be lifted off with each cutlet when serving. Cover with warm Bernaise sauce.

Bernaise Sauce:

Yield: about 1 cup

1 tablespoon chopped shallot or green onion
1 teaspoon dried tarragon
¼ teaspoon thyme
Dash of salt
Dash of pepper
¼ cup white vinegar
¼ cup California dry white wine
2 egg yolks
½ cup butter or margarine
Chopped fresh chervil and/or chopped fresh tarragon

In a small saucepan, combine shallot, dried tarragon, thyme, salt, pepper, vinegar and wine. Bring to a boil and cook until reduced by half. Let mixture cool. Beat egg yolks into mixture. Divide butter into thirds. Place egg yolk mixture over hot water. Add butter, a third at a time, and stir constantly until smooth and thickened. Garnish with chopped chervil and/or tarragon.

Veal Piccata

Yield: Serves 4

1½ pounds veal, cut into thin slices
½ cup flour
½ cup Parmesan cheese
Salt
Pepper
¼ cup butter or margarine
Juice of 3 to 4 lemons
½ cup beef broth (preferably homemade)
¼ cup California dry white wine
1 egg yolk, beaten
Parsley
Lemon slices

Lightly pound very thin veal even thinner between sheets of waxed paper. Mix flour, Parmesan cheese, salt and pepper. Dip veal in flour mixture and sauté in melted butter mixed with juice of 2 lemons. Sauté veal about 2 minutes on each side. Sprinkle more lemon juice over veal. Remove to hot platter and place in oven to keep warm. Mix beaten egg yolk with a little broth and wine. Add remaining broth and wine to pan drippings, scraping loose all particles. Add egg mixture; bring to a boil, stirring vigorously. Pour over veal and garnish with parsley and lemon slices.

Leg of Veal with Prosciutto

Yield: Serves 4

1 (2-pound) leg of veal
2 carrots, cut into strips
½ pound prosciutto, cut into ¼-inch wide strips
4 tablespoons butter
1 tablespoon olive oil
2 sage leaves
1 cup California dry white wine

Make lengthwise incisions all around veal. Place the prosciutto and carrot strips in the incisions, and tie with string, if necessary. In a large Dutch oven heat butter and oil over a low flame. Brown veal on all sides, then add sage and wine. Cover and continue cooking for about 2½ hours, basting frequently. Remove string, cut veal into slices, top with sauce from pan and serve.

Note:
Can substitute lamb and prepare in the same manner.

Veal in Wine Sauce

Yield: Serves 4 to 6

1 pound thinly sliced veal scallops
½ cup flour
1½ tablespoons vegetable oil
5 tablespoons butter or margarine
1 (4-ounce) package sliced cooked ham, cut into strips
2 tablespoons minced shallots
⅓ pound mushrooms, sliced
2 teaspoons beef stock base in 1½ cups water
½ cup California dry white wine
¼ teaspoon thyme leaves
¼ teaspoon white pepper
Salt
1 (14-ounce) can artichoke hearts, drained
1 cup Jack or other white cheese, shredded

Dredge veal in ¼ cup flour. Brown in hot oil mixed with 2 tablespoons of the butter; remove veal from pan and reserve. Add shallots and mushrooms to pan and cook until moisture evaporates. Remove pan from heat and stir in remaining ¼ cup flour; gradually add beef stock, wine, thyme and pepper. Return to heat and cook, stirring until mixture boils and thickens. Salt to taste. Arrange artichoke hearts on bottom of greased 2-quart casserole. Place veal on top of artichoke hearts, top with mushroom sauce, ham and cheese. Cover casserole and bake in a preheated 400 degree oven for 20 minutes. Uncover and bake 5 minutes more. Serve immediately.

Note:
You may substitute boneless chicken breasts for veal.

Veal Sweetbreads in Champagne Sauce

Yield: Serves 2

1 pound veal sweetbreads
Salt and pepper
2 tablespoons vegetable oil
1 cup California dry champagne
2 shallots, chopped
¼ cup mushrooms
1 cup whipping cream or heavy cream
2 tablespoons butter, softened
1 tablespoon chopped fresh tarragon

Soak the sweetbreads in ice water for 2 hours. Then place the sweetbreads in boiling water and blanch for 3 minutes. Cool in ice water and pat dry. Remove all of the membrane from the outside of the sweetbreads. Season the sweetbreads with salt and pepper. In a saucepan, heat the oil and add the sweetbreads. Brown on both sides and place in a preheated 400 degree oven for 10 minutes. Remove from the oven and keep warm. Using the same saucepan, add the champagne and bring to a boil. Add the shallots, mushrooms and the cream. Let reduce until slightly thickened. Add the softened butter and the fresh herbs and bring just to a boil. Pour sauce over the sweetbreads and serve.

Stuffed Breast of Veal

Yield: Serves 4

1 breast of veal (approximately 3 pounds), with pocket cut
3 tablespoons butter or margarine
2 cloves garlic, minced
3 tablespoons minced parsley
2 stalks celery, diced
1 medium onion, chopped
4 slices bread, crusts removed
½ cup milk
1 (10-ounce) package frozen spinach, thawed and well drained
1 pound lean ground pork
2 eggs
Dash nutmeg
1 teaspoon salt
1 teaspoon pepper
1 cup chicken broth (preferably homemade)

Preheat oven to 350 degrees. In a large skillet, sauté garlic, parsley, celery and onion in butter. Remove from heat. Soak bread in milk; drain and squeeze dry. Add bread, spinach, ground pork, eggs, nutmeg, salt and pepper to cooled mixture in skillet. Mix well. Stuff pocket of veal breast with mixture; sew opening closed with heavy thread. Place veal in large roasting pan. Pour chicken broth over veal. Cover and bake at 350 degrees for approximately 1½ hours or until juices run yellow when veal is pierced. Remove to platter and carve.

Lamb Noisettes

Yield: Serves 2 to 4
depending on amount of meat

- 6 tablespoons butter or margarine
- 1 large onion, chopped
- 1½ tablespoons flour
- ½ cup California dry white wine
- 1 cup cream
- ½ teaspoon salt
- ¼ teaspoon white pepper
- Dash nutmeg
- ¼ cup butter, or margarine
- Rack of lamb, boned and cut into 1½-inch pieces
- Butter or margarine to sauté meat

In a large saucepan, melt 6 tablespoons butter; sauté onion until it is transparent but not brown. Add flour, stirring until smooth. Add wine, cream, salt, pepper and nutmeg. Simmer mixture for 5 minutes, stirring frequently. Add ¼ cup butter just as you remove from heat. Place mixture in blender and whip. Salt meat lightly and sauté in butter until just done. Serve with sauce covering meat.

Note:
Boneless breast of chicken can be used instead of lamb.

ERNA'S ELDERBERRY HOUSE

Filet of Lamb in Tomato Sauce with Fennel

Yield: Serves 4

2 pounds beefsteak tomatoes
2 large onions, chopped
3 cloves garlic, minced
2 tablespoons virgin olive oil
2 tablespoons tomato paste
2 tablespoons sugar
Salt and pepper
Fresh thyme
3 stalks fennel
2 tablespoons fresh lemon juice
8 lamb filets
1 tablespoon virgin olive oil
4 tablespoons Pernod liqueur
Salt and pepper

Core and peel tomatoes and cut into quarters; deseed. Chop tomato flesh into small cubes and allow to drain in a colander while other ingredients are prepared. In a saucepan, sauté onion and garlic in olive oil until onions are transparent. Add tomato paste and cook over low heat for 5 minutes, stirring constantly. Blend in drained tomato cubes, sugar, salt, pepper and thyme to taste. Partially cover saucepan and simmer sauce ingredients for approximately 20 minutes or until almost all of the liquid has evaporated. Puree mixture in a blender or food processor and keep sauce warm. Meanwhile, clean fennel and cut into narrow strips. Place prepared fennel in a small saucepan; cover with water and add lemon juice. Bring to a boil, and cook for 6 to 8 minutes, or until fennel tests tender-crisp. Drain and keep warm. Clean lamb filets of all fat and skin. In a skillet, brown well on both sides in 1 tablespoon hot olive oil. Carefully pour the Pernod over lamb and flame. Continue browning the meat for another 3 minutes or so—center of each filet should still be pink. Lightly salt and pepper meat and cut filets into medium-thick slices. Spoon some of warm tomato sauce onto each individual serving plate. Place slices of filet over sauce and arrange warm fennel strips in an attractive decorative circle around meat. Serve with lemon-flavored rice.

Roast Lamb with Coffee and Cream

(Unique and wonderful!)

Yield: Serves 6

1 leg of lamb, skin removed
2 to 3 cloves garlic, sliced
Salt, pepper and dry mustard to taste
2 to 3 ounces salt pork, thinly sliced
2 cups strong coffee mixed with cream
1 cup California Port wine

Rub the skinned leg of lamb with the garlic cloves, then insert garlic slices into the lamb. Season well with salt, pepper and dry mustard. Place thin slices of salt pork over the lamb and roast in a preheated 400 degree oven for ½ hour until the lamb is well browned. Remove the pork and discard. Pour coffee and cream over the lamb and reduce heat to 325 degrees. Roast for 2 hours, basting as often as possible. Pour excess fat from basting sauce and add Port wine to juices, continue basting and baking for ½ hour more. Carve the lamb; then replace the slices on the leg bone as well as you can. Serve the gravy separately.

Barbecued Butterflied Leg of Lamb

Yield: Serves 6 to 8

1 cup catsup
1 cup water
¼ cup Worcestershire sauce
¼ cup cider vinegar
Few drops Tabasco sauce
¼ cup brown sugar, firmly packed
1 teaspoon celery salt
1 teaspoon chili powder
1 teaspoon salt
1 leg of lamb (about 6 pounds), boned, trimmed and butterflied

Combine catsup, water, Worcestershire sauce, vinegar, Tabasco, brown sugar, celery salt, chili powder and salt in a 2-quart pan. Bring to a simmer, but DO NOT BOIL. Remove from heat and pour over lamb. Marinate overnight in the refrigerator. The following day, remove lamb from marinade, reserving marinade for basting. Barbecue lamb 8 to 10-inches from hot coals for about 50 minutes. Turn often and baste every 10 to 15 minutes. Do not overcook. The meat should be crisp on the outside and pink on the inside.

Leg of Lamb with Apricot Sauce

(Wonderfully spicy!)

Yield: Serves 4 to 6 depending on size of roast

1 leg of lamb (5 to 6 pounds)
3 to 4 cloves garlic, sliced
2 large onions, chopped
1 clove garlic, minced
2 tablespoons butter or margarine
2 cups apricot jam
1 teaspoon salt
Dash cayenne pepper
2 tablespoons curry powder
3 tablespoons cider vinegar
¼ cup brown sugar

Apricot Sauce:

In a medium saucepan, lightly brown onions and garlic in butter. Add apricot jam, salt, cayenne pepper, curry powder, vinegar and brown sugar. Simmer gently for 30 to 45 minutes. Add a little water if sauce becomes too thick.

Method:

Stud leg of lamb with sliced garlic cloves. Cook to desired doneness. During the last 45 minutes of cooking time, baste with apricot sauce. Serve remaining sauce with lamb at table.

Kouzou Kzartma
(Armenian Baked Lamb Shanks)

Yield: Serves 4

2 to 3 tablespoons salad oil
4 lamb shanks
1 onion, sliced
2 cloves garlic, minced
½ cup parsley, chopped
1 teaspoon rosemary
1 (6-ounce) can tomato paste
1 (15-ounce) can tomato sauce
1 cup California Burgundy wine
Salt and pepper to taste
1 cup water

Brown lamb shanks in oil; remove from pan and reserve. Add onion and garlic to pan drippings and sauté until onion is soft. Add parsley, rosemary, tomato paste, tomato sauce, Burgundy wine, salt, pepper and water to pan. Simmer sauce for about 10 minutes. Meanwhile, arrange browned lamb shanks in roasting pan to fit; pour sauce over meat. Cover and bake in a preheated 350 degree oven for 1½ to 2 hours.

Lamb Shanks with Dill

Yield: Serves 4

4 lamb shanks
1 medium onion, sliced
1 (14-ounce) can whole tomatoes
¼ cup brown sugar
1 cup California dry white wine
1 tablespoon dry dill weed
½ teaspoon oregano
1 teaspoon rosemary
1 clove garlic, minced

Arrange lamb shanks in large casserole or roasting pan. Cover with onion slices. Mix tomatoes, brown sugar, wine, dill weed, oregano, rosemary and garlic; pour sauce over shanks. Bake in a preheated 300 degree oven for 3 hours. Uncover and let brown for 20 minutes. Serve with white rice.

Barbecue Lamb Shanks

Yield: Serves 4

4 lamb shanks
2 to 3 tablespoons vegetable oil
1 large onion, sliced
1 cup catsup
1 cup California dry red wine
2 teaspoons salt
2 tablespoons Worcestershire sauce
½ cup cider vinegar
¼ cup brown sugar
2 tablespoons dry mustard

Brown shanks in oil; place in roasting pan. Arrange sliced onions over shanks. Mix catsup, red wine, salt, Worcestershire sauce, vinegar, brown sugar and dry mustard; pour over onion-topped shanks. Cover and bake in a preheated 350 degree oven for 1½ to 2 hours, basting occasionally.

Cous-Cous
(Moroccan Lamb Stew)

Yield: Serves 6 to 8

3 onions, chopped
8 to 9 pound leg of lamb, cut into cubes, making 5 pounds
4 to 5 large tomatoes, chopped or 1 (29-ounce) can whole tomatoes, drained and chopped
1 tablespoon salt
1 teaspoon cayenne, or to taste
1 bay leaf
½ to 1 cup parsley, minced
½ cup California dry white wine
½ cup California raisins
½ cup dried apricots
½ cup dried pitted prunes
½ cup dried peaches, cut into fourths
½ teaspoon coriander
½ teaspoon turmeric
1 tablespoon honey
2 tablespoons California brandy
½ cup toasted pine nuts, or toasted, blanched, slivered almonds
1 cup drained garbanzo beans or chick peas

In a large Dutch oven, brown onions lightly in the oil. Remove from pan; reserve. In the same pan, brown meat. Return onions to the pan and add tomatoes, salt, cayenne, bay leaf, parsley, wine, raisins, dried apricots, prunes and peaches, coriander, turmeric, honey and brandy. Stir well to combine. Cover tightly and bake in a preheated 350 degree oven for 60 minutes or until meat tests tender. Remove Dutch oven from oven and stir in the garbanzo beans or chick peas. Cover for 5 minutes to heat through. Serve stew over Cous-Cous or cooked rice.

Note:
Cous-Cous is a Moroccan pasta-type product that can be found in the pasta-rice section of your grocery or the gourmet food section, or a Middle East deli.

Barbecued Pork Chops

Yield: Serves 4

½ cup apricot jam
½ teaspoon garlic salt
½ teaspoon Tabasco sauce
1 tablespoon dehydrated onions
1 tablespoon soy sauce
1 tablespoon water
8 thinly sliced pork chops

In a medium sized bowl, combine jam, garlic salt, Tabasco sauce, dehydrated onions, soy sauce and water. Pour marinade over chops and chill at least 1 hour. Grill chops over coals 25 to 30 minutes, turning often and basting with marinade. Heat remaining marinade and serve with meat.

Note:
Other flavors of jams or jellies can be used such as pineapple, peach, currant, apple or orange marmalade.

Barbecued Ribs and Sauce

Yield: Serves 3 to 4

4 pounds country-style pork ribs, cut into individual pieces
1 tablespoon butter
1 clove garlic, minced
1 cup catsup
2 tablespoons brown sugar
1 tablespoon Worcestershire sauce
1 teaspoon celery seed
⅓ cup chili sauce
2 tablespoons chopped onion
1 tablespoon prepared mustard
¼ teaspoon salt
3 thin lemon slices
Dash Tabasco sauce

Simmer ribs in enough salted water to cover, for 45 minutes to 1 hour. Drain ribs and place in a shallow baking pan. Melt butter; add garlic and sauté for 5 minutes. Add catsup, brown sugar, Worcestershire sauce, celery seed, chili sauce, chopped onion, mustard, salt, lemon slices and Tabasco. Bring to a boil, stirring frequently, and pour boiling sauce over ribs. Bake in a preheated 350 degree oven for 20 minutes, basting often. Ribs may also be barbecued, but be careful, as sauce tends to burn easily.

Chinese Marinated Pork Roast or Ribs

Yield: Serves 2 to 4

½ teaspoon salt
⅓ cup soy sauce
2 tablespoons California dry sherry
¼ cup sugar
2 teaspoons red food coloring (optional)
3 tablespoons chopped fresh ginger
6 cloves garlic, minced
1 teaspoon Five Spice powder (available in Oriental section)
Pork loin roast (about 3 pounds) or 3 to 4 pounds pork spareribs

Combine salt, soy sauce, sherry, sugar, food coloring, ginger, garlic and Five Spice powder. Pour over roast or ribs; marinate in the refrigerator overnight. Bake in a preheated 350 degree oven until well done (about 30 minutes per pound), (internal temperature of 170 degrees).

Note:
Ribs may be barbecued or baked.

Roast Pork with Currant Jelly Glaze

Yield: Serves 6 to 8

4 to 5 pound, center cut, pork loin roast
1 (10-ounce) jar currant jelly
⅓ cup light corn syrup
2 tablespoons cider vinegar
½ teaspoon dry mustard
¼ teaspoon ginger

Have meat retailer loosen the chine (back) bone by sawing across the rib bones. Place roast, fat side up, on rack in open roasting pan. Insert roast meat thermometer so bulb is in thickest part of roast, not touching bone. Bake in a preheated 325 degree oven for 2 to 2½ hours, or until meat thermometer reaches an internal temperature of 170 degrees. While roast is cooking, prepare glaze. Combine currant jelly, corn syrup, vinegar, mustard and ginger in saucepan. Bring to a simmer; simmer for 2 minutes. Brush glaze over roast 2 or 3 times during the last 30 minutes of roasting.

Raclette Sausage Rolls

Yield: Serves 1 to 2 sausages per person

1½ to 2 pounds sausages which require little additional cooking, such as garlic sausage, German veal franks, old-fashion dinner franks or Smoky Links
1 pound Muenster or Gruyere cheese
12 soft French rolls
Butter
1 (16-ounce) jar sweet-sour red cabbage

Start charcoal or wood in outdoor barbecue. When coals are ready for cooking, arrange sausages on skewers and cook over coals until lightly browned and sizzling. Meanwhile, place cheese on a foil or metal pan and heat at the edge of the grill until melted and slightly crusty. Split and butter rolls and warm on the grill. To serve - place 1 or 2 sausages in each roll; spread with cheese and garnish with a spoonful of red cabbage. Serve with a selection of mustards.

Curry Steak Marinade

Yield: About ½ cup

⅓ cup vegetable oil
2 cloves garlic, crushed
2 dashes Aromatic Bitters
2 teaspoons Worcestershire sauce
1 teaspoon salt
½ teaspoon cracked pepper
1 to 2 teaspoons curry powder to taste

Combine oil, garlic, Aromatic Bitters, Worcestershire sauce, salt, pepper and curry powder. Marinate steak of your choice for at least 1½ hours. Baste steak with marinade while broiling or barbecuing to desired doneness.

Fluffy Mustard Sauce

Food Processor
(An excellent sauce to use with either hot or cold ham, or as a sandwich spread)

Yield: about 1½ cups

2 egg yolks
½ teaspoon salt
Dash of white pepper
2 teaspoons cider vinegar
1 cup vegetable oil
1½ teaspoons fresh lemon juice
2 tablespoons Dijon mustard
1 tablespoon honey

In a food processor, using plastic or metal blade, process egg yolks, salt, white pepper and cider vinegar for 3 seconds. With motor running, very slowly pour ¼ cup of the oil through the feed tube. Alternately add the remaining oil slowly, ¼ cup at a time, and the lemon juice. Turn off motor; add mustard and honey; process for 2 seconds. Refrigerate until serving time.

Barbecue Sauce for Lamb

Yield: 1½ cups

1 cup catsup
⅓ cup vegetable or olive oil
2 cloves garlic, minced
2 tablespoons Worcestershire sauce
½ teaspoon dry mustard
4 tablespoons mint flakes
Salt and pepper to taste

Mix catsup, oil, garlic, Worcestershire sauce, dry mustard, mint flakes, salt and pepper together. Allow mixture to mellow for 1 hour. Use to baste as you barbecue lamb.

Mint Sauce

(Excellent with hot or cold lamb)

Yield: ½ cup

3 tablespoons fresh mint
4 tablespoons white sugar
6 tablespoons cider vinegar

Select fresh, tender mint leaves; wash, pat dry and chop finely. In a small bowl combine mint, sugar and mix well. Allow to stand for a few minutes. Add vinegar to the mixture; cover and let stand for 24 hours or more at room temperature to allow flavors to mellow. Serve as an accompaniment sauce for a lamb dish.

Fresno Raisin Sauce

(Great over ham)

Yield: 1 cup

½ cup brown sugar
2 tablespoons cornstarch
1 teaspoon dry mustard
¼ teaspoon grated lemon peel
1½ cups water
2 tablespoons cider vinegar
2 tablespoons fresh lemon juice
½ cup California raisins

In a saucepan, mix brown sugar, cornstarch, dry mustard and lemon peel together; add water, vinegar and lemon juice and bring to a boil, stirring until sugar dissolves. Add raisins; reduce heat and simmer for 5 minutes. Serve sauce hot over ham, or chill to serve as a relish.

Spiced-Fruit Sauce for Baked Ham

Yield: 1½ cups

¼ cup butter
1 tablespoon flour
¼ cup orange juice
⅓ cup brown sugar
2 tablespoons sugar
¼ teaspoon cinnamon
¼ teaspoon nutmeg
⅛ teaspoon ground cloves
½ cup apple butter

In a small saucepan melt butter. Add flour, orange juice, brown sugar, sugar, cinnamon, nutmeg, cloves and apple butter. Mix and bring to a boil, stirring constantly. Serve hot with ham.

Variety Ham Glazes

Pineapple Glaze:

1 cup shredded pineapple, well drained
1 cup brown sugar
½ cup finely sifted bread crumbs

Mix together the pineapple, brown sugar and sifted bread crumbs. Pack over the top and sides of the baked ham, and bake for 1 more hour.

Apple Sauce Glaze:

1 cup apple sauce
½ teaspoon cinnamon

Mix together the apple sauce and cinnamon. Remove ham from oven, before last hour of baking. Score the fat, and spread the apple sauce mixture over the top and the sides. Bake for 1 more hour.

Peach Glaze:

2 (15-ounce) cans peach halves, drained and quartered (reserve juice)
Whole cloves
½ cup brown sugar
1 tablespoon ground cloves

Place peach quarters over the entire surface of the ham and secure with whole cloves. Bake ham. In a saucepan, combine reserved juice, brown sugar and ground cloves and bring to a boil. Let cook, stirring, for 5 minutes. Use the mixture to baste the ham during the last hour of baking.

Note:
These coatings are to be used on the smoked variety or Virginia-style ham, that have the skin removed and are at least partially cooked.

Notes

Buddhist Temple
Fresno

In 1889, a Buddhist Priest came from San Francisco to form a young man's organization. The first Buddhist temple was constructed in 1901, and the first service of the new Bukkyo Sein Kai was held in the little wooden structure in 1902. In 1920, this new three-story building was dedicated and renamed the Fresno Buddhist Church.

With the opening up of the state by the railroads, land in the Valley could be had for little money. An investor could purchase large-scale holdings and offer smaller, watered lots at a price that would ensure a profit. This was the Colony system. Much like the modern concept of sub-dividing lots, the Colonies were on a much larger scale, the sub-dividing of areas. These men would advertise throughout the world, offering the future to would-be immigrants. Each group of immigrants brought their customs, religion and hard work to the San Joaquin, and each area offered has grown into a town or an area of a present-day city.

By August, 1875, two San Francisco financiers were offering 192 acre lots in the Central California Colony. The first purchaser was even given a cow and grain, and soon thirty-six adults and eighteen children had settled in the area.

There were many Colonies in the Valley. A few of the most pronounced were:

The Irish Colony	at Woodville	1868
The Alabama Colony (Southerners)	Madera	1868
The Portuguese Colony	Hanford	1869
The Malaga Colony (Scandinavians)	Malaga	1869-1870
The Armenian Colony	Fresno	1874
The Scandinavian Colony	Clovis	1879
The Swiss Colony	Bakersfield	1880
The American Colony	South-West Malaga	1882
The Japanese Colony	Livingston	1906

Eventually, nearly every ethnic group in the world settled in the Valley. With each group came schools, churches and new customs, each adding to the rich heritage of the San Joaquin.

Compliments of **Spalding Wathen**

Salads & Dressings

Cranberry Cube Salad

(A very rich and pretty cranberry mold) Yield: Serves 12

2 (3-ounce) packages cream cheese, softened
¼ cup Italian-style salad dressing
¼ cup fresh lemon juice
⅛ teaspoon salt
1 cup drained, crushed pineapple
1 cup diced walnuts
1 cup diced or sliced bananas
1½ cups heavy cream, whipped
1 (1-pound) can jellied cranberry sauce, chilled and cut into cubes
1 package whipped topping mix for decoration (optional)
Extra jellied cranberry sauce for decoration (optional)

In a large mixing bowl, beat cream cheese, salad dressing, lemon juice and salt until smooth. Stir in pineapple, walnuts and bananas. Whip cream and fold into mixture. Lightly fold in the cranberry chunks. Turn into a 9x5x3-inch bread pan that has been lined on all sides with a double thickness of waxed paper or parchment paper. Cover and freeze. To unmold, place pan in warm water only to loosen. Turn out onto a chilled platter. Place in refrigerator for about 30 minutes or longer before serving. Slice to serve.

Optional Decoration:

Prepare 1 package whipped topping mix according to package directions. Reserve ½ cup of prepared mix. Spread the rest over sides and top of frozen salad. Pipe on a decorative edging with reserved whipped topping using a cake decorator tip #30. Decorate top with bells or other appropriate shapes cut from jellied cranberry sauce. Freeze to set decorations.

Pretzel Salad

Yield: Serves 12 to 15

- 2⅔ cups pretzels, broken into small pieces
- 1½ cups butter or margarine, melted
- 4 (3-ounce) packages cream cheese, softened
- 1¼ cups sugar
- 1 (9-ounce) container frozen whipped topping, thawed
- 1 (6-ounce) package strawberry Jello
- 1¾ cups pineapple juice or water
- 3 tablespoons tequila
- 1 tablespoon Grand Marnier
- 1 (16-ounce) package frozen whole unsweetened strawberries, sliced if desired, or 2 to 3 cups fresh whole unsweetened strawberries, sliced if desired

Toss the pretzels and melted butter together and pat into the bottom of a 9x13-inch baking dish. Bake in a preheated 400 degree oven for 10 minutes. Cool to lukewarm. Cream the cheese and sugar together. Spread over the top of the lukewarm baked pretzels. Spread whipped topping on top of the cheese. Chill. In a large mixing bowl, dissolve Jello in the boiling water or pineapple juice. Add the tequila and Grand Marnier and stir. Stir in the strawberries and allow to thicken almost to the jelled point. Spread over the top of the cream layer and refrigerate until thoroughly chilled.

Apple-Grape Salad

(Wonderful salad for summer, light and cool in appearance and taste)

Yield: Serves 4

- 2 to 3 medium tart apples, cored and quartered
- ½ pound dark red or purple California grapes, halved and seeded
- 1 stalk garden mint (leaves only)
- 2 teaspoons sugar
- 2 tablespoons lemon juice
- 2 tablespoons California brandy

Cut apples crosswise in thin slices. Arrange apples, grapes and mint leaves in glass serving bowl. Sprinkle with sugar, lemon juice and brandy. Toss lightly. Cover; chill 1 hour.

Avocado and Orange Tossed Salad

(The extra dressing would be equally good on fruit or lettuce salads.)

Yield: Serves 10

½ cup vegetable oil
1½ teaspoons finely shredded orange peel
¼ cup orange juice
1½ teaspoons finely shredded lemon peel
2 tablespoons fresh lemon juice
2 tablespoons red wine vinegar
4 teaspoons sugar
½ teaspoon dry mustard
¼ teaspoon salt
2 large oranges
1 small red onion, sliced and separated into rings
1 large avocado
8 cups mixed greens, torn into bite-sized pieces

In a screw-top jar combine oil, orange peel and juice, lemon peel and juice, vinegar, sugar, mustard and salt. Cover and shake well. Peel oranges, removing the white membrane. Slice the oranges crosswise; cut each slice into thirds. In a bowl combine orange slices and onion. Pour dressing over all; stir to coat well. Cover and refrigerate. At serving time, drain orange mixture, reserving dressing. Peel, seed and slice the avocado lengthwise. In a large salad bowl, arrange the orange, onion and avocado atop the mixed greens. Drizzle with desired amount of the reserved dressing. Toss to coat well.

Note:
Remaining dressing will keep in refrigerator for several days.

California Style Salad

Yield: Serves 6 to 8

2 Golden Delicious apples, unpeeled and sliced
2 tablespoons fresh lemon juice
3 cups torn Bibb lettuce, washed
3 cups torn, washed fresh spinach
½ cup coarsely chopped pecans
½ cup crumbled bleu cheese
6 slices bacon, fried crisply and crumbled
½ cup fresh sliced mushrooms
½ cup thinly sliced red onion

Lightly toss apple, lemon juice, lettuce, spinach, pecans, bleu cheese, crumbled bacon, mushrooms and red onion in a large salad bowl. Chill.

Dressing:

¼ cup red wine vinegar
⅓ cup vegetable oil
1 teaspoon Worcestershire sauce
1 clove garlic, bruised
½ teaspoon salt
¼ teaspoon dried oregano
½ teaspoon sugar
Dash of pepper

Place vinegar, oil, Worcestershire, garlic, salt, oregano, sugar and pepper in a small jar and shake well until blended. Chill for at least 1 hour.

Method:

When ready to serve salad, remove garlic from dressing. Pour just enough dressing over chilled salad to lightly coat. Toss.

Skinny Orange and Almond Salad

(Each serving has approximately 93 calories.) Yield: Serves 6

6 cups mixed greens: romaine lettuce, Boston lettuce, iceberg lettuce, red leaf lettuce, watercress, spinach
1½ cups orange segments
½ cup sliced blanched, toasted almonds

Toss and serve with "Skinny Gourmet Salad Dressing".

Skinny Gourmet Salad Dressing

(Each tablespoon of dressing contains approximately 28 calories.) Yield: Serves 6

¼ cup safflower oil
¼ cup tarragon vinegar
⅓ cup chicken consommé
⅓ cup orange juice
1 tablespoon chopped parsley
Pinch of dry mustard
⅛ teaspoon black pepper
1 teaspoon honey

Combine oil, vinegar, chicken consommé, orange juice, parsley, mustard, pepper and honey in a small jar and shake. Chill well.

Sweet and Sour Asparagus

Yield: Serves 4

1 pound fresh asparagus spears
⅓ cup red wine vinegar
¼ cup water
¼ cup sugar
½ teaspoon salt
3 whole cloves
1 stick cinnamon
¼ teaspoon celery seed

In a large covered frying pan, cook asparagus in a small amount of water until tender crisp. Drain and set aside. Meanwhile, combine vinegar, water, sugar, salt, cloves, cinnamon and celery seed in a small saucepan. Heat slowly until sugar dissolves. Pour over asparagus while still warm. Refrigerate 4 to 6 hours. Drain asparagus before serving and place on a bed of lettuce.

Note:
May also be served as a cold vegetable.

Valley Fruit Toss

Yield: Serves 10 to 12

- 1 head iceberg lettuce, broken into bite-size chunks
- 2 cups California seedless green or red grapes
- 2 medium oranges, peeled, broken into sections with each section quartered
- 4 medium peaches or nectarines, peeled and sliced
- 1 pint strawberries, hulled and halved
- 2 kiwi, peeled, sliced and quartered
- 1 cup light corn syrup
- 1 cup water
- 1 teaspoon grated lemon peel
- 2 to 3 tablespoons fresh lemon juice
- 2 tablespoons corn starch
- 4 tablespoons water
- ½ cup crumbled bleu cheese
- ½ cup chopped cashew nuts

Place lettuce in the bottom of a large bowl. Add grapes, oranges, peaches or nectarines, strawberries and kiwi. Chill. In a medium saucepan combine syrup, water, lemon peel and juice. Heat to a boil, stirring constantly; boil for 5 minutes. In a separate small bowl, mix cornstarch and water together until smooth. Add mixture to the boiling dressing and boil for 1 additional minute. Remove from heat and cool. When ready to serve, add dressing sparingly, using just enough to coat the fruit; toss. Just before serving, sprinkle bleu cheese and cashews on top of the salad.

Beet Salad with Apples

(This is a beautiful holiday or buffet salad.) Yield: Serves 6

1 (15-ounce) jar sliced pickled beets
3 large tart red apples, unpeeled
3 or 4 tablespoons mayonnaise
1 tablespoon sugar
1 teaspoon fresh lemon juice
⅛ teaspoon salt
Fresh ground pepper
2 tablespoons fresh chopped parsley
¼ cup coarsely chopped nuts

Drain the pickled beets and blot dry; cut slices into strips ¼-inch thick. (Handle beets carefully as the juice will stain.) Cut apples into sixths, core and slice thinly. In a large serving bowl, lightly mix beets, apples, mayonnaise, sugar, lemon juice, salt, pepper and nuts together. Garnish top with the chopped parsley and chill for several hours before serving.

Chilled Broccoli Salad

Yield: Serves 8 to 10

8 cups fresh broccoli florets (about 2 bunches)
4 cups small fresh button mushrooms
Juice of 1 lemon
2 cups small pitted black olives, drained
1 cup sweet red pepper, diced or ½ cup red pimiento, drained and diced
¼ cup red wine vinegar
¾ cup peanut or vegetable oil
1 teaspoon fresh basil, finely chopped or ½ teaspoon dried basil
½ teaspoon fresh ground pepper
½ teaspoon Worcestershire sauce
1 tablespoon sugar
¼ teaspoon lemon juice
2 tablespoons finely chopped green onions
1 cup crumbled bleu or feta cheese

Remove most of the stem from the broccoli florets. Steam broccoli for 3 to 5 minutes. Drain and immerse in cold water. Broccoli should be crisp and green. Drain again and chill in refrigerator. Clean and blot dry mushrooms; remove stems. Sprinkle with juice of lemon and chill. When all vegetables are well chilled, place in a large glass salad bowl. Add olives and red pepper. In a 1-quart jar, combine vinegar, oil, basil, pepper, Worcestershire sauce, sugar, lemon juice and onions. Shake well to blend thoroughly. About 3 to 4 hours before serving, toss salad ingredients with enough dressing to coat the vegetables, and refrigerate. Just before serving, stir in the cheese.

Colorful Calico Coleslaw

Yield: Serves 8 to 10

4 cups finely shredded cabbage
1½ cups chilled canned niblet corn, well drained
½ cup finely chopped onion
¼ cup chopped green pepper
¼ cup chopped pimiento

In a medium-sized bowl, combine cabbage, corn, onion, green pepper and pimiento. Cover, and chill thoroughly.

Dressing:

½ to ¾ cup mayonnaise
1 teaspoon salt
2 tablespoons cider vinegar
1 teaspoon sugar

In a small bowl, mix mayonnaise, salt, vinegar and sugar together. Cover and chill.

Method:

Just before serving, drain salad and add desired amount of dressing. Toss lightly.

Macaroni Slaw

(A different tasty approach to coleslaw) Yield: Serves 6 to 8

1 medium head green cabbage, shredded
1½ cups small macaroni, cooked, drained and cooled
½ pound Swiss cheese, shredded
1 cup chopped green onions
½ cup chopped celery
¼ cup minced pimiento
1 to 1½ cups mayonnaise
¼ cup red wine vinegar
Salt and pepper to taste

In a large salad bowl, combine cabbage, macaroni, Swiss cheese, onions, celery and pimiento. In a small mixing bowl, add mayonnaise and vinegar and mix. Add to the cabbage mixture. Toss and season with salt and pepper to taste. Chill for at least 1 hour before serving. Garnish with additional pimiento if desired.

Romaine Salad with Cashews

(This salad serves a large group.) Yield: Serves 12

3 heads romaine lettuce
1 cup salted cashew nuts
½ cup thinly sliced sweet red onion
½ cup canned garbanzo beans, rinsed and drained well

Wash lettuce and drain well; tear into bite-sized pieces and place in a large salad bowl. Add cashews, onion, and garbanzo beans. Toss lightly and chill.

Dressing:

¼ cup cider vinegar
1 tablespoon Dijon-style mustard
Salt and freshly ground pepper to taste
Pinch of ground cumin
Pinch of ground cardamom
½ cup to ¾ cup light olive oil

In a small jar, combine vinegar, Dijon-style mustard, salt, pepper, cumin, cardamom and olive oil. Shake. Adjust seasoning as needed and chill.

Method:
Just before serving, stir dressing well and add desired amount to the salad and toss lightly.

Spinach Berry Salad

Food Processor
(This dressing is so special that it can be used on any fresh fruit salad.)

Yield: Serves 10 to 12

3 bunches spinach
1 pint fresh strawberries (mandarin oranges may be substituted)
1 cup sugar
2 tablespoons sesame seeds
3 tablespoons poppy seeds
2 teaspoons dry mustard
1 teaspoon salt
3 tablespoons minced green onions, or 1 tablespoon dried minced onions
⅔ cup cider vinegar
2 cups salad oil

Prepare spinach by washing well and removing stems; tear into bite-sized pieces and spin or blot dry. Chill. Wash, hull and halve strawberries. Place strawberry halves on a paper towel-lined plate and chill. Combine sugar, sesame seeds, poppy seeds, dry mustard, salt, onions and vinegar in a blender or food processor fitted with metal blade. Add oil through feed tube while blending. Turn on/off several times to thoroughly mix, scraping down sides of bowl. Chill. At serving time, arrange spinach and strawberries in a large chilled salad bowl. Toss with just enough dressing to coat spinach leaves lightly.

Curried Spinach Salad

Yield: Serves 10 to 12

2 pounds fresh spinach, cleaned, well-drained with stems removed
2 Red Delicious apples, unpeeled, seeded and sliced
⅔ cup dry roasted Spanish peanuts
½ cup California seedless raisins
⅓ cup thinly sliced green onions
2 tablespoons toasted sesame seeds
½ cup white wine vinegar
⅔ cup vegetable oil
1 to 1½ teaspoons curry powder
1 teaspoon salt
1 teaspoon dry mustard
¼ teaspoon hot red pepper sauce

Tear prepared spinach into bite-sized pieces. Dry well on paper toweling, or spin dry. Chill. Place apples in a large salad bowl. Add peanuts, raisins, onions and sesame seeds. In a small jar, combine vinegar, oil, curry, salt, mustard and red pepper sauce; shake vigorously. Add spinach to the bowl and toss with just enough dressing to coat leaves.

Note:
Diced chicken can be added to this salad to make it a meal.

Layered Spinach Salad

Yield: Serves 10

2 large bunches spinach, washed, drained, stems removed and torn into bite-sized pieces
1 bunch green onions (about 6 to 7), chopped
4 hard-cooked eggs, sliced
1 to 2 pounds fresh mushrooms, sliced
1 cup dairy sour cream
1½ cups mayonnaise
6 ounces grated Parmesan cheese
4 tablespoons sugar
10 slices bacon, fried crisp

In a large salad bowl, layer spinach, onions, eggs and mushrooms. Mix sour cream and mayonnaise together and spread over top of the salad. Combine Parmesan and sugar; sprinkle on top of the mayonnaise mixture. Crumble the bacon on top. Cover and refrigerate overnight. Can serve tossed or untossed, according to preference.

Spinach Salad Flambé

Yield: Serves 8 to 10

- 2 large bunches spinach (about 12-ounces each), washed, drained and dried thoroughly, and stems removed
- 6 hard-cooked eggs, sliced
- ¼ teaspoon salt
- ½ teaspoon ground fresh pepper
- 12 slices bacon, fried crisp and chopped
- ¾ cup bacon drippings
- ½ cup malt vinegar
- ¼ cup fresh lemon juice
- 4 teaspoons sugar
- 1 teaspoon Worcestershire sauce
- 1½ ounces 100-proof California brandy

Tear prepared spinach into bite-sized pieces and place in a large salad bowl. Add egg slices, salt and pepper. In a small saucepan, mix bacon pieces, bacon drippings, vinegar, lemon juice, sugar and Worcestershire sauce and heat until very hot. In a separate saucepan, heat the brandy carefully, and add to the bacon mixture. Ignite (with caution) and pour the flaming dressing over the spinach and toss gently. Serve on warmed salad plates.

Tomato-Shrimp Vinaigrette Salad

Yield: Serves 6 to 8

½ teaspoon salt
¼ teaspoon ground pepper
1 clove garlic, pressed
¼ teaspoon Dijon-style mustard
½ cup vegetable or olive oil
⅓ cup red wine or malt vinegar
2 tablespoons minced green onion
2 tablespoons finely minced parsley
¼ teaspoon dry basil
1 tablespoon capers, drained
1 tablespoon dill pickle relish
4 to 6 large tomatoes
1 pound cooked salad-sized shrimp

Combine salt, pepper, garlic, mustard, oil, vinegar, green onion, parsley, basil, capers and dill pickle relish in shaker-bottle. Shake well and chill. At serving time, attractively arrange well-drained lettuce leaves around the edge of a deep serving platter. Cut 4 to 6 tomatoes into slices and arrange them, slightly overlapping, on the platter. Soak cooked shrimp in ice water for about 15 minutes. Remove, drain and blot dry thoroughly. Sprinkle shrimp over tomato slices and then pour salad dressing over all.

Summer Time Gazpacho

Yield: Serves 6 to 8

2 medium cucumbers, peeled and sliced
1 tablespoon salt
10 medium-sized fresh mushrooms, sliced
4 whole green onions, sliced
⅓ cup minced fresh parsley
3 large tomatoes, peeled and chopped
1 medium green bell pepper, thinly sliced into ½-inch rings
½ pound Swiss cheese, cut into thin julienne strips

Slice cucumbers into a small bowl and sprinkle with salt. Set aside and allow to stand at room temperature for 30 minutes. Rinse and drain cucumbers and pat them dry with paper toweling. Place cucumbers in large bowl; add mushrooms, green onions, parsley, tomatoes and green pepper.

Dressing:

2/3 cup vegetable oil
1/3 cup red wine vinegar
1 clove garlic, minced
1 teaspoon dried basil, crumbled
1 teaspoon salt
1/2 teaspoon pepper

Mix all ingredients together in a small bowl.

Method:

Pour dressing over salad, cover and chill for at least 4 hours. Just before serving, top with strips of Swiss cheese.

Note:

Excellent when baby shrimp are added.

White Bean Salad

(Use with VALLEY SALAD DRESSING) Yield: Serves 8

3 recipes VALLEY SALAD DRESSING (page 254)
2 (15-ounce) cans Ranch-style Navy Beans (small white), rinsed and drained
1 small stalk celery, chopped
1/3 cup chopped red bell pepper
1/3 cup chopped green bell pepper
1 tablespoon dried parsley flakes
1 1/2 teaspoons dried sweet basil
1 pinch dried dill weed
1 teaspoon salad salt, (found in gourmet section of market; can use Jane's Crazy Salt)

In a large bowl, combine dressing, beans, celery, red and green bell pepper, parsley flakes, basil, dill and salad salt. Let stand for a minimum of 2 hours in refrigerator to allow flavors to blend.

Green Vegetable

(A good variation of the 3-bean salad) Yield: Serves 6 to 8

½ cup chopped green pepper
1 (16-ounce) can French-style green beans, drained
1 (16-ounce) can small peas, drained
1 (8-ounce) can lima beans, drained
1 small red onion, thinly sliced and separated into rings
½ cup salad oil
½ to ¾ cup sugar
1 teaspoon salt
½ cup cider vinegar
½ teaspoon pepper

Place green pepper, beans, peas, lima beans and onion into a large salad bowl. In a 1-quart jar, place salad oil, sugar, salt, vinegar and pepper; shake vigorously. Toss vegetables with dressing and refrigerate overnight. Toss salad again when ready to serve.

Variation:

10-ounce packages of frozen green beans, peas and lima beans may be substituted for the canned vegetables. The green beans and limas should be just barely cooked in boiling water; the peas should be thawed.

Green Goddess Salad Dressing

Yield: 1½ cups

3 tablespoons finely chopped, canned anchovies
3 tablespoons finely chopped chives
1 tablespoon fresh lemon juice
3 tablespoons red wine vinegar
½ cup dairy sour cream
1 cup mayonnaise
⅓ cup finely chopped parsley
Dash of garlic salt
Dash of coarse black pepper

Put anchovies, chives, lemon juice, vinegar, sour cream, mayonnaise, parsley, garlic salt and pepper in a blender or food processor and process until smooth. Chill until ready to use.

Grapevines
Reedley

This farmhouse, predominantly in the Queen Anne style and distinguished by its polygonal turret at the front corner, is typical of area houses built during the late 1800's and early 1900's. To the passer-by, these occasional "lapses in time" bring a sigh of nostalgia. Ladies in white on summer porches, Chinese lanterns hanging on the branches of trees, and horse drawn buggies, all seem possible once again.

The areas most famous agricultural product is the grape. When the Spanish Friars first explored the Central Valley, looking for Mission sites, they found "wild" grape vines growing along the rich bottom land of the rivers. The vines would entangle themselves in the trees and produce little blue fruits used by the Indians.

The Franciscans had brought bundles of vine cuttings with them to "the new world", and planted them, for personal use, along the Mission highway. Vineyards soon sprang up, as the Friars shared their cuttings with the local Spanish ranchos. The grapes were called Mission grapes and produced a delightful white wine. The Muscat grape soon followed and in 1873, found its way to the Fresno area.

A rancher in Sutter County, William Thompson, imported some cuttings from England in 1872. After some experimentation and the survival of one vine, his Thompson Seedless Grape became the parent of the millions of grapes grown in the Valley today.

The climate of the Valley is perfect for the growing of grapes and the drying into raisins. The high heat and deep alluvial soil makes this the perfect spot on Earth for this huge industry.

There are some 9,537 acres of grapes in Fresno County alone, with a raisin tonnage of 37,000, and a dollar value in the millions.

Compliments of Charles B. Bonner, Gus and Greti Bonner, Susan Bonner Martin, Nicholas and Nancy Boghosian

Orzo and Artichoke Salad

Yield: Serves 4

1½ cup orzo (rice-shaped pasta)
¾ cup olive oil
1 (9-ounce) package frozen artichoke hearts, thawed, halved if large
½ cup canned chicken broth
1 large egg yolk
2 tablespoons white wine vinegar
1 teaspoon Dijon-style mustard
2 tablespoons minced fresh basil, or 1 tablespoon dried basil
2 ounces prosciutto, minced
2 ounces grated Parmesan cheese
2 tablespoons fresh lemon juice, or to taste
¼ cup minced fresh parsley leaves
4 green onions, minced
Fresh basil leaves for garnish

In a pan of boiling salted water, cook the orzo for 7 to 8 minutes, or until it is just al dente; drain it in a sieve, and refresh it under cold water. Drain the orzo well and in a bowl toss it with ¼ cup of the oil. In a small saucepan, simmer the artichoke hearts in the chicken broth for 6 to 7 minutes, or until they are just tender; drain them well, and add them to the orzo. In a small bowl, whisk together the egg yolk, vinegar, mustard, and salt and pepper to taste; add the remaining ½ cup of oil in a stream, whisking to form an emulsion. Whisk in the minced basil and pour the dressing over the orzo mixture. Add the prosciutto, Parmesan, lemon juice, parsley, onions, and salt and pepper to taste. Toss the salad, and garnish with basil leaves. Chill before serving.

Pasta Nicoise

Yield: Serves 8 to 12

24 Greek olives, pitted and halved (if these are unavailable substitute pitted green or ripe olives)
3 cups fresh green beans, cut into 1¼-inch pieces and blanched
½ cup plus 2 tablespoons fresh lemon juice
6 tablespoons olive oil
2 tablespoons Dijon-style mustard
1 tablespoon minced or crumbled dried oregano
1 large clove garlic, minced
¼ cup minced parsley
2 (6½-ounce) cans water-packed tuna (solid white or albacore), well drained and flaked
1 bunch green onions (6 to 8), chopped including tops
Salt and pepper to taste
1 pound small shell pasta, cooked and drained
4 hard-cooked eggs, sliced
Anchovy filets for garnish (optional)

In a large salad bowl combine olives, beans, lemon juice, oil, mustard, oregano and garlic. Cover and marinate in refrigerator for several hours. Add parsley, tuna, onions, salt and pepper and cooked pasta. Stir to mix. Cover and refrigerate for 3 to 4 hours more. When ready to serve, stir again, then garnish with eggs and optional anchovies.

French Potato Salad

Yield: Serves 8

2½ pounds new red potatoes, washed, with skins left on
⅓ cup chopped parsley
1 small onion, chopped
1 tablespoon champagne mustard
1½ teaspoons salt
1 teaspoon pepper
¾ teaspoon dried tarragon, crumbled
2 cloves garlic, minced
½ cup white wine vinegar
⅔ cup vegetable or olive oil

Cook potatoes in a large pan in 1 to 2-inches of boiling water until they are done but still firm. Drain, and let stand for 10 minutes and then cut into ¼ to ½-inch thick slices. Place potatoes, parsley and onion into a salad bowl. In a separate bowl or jar, blend mustard, salt, pepper, tarragon, garlic, vinegar and oil. Stir or shake until well blended. Pour over potatoes and stir. Cover and let sit at room temperature for 3 hours. Then chill 3 to 4 hours in the refrigerator. Toss salad lightly just before serving.

Armenian Cracked Wheat Salad
(Tabbouleh)

(A great summer barbeque accompaniment) Yield: Serves 4 to 6

1 cup bulgur (cracked wheat)
2 cups boiling water
2 tablespoons fresh lemon juice
1 cup chopped green onions
1 cup chopped fresh tomatoes, or halved cherry tomatoes
1 cup chopped, peeled cucumber
1 cup minced parsley
3 to 4 tablespoons chopped fresh mint or 3 tablespoons crumbled dry mint
1 teaspoon salt
¼ teaspoon thyme
⅛ teaspoon pepper
¼ cup olive oil
⅓ cup lemon juice
Romaine lettuce leaves for garnish

Combine bulgur, boiling water and lemon juice in a large mixing bowl. Let stand for 1 hour; then drain thoroughly by placing in a colander and shaking until all liquid is removed. Place drained bulgur in a salad bowl; add onions, tomatoes, cucumber, parsley, mint, salt, thyme, pepper, oil and lemon juice. Stir to blend and chill thoroughly for several hours, or overnight. Serve on a bed of romaine lettuce.

Chicken Salad Azteca

Yield: Serves 6

Chicken Preparation:

1 (7-ounce) can green chili salsa
½ teaspoon chili powder
2 tablespoons vegetable oil
2 tablespoons red wine vinegar
2 cups cooked chicken strips
1 (20-ounce) can pineapple chunks

To prepare the chicken: Measure out 2 tablespoons of the salsa and mix with the chili powder, oil and vinegar. Save the remaining salsa for the dressing. Toss this mixture with the cooked chicken; cover and refrigerate. Drain and chill pineapple. Reserve ¼ cup pineapple juice for dressing.

Azteca Dressing:

⅓ cup vegetable oil
⅓ cup red wine vinegar
Reserved green chili salsa
Reserved ¼ cup pineapple juice
½ teaspoon chili powder
½ teaspoon garlic salt
1 tablespoon minced parsley

In a jar, combine oil, red wine vinegar, reserved chili salsa and pineapple juice, chili powder, garlic salt and parsley; shake well to blend. Chill.

Salad Assembly:

1 cup chopped celery
⅓ cup chopped green pepper
2 tablespoons finely chopped parsley
Lettuce leaves
6 cups shredded lettuce
2 medium tomatoes, cut into wedges
½ cup sweet red onion rings
½ cup pitted, whole, ripe olives

To prepare salad: line a chilled salad bowl with large lettuce leaves and add shredded lettuce. Toss the chilled chicken mixture with the celery, green pepper and 2 tablespoons parsley and arrange on lettuce. Decorate with drained, chilled pineapple, tomato wedges, onion rings and ripe olives. Serve salad with Azteca dressing.

Oriental Chicken Salad

Yield: Serves 10 to 12

- 2 whole chicken breasts
- 2 to 3 sticks ginger
- 2 small heads iceberg lettuce, shredded
- 1 (8-ounce) package sliced almonds
- 4 tablespoons toasted sesame seeds
- 3 to 4 green onions, sliced into slivers
- ½ to 1 cup cooking oil (enough to cover the bottom 1-inch of a frying pan)
- ¼ to ½ of a (15-ounce) package rice stick noodles
- ½ cup sugar
- ½ teaspoon pepper
- 2 teaspoons salt
- ½ cup salad oil
- ½ cup white wine vinegar

Place chicken and ginger in a medium saucepan. Cover with water, and bring to a boil. Reduce heat and simmer until fork tender, about ½ to ¾ of an hour. Remove chicken and let cool. Skin and bone, then shred the meat. Place shredded chicken and lettuce in a large salad bowl. Add almonds, sesame seeds and green onions. Chill. Meanwhile, in a large frying pan, pour 1-inch of cooking oil. Place over high heat and when hot, add rice sticks, one handful at a time, to the oil. These sticks will puff up very quickly, so take care. When puffed up remove with a slotted spoon and drain on paper toweling. Repeat process until all noodles are fried. Add cooked rice sticks to the salad bowl.

Dressing:

Combine sugar, pepper, salt, oil and wine vinegar in a 1-quart jar, and shake until blended.

Method:

Pour the desired amount of dressing over the lettuce-rice stick mixture and toss.

Note:

You may wish to add 1 teaspoon of sesame oil to the salad dressing. If rice stick noodles are not available, fried chow mein noodles may be substituted.

Curried Chicken Toss

Yield: Serves 6 to 8

2 whole chicken breasts, cooked and cubed (approximately 6 cups)
1 large red apple, cubed with peel on
3 green onions, chopped, tops included
½ cup California golden raisins
½ cup unsalted peanuts
¼ cup shredded coconut
½ cup frozen peas, thawed, or ½ cup fresh peas, cooked slightly
½ cup mayonnaise
Juice of ½ lemon
1½ teaspoons curry powder
½ teaspoon salt
Pinch cayenne
Pinch black pepper
⅓ pound bacon, fried crisp and crumbled

Place cooked chicken, apple, onions, raisins, peanuts, coconut and peas in a large salad bowl. In a small bowl, combine mayonnaise, lemon juice, curry, salt, cayenne and black pepper. Pour dressing over chicken mixture and toss. Refrigerate salad for 2 to 3 hours to blend flavors. Just before serving, add crumbled bacon to salad and toss again.

Honeydew-Chicken-Fruit Salad

Yield: Serves 4

1 honeydew melon
1 cup cubed, cooked chicken
1 orange, peeled and sectioned
1 large nectarine, chopped
½ cup seedless California green grapes, halved
½ cup fresh dark sweet cherries, halved and pitted
¼ cup chopped celery
½ cup peach yogurt
¼ cup mayonnaise

Chill all ingredients thoroughly. Cut melon into quarters; remove seeds. Separate melon flesh from shell by cutting along the bottom between the meat of the melon and the rind; cut into pieces, leaving pieces in shell. Combine cooked chicken, orange sections, nectarine, green grapes, cherries and celery in a bowl. Toss to mix. Spoon the meat-fruit mixture onto melon quarters. Blend peach yogurt and mayonnaise and spoon over the fruit mixture on melon.

Layered Overnight Chicken Salad

(A do-ahead entree salad to serve on a busy day)

Yield: Serves 10 to 12

- 6 cups shredded iceberg lettuce
- ¼ cup bean sprouts
- 1 (8-ounce) can water chestnuts, rinsed, drained and sliced
- ½ cup sliced green onion
- 1 medium cucumber, sliced
- 4 cups cooked chicken, cut into 2 to 3-inch strips
- 2 (6-ounce) packages frozen pea pods, thawed
- 2 cups mayonnaise
- 2 teaspoons curry powder
- 1 tablespoon sugar
- ½ teaspoon dried ground ginger
- ½ cup Spanish-style peanuts
- 1 to 1½ dozen cherry tomatoes, halved

In a 4-quart serving dish, distribute lettuce. Top with layers of bean sprouts, water chestnuts, green onions, cucumber and chicken. Pat the pea pods dry and place on top. In a small bowl combine the mayonnaise, curry powder, sugar and ginger. Spread on top of the salad. Cover and refrigerate salad up to 24 hours. To serve, garnish with peanuts and tomatoes. Let each guest scoop out their serving from the bottom of the dish, or toss lightly before serving.

Coalinga

Lemon Beef Salad

Yield: Serves 4

¼ cup fresh lemon juice
2 tablespoons water
2 tablespoons sugar
1 teaspoon poppy seeds
¼ teaspoon salt
1 pound cooked roast beef, cut into strips (about 2 cups)
4 ounces fresh mushrooms, sliced (about 1 cup)
⅔ cup dairy sour cream or yogurt
1 teaspoon Dijon-style mustard
1 head red leaf lettuce
1 tomato, cut into wedges
4 small artichokes, cooked and halved

In a saucepan, mix lemon juice, water, sugar, poppy seeds and salt. Heat to boiling; reduce heat and cover. Simmer 15 minutes and cool. In a large bowl, mix lemon mixture, beef and mushrooms; cover. Refrigerate at least 3 hours, no longer than 24 hours. Drain beef mixture and reserve 3 tablespoons marinade. Stir reserved marinade into sour cream or yogurt; stir in mustard. Arrange beef, mushrooms, tomato and artichokes on bed of lettuce. Serve dressing on the side.

Zesty Chicken Pasta Salad

Yield: Serves 6

1 whole chicken breast
¾ cup vegetable or olive oil
4 tablespoons red wine vinegar
1 teaspoon salt
½ teaspoon coarsely ground pepper
¼ teaspoon Dijon-type mustard
8 ounces small shell pasta
4 to 6 green onions, chopped, including tops
1 cup pitted olives, minced (black or green or a combination of both)
2 stalks celery, minced
1 to 2 green bell peppers, chopped
1 to 2 red bell peppers, chopped
⅓ pound crumbled feta cheese
4 slices bacon, fried and crumbled

In a medium saucepan, poach chicken in enough water to cover for 15 minutes, or until done; cool, skin and bone. Cut chicken into bite-sized pieces and place in a salad bowl. In a small bowl combine oil, vinegar, salt, pepper and mustard and stir until blended. Pour ½ of the dressing mixture over the chicken; cover and refrigerate. Cook shells according to package directions, drain and cool. Add shells to chicken and stir to blend. Add onions, olives, celery, green and red peppers, cheese and bacon. Pour remaining dressing over the mixture and toss. Chill until ready to serve.

Bengal Seafood Salad

Yield: Serves 6

1 cup mayonnaise
¼ cup sour cream
½ teaspoon curry powder, or more according to preference
1 cup crab meat
1 cup shrimp
1 (20-ounce) can pineapple chunks, drained
½ cup water chestnuts, sliced
¼ cup finely chopped green onions
1 cup celery, sliced
2 tablespoons chutney
2 tablespoons California golden raisins
Juice of 1 lemon
⅓ cup chopped pine nuts or almonds
2 to 3 tablespoons pine nuts or almonds for garnish

Blend mayonnaise, sour cream and curry powder thoroughly, and refrigerate for at least 3 hours to allow flavors to mellow. Place crab and shrimp in a large salad bowl. Drain pineapple well and then pat with paper toweling to absorb all liquid. Add pineapple, water chestnuts, onions, celery, chutney, raisins and lemon juice to the salad bowl and toss. Chill. When ready to serve, add the ⅓ cup of nuts and just as much dressing as needed to lightly coat ingredients. Toss salad and garnish with remaining nuts.

Shrimp Extraordinaire

Yield: Serves 6

1 pound medium-sized shrimp, cooked, shelled and deveined
½ pound fresh whole mushrooms, cut in half
1 (8½-ounce) can artichoke hearts, rinsed, drained and coarsely chopped
1 cup (1-inch) carrot sticks
1 medium onion, thinly sliced and separated into rings
¾ cup (1-inch) celery sticks
1 (2-ounce) jar pimiento, drained and diced
3 cloves garlic, minced
1¼ cups white distilled vinegar
¾ cup water
¼ cup vegetable oil
1 teaspoon lime juice
2 (.6-ounce) packages dry Italian Salad Dressing mix
1 teaspoon salt

In a 3½-quart mixing bowl, combine shrimp, mushrooms, artichoke hearts, carrots, onion rings, celery and pimiento. In a jar, combine vinegar, water, oil, lime juice, salad dressing mix and salt; shake vigorously to mix. Pour dressing over salad ingredients and toss to combine. Cover tightly and chill 4 to 6 hours, stirring every 2 hours. Serve in your prettiest glass bowls.

Coastal Shrimp Salad

Yield: Serves 4

½ pound fresh, cooked baby shrimp, or 2 (4½-ounce) cans deveined shrimp
3 tablespoons tarragon vinegar
½ teaspoon dried tarragon, crushed
¼ teaspoon salt
¼ teaspoon ground dried ginger
½ teaspoon minced lemon peel
1 tablespoon instant minced onions
2 teaspoons dried chervil
1 cup dairy sour cream
1 large ripe avocado
1 cup halved cherry tomatoes
1 large cucumber
Chervil for garnish (optional)

Rinse and drain the shrimp, blot dry completely and place in a large bowl. Combine tarragon vinegar, tarragon, salt, ginger, lemon peel, minced onion and chervil and pour over the shrimp. Cover and marinate for 2 to 3 hours in the refrigerator. Drain off excess marinade and reserve. Stir sour cream into shrimp mixture. Halve and peel the avocado; remove seed and dice. Add avocado and tomatoes to shrimp mixture, tossing lightly. Slice unpeeled cucumber lengthwise into very thin slices; remove excess seeds carefully. Arrange cucumber slices on each of four chilled salad plates. Heap shrimp mixture over slices. Garnish with optional chervil and sprinkle on reserved marinade if desired.

Bleu Heaven Salad Dressing

Yield: 2½ cups

1 cup mayonnaise
1 cup dairy sour cream
¼ cup finely minced parsley
1 large clove garlic, minced
2 tablespoons red wine vinegar
2 tablespoons fresh lemon juice
1 teaspoon salt
¼ pound bleu cheese, crumbled
1 tablespoon anchovy paste (optional)

Blend mayonnaise, sour cream, parsley, garlic, vinegar, lemon juice, salt, bleu cheese and optional anchovy paste in a blender or food processor. Refrigerate. This dressing will keep for several days.

Note:
For a dressing with more texture, stir in the crumbled bleu cheese after the processing step.

Chutney Salad Dressing

Food Processor

Yield: 1½ cups

½ cup wine vinegar
6 tablespoons chutney
1 garlic clove, crushed
4 tablespoons French-style mustard
3 or 4 teaspoons sugar
1 cup oil
Salt and pepper to taste

Combine vinegar, chutney, garlic, mustard and sugar in the food processor; mix until smooth. With machine running slowly, pour in oil. Process until thick and smooth.

Cole Slaw Dressing

Food Processor
(This dressing should be made 1 day before serving.)

Yield: 1½ cups

½ cup mayonnaise
½ cup dairy sour cream
1 teaspoon prepared mustard
¼ teaspoon paprika
¼ teaspoon salt
2 tablespoons vegetable oil
3 tablespoons sugar
2 tablespoons minced onion
¼ clove garlic, mashed
2 tablespoons red wine vinegar
Dash Tabasco sauce

Process mayonnaise, sour cream, mustard, paprika, salt, oil, sugar, onion, garlic, vinegar and Tabasco in blender or food processor. Chill for at least 24 hours to allow flavors to mellow.

Grapefruit French Dressing

(A good dressing for a green salad with oranges or any fresh fruit salad)

Yield: ½ cup

¼ cup fresh grapefruit juice
6 tablespoons vegetable oil
¼ teaspoon salt
¼ teaspoon paprika
¼ cup red currant jelly

In a small jar, combine grapefruit juice, oil, salt, paprika and jelly and shake well. Cover, and keep in refrigerator until ready to use. Dressing will keep for several days.

Note:
Add 1 to 2 tablespoons of red wine vinegar if a more tart dressing is desired.

A Great Salad Dressing

Food Processor

Yield: 1¼ cups

1¼ teaspoons salt
Pinch of sugar
⅛ teaspoon dried tarragon
⅛ teaspoon dry mustard
¼ teaspoon coarse black pepper
2 tablespoons dry California red wine
1¼ teaspoons water
1½ tablespoons distilled white vinegar
1½ tablespoons red wine vinegar
¼ teaspoon Worcestershire sauce
¼ medium onion, peeled and chopped
1 clove garlic, peeled and minced
1 cup vegetable or olive oil, or a combination of both

In a food processor work bowl fitted with the metal blade, combine salt, sugar, tarragon, mustard, pepper, wine, water, white and red vinegar, Worcestershire sauce, onion and garlic. Pulse on/off quickly 3 or 4 times, scraping down sides of work bowl with spatula. Turn processor back on; very slowly add the oil through the feed tube and mix well until blended. Refrigerate.

Valley Salad Dressing

Yield: ½ cup

2 tablespoons olive oil
2 tablespoons red or white wine vinegar
½ to 1 small clove garlic, mashed
⅛ teaspoon Worcestershire sauce
⅛ teaspoon dry mustard
¼ teaspoon onion salt
Cracked pepper to taste
Grated Parmesan cheese to taste

In a small bowl, combine oil, vinegar, garlic, Worcestershire sauce, dry mustard and onion salt. Blend with the back of a spoon and let sit for 5 to 10 minutes. Pour over salad greens or whatever you are dressing; grind fresh cracked pepper over all and top with a generous amount of Parmesan cheese. Toss gently.

Note:
This dressing can be used with any greens combination, vegetables or beans that you are making into a salad. It is especially good with White Bean Salad.

Creamy Caesar Salad Dressing

Yield: 2½ cups

1 teaspoon salt
1 teaspoon dry mustard
½ teaspoon white pepper
½ teaspoon garlic powder
½ teaspoon paprika
½ teaspoon celery salt
¼ cup grated Parmesan cheese
⅛ cup red wine vinegar
Juice of 1 lemon
2 cups vegetable oil
1 teaspoon Worcestershire sauce
2 ounces anchovies, finely chopped
1 egg, well beaten

In a large bowl, mix together salt, mustard, white pepper, garlic powder, paprika, celery salt and grated Parmesan. Add the beaten egg to this mixture and mix thoroughly; while beating continuously, add vegetable oil, juice of lemon, wine vinegar, anchovies and Worcestershire sauce.

Desserts

Autumn Harvest Cake

Yield: Serves 10 to 12

½ cup vegetable shortening
¼ cup water
2 cups sugar
1 (8-ounce) can applesauce
1 (1-pound, 1-ounce) can pumpkin pie filling
2 eggs
2½ cups sifted all-purpose flour
2 teaspoons salt
1 tablespoon soda
1½ teaspoons cinnamon
½ cup finely chopped walnuts
½ cup finely chopped dates
½ cup finely chopped California golden raisins

In a large mixer bowl, cream shortening, water and sugar thoroughly on medium speed Add applesauce and pumpkin pie filling and beat 2 minutes. Add eggs, one at a time, beating after each addition. Sift flour, salt, soda and cinnamon together. Gradually add the creamed mixture. Beat at medium speed for 3 minutes after all flour is added. Blend in nuts, dates and raisins. Pour batter into 2 greased and floured 9-inch cake pans. Bake in a preheated 350 degree oven for 35 to 40 minutes, or until toothpick inserted in center of cake comes out clean. Cool in pans on rack for 5 minutes. Cake may be removed from pan, cooled thoroughly and served with whipped cream or ice cream, or cut into serving pieces from the pan.

Variation:

May be frosted with cream cheese frosting or buttercream frosting, and served as a layer cake.

To cut a frosted layer cake, dip blade of knife in warm water occasionally. Slice with up-and-down motion.

Praline Applesauce Cake

Yield: makes 24 servings

Cake:

2¾ cups sifted cake flour
1⅓ cups sugar
1½ teaspoons baking soda
¼ teaspoon baking powder
1½ teaspoons cinnamon
½ teaspoon ground cloves
½ teaspoon salt
½ cup vegetable shortening
1¾ cups applesauce
2 eggs
1½ cups California raisins

Into a large mixer bowl, sift together the flour, sugar, baking soda, baking powder, cinnamon, cloves and salt. Add shortening and applesauce and beat 2 minutes at medium speed, with an electric mixer. Add eggs and beat 2 minutes longer or until thoroughly blended. Fold in the raisins. Pour batter into a greased and lightly floured 9x13x2-inch baking pan. Bake in a preheated 350 degree oven for 35 minutes or until center springs back when lightly pressed. Remove from oven and cool in pan on a wire rack for 15 minutes. Meanwhile prepare the Praline Topping.

Praline Topping:

½ cup (1-stick) butter or margarine
¾ cup brown sugar, packed
¼ cup whipping or heavy cream
1½ cups chopped pecans
⅔ cup flaked coconut

Cream butter with brown sugar until light and fluffy. Add cream and beat until smooth. Stir in pecans and coconut. Spread Praline Topping evenly over warm cake. Put under broiler, 6-inches from heat source, for 3 or 4 minutes or until topping bubbles up and turns golden brown. Cool on wire rack. Cut into squares.

Cocoa Apple Cake

Yield: Serves 12 to 16

3 eggs
2 cups sugar
1 cup (2-sticks) butter or margarine
½ cup water
2½ cups all-purpose flour
2 tablespoons cocoa, unsweetened
1 teaspoon baking soda
1 teaspoon cinnamon
1 teaspoon allspice
1 cup finely chopped walnuts
½ cup semi-sweet chocolate chips
2 cups grated apples (peeled and cored)
1 tablespoon vanilla

In a large mixing bowl, cream together eggs, sugar, butter or margarine and water until fluffy. Sift flour, cocoa, soda, cinnamon and allspice together and mix with creamed mixture. Fold in walnuts, chocolate chips, apples and vanilla. Spoon into a greased and floured 10-inch tube pan or a 10-cup bundt pan. Bake in a preheated 325 degree oven for 60 to 70 minutes or until cake tests done. Cool before removing from pan.

Grommon's Sacher Torte

Yield: Serves 10

2 ounces unsweetened chocolate
3 tablespoons vegetable oil
¼ teaspoon salt
½ cup hot strong coffee
1 cup sugar
1 egg
¼ cup buttermilk
1 teaspoon soda
1 teaspoon vanilla
1 cup all-purpose flour
½ cup apricot preserves
2 tablespoons California brandy or 1 teaspoon brandy extract
Chocolate frosting (recipe follows)

Preheat oven to 350 degrees. In the top of a double-boiler, stir chocolate, oil, salt and coffee over barely simmering water until blended. Cool slightly. Pour mixture into the large bowl of an electric mixer and add sugar, egg, buttermilk, soda and vanilla; beat on medium speed until well blended. Add flour and continue beating for 5 minutes, occsionally scraping sides down with a rubber spatula. Pour into a greased and floured 8-inch cake pan. Place in the preheated oven and bake just until cake begins to pull from sides of pan, about 30 minutes. Set on a rack to cool, then remove from pan. (At this point you may wrap cool cake and freeze as long as 1 week. Thaw uncovered, at room temperature before proceeding.) Cut cake in half horizontally to make 2 layers. Combine apricot preserves and brandy; spread evenly over bottom layer of cake. Set top layer in place and put cake on rack.

Chocolate Frosting:

5 squares (5-ounces) semi-sweet baking chocolate

4 teaspoons solid vegetable shortening

In the top of a double-boiler, over barely simmering water, stir semi-sweet chocolate and vegetable shortening together until melted.

Method:

Slowly pour chocolate frosting onto center of cake so it flows over the entire surface. With a spatula, guide icing down over sides of the cake to coat smoothly. Chill until the icing is set, at least 30 minutes. Using a wide spatula, loosen the cake from rack and gently slide onto a serving plate. (If the cake is made ahead, cover without touching and chill up to 6 hours; return to room temperature to serve.)

The easiest way to make chocolate curls is to be sure the chocolate is at room temperature, then pare off a thin curl with a swival bladed vegetable peeler.

La Torte Cacao

Food Processor Yield: Serves 12
(A special dessert for a special occasion!)

1⅓ cups cake flour
¾ teaspoon baking soda
¼ teaspoon salt
1½ cups sugar
12 tablespoons (1½-sticks) unsalted butter, room temperature
Butter for pans
2 large eggs, room temperature
3 ounces unsweetened chocolate, melted
⅔ cup milk
4 teaspoons vanilla extract
6 ounces semi-sweet chocolate
2½ cups whipping or heavy cream
¼ cup powdered sugar
⅓ cup creme de cacao (optional)
3 tablespoons cold water
1 (0.25-ounce) package unflavored gelatin

Preheat oven to 350 degrees. Butter three 8-inch round cake pans; line them with parchment paper or waxed paper and butter the paper. Set aside. In a food processor work bowl, using the metal blade, mix the flour, soda and salt, processing for 10 seconds. Set aside. Use the metal blade to process 1¼ cups of the sugar with 8 tablespoons of the butter for 2 minutes, stopping once or twice to scrape the bowl. Add the eggs and pulse 4 or 5 times to mix. Add the melted unsweetened chocolate and pulse 4 or 5 times, scraping the bowl once. Add the milk and 2 teaspoons of the vanilla; pulse 4 or 5 times, scraping the bowl once. Add the reserved flour mixture; pulse 3 or 4 times, just until the flour disappears. Divide the batter evenly among the 3 prepared cake pans. Bake in the center of the preheated oven for 20 minutes or until the cakes have shrunk slightly from the sides of the pans. Remove to wire racks to cool for 10 minutes, then invert the cakes onto the racks to finish cooling. Meanwhile, in the top of a double-boiler over hot water, stir together the semi-sweet chocolate, ½ cup of the heavy cream, the remaining 4 tablespoons of butter and the remaining cup of sugar. Stir until the sugar has dissolved and the mixture is smooth. Set in a pan of ice water and stir occasionally until thick and cool. Set aside. In a chilled 3-quart bowl, beat the remaining 2 cups of heavy cream until it just begins to hold its shape.

Add the powdered sugar, the remaining 2 teaspoons of vanilla and the creme de cacao, if used; beat until stiff. Refrigerate until needed. Put the cold water in a small saucepan. Sprinkle the gelatin over it and let stand for 5 minutes to soften. Stir the mixture over moderate heat just until it begins to boil. Set aside to cool for 5 to 10 minutes. Whisk the gelatin mixture into the reserved whipped cream mixture. Refrigerate until needed. To assemble the cake, first split each layer in half horizontally to make 6 layers. Place 1 of the layers on a serving plate. Spread about ⅕ of the cream mixture over the cake layer. Top with another layer and spread with about ⅓ of the reserved chocolate mixture. Continue stacking the layers, alternating the fillings, finishing with chocolate on the top. Refrigerate the remaining cream mixture and the cake for 1 hour. Spread the remaining cream mixture around the side of the cake, reserving about ½ cup for garnishing if desired. Refrigerate.

Chocolate Dessert Shells

Yield: Makes 6 cups

½ of a 1-ounce bar of milk chocolate

1 tablespoon shortening

In a small saucepan melt the chocolate and shortening over low heat. Place 6 foil cups in muffin tins. Spoon about 1 tablespoon chocolate mixture into each cup; spread evenly with narrow metal spatula over bottom and up the sides of the cups. Refrigerate or freeze until firm. Chill to store.

Note:
Fill shells with liqueur or cream filling.

Grandma's Prune Cake

(An old family recipe) Yield: Serves 12

1 teaspoon soda
1 cup buttermilk
1 cup sugar
2 cups all-purpose flour
½ teaspoon ground cloves
1 teaspoon ground cinnamon
¼ teaspoon salt
3 tablespoons unsweetened cocoa
1 cup vegetable oil
1 egg
1 teaspoon vanilla
1 cup dried prunes, snipped and steamed
1 cup walnuts, chopped (optional)

Combine soda and buttermilk, set aside. In a medium bowl, combine the sugar, flour, cloves, cinnamon, salt and cocoa; set aside. In a large mixing bowl, combine the oil, egg, vanilla and buttermilk/soda mixture and beat until well blended. Add the dry ingredients to batter and mix well. Stir in prunes and walnuts. Grease and flour a 9-inch or 10-inch bundt pan. Spoon batter into prepared pan. Bake in a preheated 350 degree oven (9-inch pan for 40 to 45 minutes; 10-inch pan for 30 to 35 minutes) or until cake tests done. When cooled, a chocolate glaze can be added.

Chocolate Glaze: Yield: about ½ cup glaze

1 tablespoon butter or margarine
2 tablespoons all-purpose unsweetened ground chocolate or cocoa
2 tablespoons water
¼ teaspoon vanilla extract
⅔ cup powdered sugar

Combine butter, cocoa and water in a small saucepan. Cook over low heat, stirring constantly, until mixture thickens. DO NOT BOIL. Remove from heat; add powdered sugar and stir until smooth, add additional hot water, ½ teaspoon at a time, if a thinner consistency is needed. Pour over top of cooled cake.

Pumpkin Cake Roll

Yield: Serves 12

¾ cup all-purpose flour
2 teaspoons cinnamon
1 teaspoon baking powder
1 teaspoon ground ginger
½ teaspoon salt
½ teaspoon nutmeg
3 eggs
1 cup sugar
⅔ cup canned pumpkin
1 teaspoon fresh lemon juice
1 cup chopped walnuts
Sifted powdered sugar

Filling:

2 (3-ounce) packages cream cheese, softened
¼ cup butter or margaine
½ teaspoon vanilla
1 cup sifted powdered sugar

Grease and lightly flour a 10x15x1-inch jelly roll pan. Stir together flour, cinnamon, baking powder, ginger, salt and nutmeg. In a small bowl with electric beater, beat eggs at high speed for 5 minutes until thick and lemon-colored. Gradually add sugar and beat until sugar is dissolved. Stir in the pumpkin and lemon juice. Fold dry ingredients into pumpkin mixture. Spread evenly into prepared pan. Sprinkle walnuts over top. Bake in a preheated 375 degree oven for 12 to 15 minutes or until cake tests done. Immediately loosen edges of cake from pan. Turn out onto a towel sprinkled with powdered sugar. Starting with the narrow end, roll cake and towel together and place on a wire rack to cool. For filling; beat cream cheese, butter or margarine and vanilla until smooth. Beat in 1 cup of powdered sugar, or more if needed. After the cake has cooled, unroll carefully and spread with filling. Roll back up and chill until serving time. To serve, slice in ½ to 1-inch slices.

Zucchini Fruitcake

Yield: 2 large (8½x4½x2½-inch) loaves
or 5 small (3¼x5¾-inch) loaves

3 eggs
1 cup vegetable oil
2 cups packed brown sugar
1 tablespoon vanilla
3 cups all-purpose flour
1 tablespoon cinnamon
2 teaspoons soda
2 teaspoons ground allspice
1 teaspoon salt
1 teaspoon ground nutmeg
1 teaspoon ground cloves
½ teaspoon baking powder
2 cups coarsely shredded zucchini
2 cups chopped walnuts
2 cups California raisins
1 cup dried currants
2 cups mixed dried fruits, chopped coarsely
California brandy or rum

Beat eggs, oil, brown sugar and vanilla until well blended. In a separate bowl, thoroughly mix flour, cinnamon, soda, allspice, salt, nutmeg, cloves and baking powder. Combine the dry ingredients into the creamed mixture until well blended. Stir in zucchini, walnuts, raisins, currants and dried fruit. Mix just until blended. Line the bottoms of 2 large loaf pans or 5 small loaf pans with parchment paper and grease with shortening. Spoon mixture into prepared pans. Bake in a preheated 325 degree oven about 1 hour and 10 minutes (less time is required for small loaves), or until done. Let cool in pans on racks. If desired, spoon 4 tablespoons of brandy or rum over each loaf while still warm, less for smaller loaves. When completely cool, remove fruitcake from pans; wrap each loaf well in foil and freeze (or allow the wrapped loaves to age in refrigerator at least 2 weeks before serving).

Apricot Cheesecake

Food Processor Yield: 8 to 10 servings

3 graham crackers (2½-inches square), broken into pieces
1 tablespoon butter, softened
1 cup loosely packed dried apricots, cooked according to package directions, and drained
Peel from ¼ lemon, cut into strips
3 (8-ounce) packages cream cheese, softened and each package cut into quarters
4 eggs
1 cup sugar
½ cup dairy sour cream
Apricot Glaze (optional—recipe follows)

Preheat the oven to 350 degrees. In a processor bowl fitted with the metal blade, process the graham crackers until they are crushed. You should have about ¼ cup of crumbs. Butter an 8-inch springform pan and coat it with the crumbs. Still using the metal blade, process the apricots and the lemon peel for 15 seconds, or until puréed. Add 1 package of the cream cheese and 1 egg and process until smooth, about 15 seconds, scraping down the side of the bowl as necessary. Repeat this procedure 2 more times, processing 1 package of cream cheese and 1 egg until smooth each time. Add the remaining egg, the sugar and the sour cream and process for 5 seconds. Scrape down the side of the bowl. Process for 10 seconds more. Pour this batter into the prepared springform pan and pake in the preheated oven for 50 to 55 minutes, or until the center of the cake is just firm. Cool in the pan on a wire rack away from any draft. When cool, cover the pan and refrigerate the cake overnight. If you are using the Apricot Glaze, spoon and spread it over the top of the cheesecake before you unmold it. Remove the side of the pan just before serving.

Apricot Glaze:

½ cup apricot preserves
1 tablespoon California brandy

In a small saucepan, heat the apricot preserves over moderate heat until melted. Stir in the brandy. Strain the mixture through a strainer into a small bowl.

Macadamia Nut Cheesecake

Yield: Serves 12

Crust:

1 cup (2-sticks) butter, room temperature
½ cup brown sugar, packed
2 cups all-purpose flour
1 cup macadamia nuts, chopped

In a medium-sized bowl, mix the butter, brown sugar, flour and nuts together until thoroughly blended. Spread ¼-inch thick on a cookie sheet. Bake in a preheated 400 degree oven for 15 minutes or until golden brown. Allow to cool slightly; break up with a fork to crumble. Pat crumbs into the bottom and up sides of a buttered 10-inch springform pan. Set aside.

Filling:

2 (8-ounce) packages cream cheese, softened
3 eggs
1 cup sugar
2 cups (1-pint) dairy sour cream
1 teaspoon vanilla extract

In a large mixer bowl, mix the cream cheese. Add the eggs, one at a time, mixing thoroughly after each addition. Add the sugar, sour cream and vanilla and mix until smooth. Pour cheesecake mixture into the prepared pan. Bake at 350 degrees for 30 minutes. Turn off the oven and keep the cake in the oven for an additional 1½ hours. Cool slightly, then refrigerate.

Topping:

1 (21-ounce) can cherry pie filling

Just before serving, top with the cherry pie filling, then remove the side of the springform pan.

Currant Cheesecake

Yield: 12 servings

Crust:

1¼ cups graham cracker crumbs
¼ cup (½-stick) butter, melted
3 to 4 tablespoons sugar

Combine crumbs, butter and sugar in a large bowl and blend well. Press into the bottom of a 10-inch springform pan.

Filling:

½ cup dried currants
¼ cup California port wine
3 (8-ounce) packages cream cheese, room temperature
¾ cup sugar
4 eggs
Finely grated peel of 2 lemons (about 1½ tablespoons)
½ teaspoon vanilla

Preheat oven to 325 degrees. Combine currants and port wine in a small saucepan and bring to a boil over medium-high heat. Remove from heat and let stand for 10 minutes.

Method:

Combine cream cheese and sugar in a large bowl and beat until smooth. Add eggs, one at a time, beating well after each addition. Stir in lemon peel and vanilla. Add currant mixture and blend well. Turn mixture into prepared crust. Bake until set, about 40 minutes. Let cool to room temperature, then cover and refrigerate overnight. Remove sides of springform pan carefully. Serve cheesecake slightly chilled or at room temperature.

Almond Pear Pie

(A pronounced almond flavor— a must for almond lovers!)

Yield: 8 servings

Pastry for 1 (9-inch) pie shell

Custard Filling:

¼ cup + 2 tablespoons sugar
¼ teaspoon salt
1½ tablespoons cornstarch
1½ cups milk
3 egg yolks, slightly beaten
¾ teaspoon vanilla
¼ teaspoon almond extract
¼ cup almond paste
1 (1-pound, 14-ounce) can pear halves, well drained
⅓ cup apricot preserves, melted
½ cup whipping or heavy cream
2 tablespoons powdered sugar

Bake shell about 8 minutes or until golden brown in a preheated 450 degree oven. Cool on rack. Make filling: In a small saucepan (a teflon or heavy non-stick pan is best to use so custard does not scorch) mix sugar, salt and cornstarch with wooden spoon. Stir in milk. Cook, stirring over medium heat until mixture thickens and begins to boil; boil 1 minute. Stir a little hot mixture into egg yolks and when slightly warmed, stir yolk mixture back into saucepan. Cook, stirring constantly, until mixture is thick and bubbly. Stir in vanilla and almond extracts. Remove from heat. Pour into a medium bowl; place waxed paper directly on surface. Refrigerate for 1 hour to cool. To assemble: Roll almond paste between 2 sheets of waxed paper into a 6-inch circle. Remove top sheet. Invert paste on bottom of baked pie shell; remove remaining paper. Spread with custard. Arrange well-drained pears around edge. Brush with melted preserves. Chill. In a small bowl, beat heavy cream with powdered sugar until stiff. Fill pastry bag with whipped cream using a number 6 star tip; pipe swirls between pear halves and in the center of pie. Refrigerate 2 hours. To serve, cut pie into wedges.

Fruit Pie

Yield: 2 pies

2 (9-inch) pie shells, baked
1¾ cup sugar
1 (16-ounce) can sour cherries
4 tablespoons flour
1 (20-ounce) can pineapple chunks or fresh pineapple
1 (3-ounce) package orange Jello
3 bananas, sliced
1 cup chopped walnuts
1 cup heavy cream
½ cup shredded coconut

Combine sugar, flour, cherries and pineapple in juices; cook until thickened over low heat; add dry Jello and stir to dissolve. Cool. Add bananas and nuts and pour into 2 baked pie shells. Refrigerate until chilled and set. To serve, whip cream and pile on top of pie; sprinkle coconut on the top.

Ice Cream Pie

Yield: Serves 6

Meringue Shell:

½ teaspoon baking powder
3 egg whites
1 cup sugar
½ teaspoon vanilla extract
14 Ritz or Hi-Ho crackers, crushed
⅔ cup chopped nuts; walnuts, almonds or pecans
1 quart ice cream, any flavor
Fresh fruit slices or whole fresh berries (optional)
Chocolate sauce (optional)

In a narrow bowl, add the baking powder to the egg whites. Beat until they begin to hold their shape. Add sugar and vanilla gradually while still beating, and beat meringue to the firm-peak stage. Fold in crushed crackers and nuts. Spoon into a 9-inch buttered pie pan. Bake in a preheated 325 degree oven for 30 minutes. Cool completely. Before serving fill with scoops of your favorite ice cream. Add optional fresh fruit and drizzle with chocolate sauce if desired.

Ma's Spice Pie

Yield: Serves 8

¾ cup sugar
4 tablespoons all-purpose flour
1 teaspoon cinnamon
½ teaspoon cloves
½ teaspoon allspice
½ teaspoon nutmeg
Dash salt
1½ cups milk
3 egg yolks
1 tablespoon butter
1 (8-inch) baked pie shell

Mix sugar, flour, cinnamon, cloves, allspice, nutmeg and salt together in a saucepan. Add milk and beaten egg yolks. Cook over low heat until thick, stirring constantly. Add butter and stir well to incorporate; let cool about 15 minutes. Pour into baked shell.

Meringue Topping:

3 egg whites
¼ teaspoon cream of tartar
6 tablespoons sugar
¾ teaspoon vanilla

Beat egg whites and cream of tartar together until very frothy; gradually add sugar and vanilla and beat until soft peaks form. Cover pie filling with meringue and bake for 10 minutes in a preheated 300 degree oven, or until brown. Cool completely before serving.

Lemon Chess Pie

Yield: Serves 8

2 cups sugar
1 tablespoon all-purpose flour
1 tablespoon yellow cornmeal
4 eggs, well beaten
¼ cup fresh lemon juice (may add 1 more tablespoon if desired)
¼ cup melted butter (do not substitute margarine)
¼ cup milk
1 (8-inch) unbaked pie shell
Grated peel of 1 lemon

Combine sugar, flour and cornmeal together in a medium mixing bowl. Add eggs, lemon juice, melted butter and milk and stir well. Pour mixture into the unbaked pie shell. Bake in a preheated 425 degree oven for 10 minutes; lower heat and bake an additional 30 to 40 minutes at 325 degrees. Best if served at room temperature or slightly warm.

Note:
This filling may be baked in tiny tartlet shells.

Valley Grape Pie

Yield: Serves 6

Crust:

1½ cups graham cracker crumbs
3 tablespoons sugar
⅓ cup melted butter

Combine cracker crumbs with sugar and melted butter; toss with fork until well blended. Reserve ¼ cup of the crumb mixture. Press the rest evenly into bottom and sides of a buttered 9-inch pie pan. Bake in a preheated 350 degree oven for about 8 minutes. Cool.

Filling:

3 tablespoons cornstarch
¼ cup cold water
⅔ cup sugar
1 quart California Thompson seedless grapes, stems removed
1 tablespoon fresh lemon juice
1 cup (½-pint) dairy sour cream
1 tablespoon sugar
1 teaspoon vanilla extract

In a saucepan, dissolve cornstarch in cold water; stir in sugar and when dissolved, add grapes. Bring to a boil, stirring carefully, then reduce heat and simmer about 5 minutes. Remove from heat and stir in lemon juice and cool. To serve, turn cooled grape filling into pie shell; blend sour cream with the 1 tablespoon sugar and vanilla and spread evenly over top. Sprinkle with reserved crumbs.

Selma Raisin Pie

Yield: 1 pie—serves 8

Pie crust dough (enough dough to make a 9-inch crust, top and bottom)
1 egg
1 cup dairy sour cream
1 tablespoon vinegar
1 cup ground California raisins (use 1½ cups raisins)
1 cup sugar
½ teaspoon cinnamon
½ teaspoon ground cloves
Pinch of salt

Preheat oven to 450 degrees. Prepare pie crust. In a large mixing bowl, beat egg and stir in sour cream, vinegar and raisins. Set aside. Mix together sugar, cinnamon, ground cloves and salt. Stir into cream-raisin mixture. Pour mixture into prepared pie crust, add top crust and seal. Bake in 450 degree oven for 10 minutes, then reduce heat to 350 degrees and bake for 25 to 30 minutes more. Serve when cold.

Note:
Serve as you would a mincemeat pie.

Pumpkin Pecan Pie

(An interesting variation of textures and flavors creates new interest for an old favorite.)

Yield: Serves 6 to 8

3 eggs, slightly beaten
1 cup freshly cooked or canned pumpkin
1 cup sugar
½ cup dark corn syrup
1 teaspoon vanilla extract
½ teaspoon cinnamon
¼ teaspoon salt
1 cup pecan halves
1 (9-inch) unbaked pie shell

Mix eggs, pumpkin, sugar, corn syrup, vanilla, cinnamon and salt in a large bowl until thoroughly combined. Stir in the pecan halves and pour into the unbaked pie shell. Bake in a preheated 350 degree oven for 30 to 40 minutes or until a knife inserted in the center comes out clean. Place on wire rack to cool. Serve with dollops of whipped cream if desired.

Wheat Westlands

The first wheat was grown in Fresno County in 1839. The Spanish-California cattlemen planted wheat for home consumption, and by 1868 wheat was planted throughout the Valley. In 1870, the first commercial wheat was planted, and on October 27, 1870, the first trainload of grain left the San Joaquin Valley. The Valley soon became a major producer and in 1874, produced more wheat than any other state in the Union.

The main industry in the Valley is agriculture. In Fresno County alone there are some 2 million, 72 thousand and 188 acres (2,072, 188) in land and farms, employing over fifty-nine thousand people.

It is the climate that makes everything possible. Fresno sits at an elevation of three-hundred and twenty-eight feet above sea level. The prevailing winds are from the northwest at an average speed of 6.4 miles per hour. The county receives around 10.52 inches of rain each year with a humidity factor of 58%. The average temperature in January is a minimum of 36.8 to a maximum of 52.2. In July, the minimum is 64 (accounting for the beautiful Summer nights) and a maximum average is 97.9.

As the nation's number one farm county, Fresno produces close to 200 commercial crops. The leading crops are: cotton, grapes, cattle and calves, tomatoes, milk, turkeys, oranges, alfalfa hay, cantaloupes and nectarines. Field crops include: barley, corn, cotton seed, rice, safflower, sorghum, sugar beets, wheat, vegetable seed, wheat seed, barley seed and alfalfa seed. Vegetable crops include: broccoli, cauliflower, Chinese vegetables, eggplant, garlic, head lettuce, onions, peppers (bell and chile), squash (summer and winter), sweet potatoes, and others. Fruit and nut crops include: almonds, apricots, avocados, boysenberries, lemons, oranges, figs, kiwi, olives, peaches, pears, pecans, persimmons, pistachio nuts, plums, pommegranates, prunes, strawberries and walnuts. Livestock and poultry include: cattle and calves, hogs and pigs, horses and mules, sheep and lambs, goats, eggs, wool, and animal waste, beeswax and honey.

Compliments of **Harris Ranch Beef Company**

Pecan Fudge Pie

Yield: Serves 8

½ cup (1-stick) butter
3 (1-ounce) squares unsweetened chocolate
4 eggs
3 tablespoons light corn syrup
1½ cups sugar
¼ teaspoon salt
1 teaspoon vanilla
1 cup chopped pecans
1 (9-inch) unbaked pastry crust

Melt butter and chocolate in the top of double-boiler or over low heat. Meanwhile beat eggs until thick and lemony in color. Beat in corn syrup, sugar, salt and vanilla. Add nuts and the slightly cooled chocolate mixture. Mix thoroughly and pour into pastry shell. Bake in a preheated 350 degree oven for 25 to 35 minutes until top is crusty and filling is set, but soft inside. DO NOT OVERBAKE. Pie should shake like a custard so it will not be too stiff when cool. Serve plain or with ice cream or whipped cream.

Creme Fraiche

(Make a day ahead or up to 10 days)

Yield: 3 cups

2 cups heavy cream or whipping cream
1 (8-ounce) container dairy sour cream

In a medium bowl or 1-quart jar, mix the cream and the sour cream until thoroughly blended. Cover bowl with plastic wrap and let stand, at room temperature, until thickened. (This will take about 6 to 8 hours on a warm day, 24 hours on a cool day.) After mixture has thickened, stir to mix well; cover and refrigerate at least 4 hours. Stir before using.

Note:
Use as a topping for fresh or poached fruit and berries, and fruit pies.

Almond Lemon Torte

Food Processor Yield: Serves 8 to 10

2 tablespoons whipping or heavy cream
1 large egg yolk
1¼ cups all-purpose flour
1½ cups sugar
½ cup cold unsalted butter, cut into 8 pieces
1 teaspoon finely grated lemon peel
1¼ cups (6-ounces) blanched almonds
3 large egg whites, room temperature
Lemon curd (recipe follows)

Preheat oven to 350 degrees. With a fork, mix the cream and egg yolk in a small bowl just until they are combined; set aside. Put the flour, ½ cup of the sugar and the butter in the processor work bowl. With the metal blade; turn the machine on/off 4 or 5 times, until the butter is in pea-sized pieces. With the machine running, add the cream-egg mixture and the lemon peel and process until the dough just begins to hold together, about 6 or 7 seconds. Remove the dough from the processor and press it into a ball. Break off a quarter of the dough, wrap in plastic wrap and refrigerate. Press the larger piece of dough into the bottom and 1-inch up the sides of a 9-inch springform pan; refrigerate. With the metal blade, process the almonds and remaining 1 cup of sugar until the almonds are finely ground, about 30 seconds. In a 2½-quart mixing bowl, beat the egg whites with an electric beater until stiff peaks form. Sprinkle the almond mixture over the top and gently fold into the egg whites. Remove the springform pan from the refrigerator and spoon the almond filling into the prepared crust, smoothing the top with a knife or spatula. Remove the reserved piece of dough from the refrigerator and roll it out on a lightly floured board to a 3x10-inch rectangle. Use a pastry cutter or wheel to cut 6 strips ½x10-inches. Place 3 parallel strips over the almond filling, one in the center and the other 2 equally spaced on either side of it; press the ends into the rim of the crust. Repeat with the remaining 3 strips, laying them perpendicular to the first 3 to form a lattice. Bake in the bottom third of the preheated oven for 40 minutes, or until the crust is golden. Place the torte on a wire rack and let cool for 10 minutes. Use a sharp, narrow-pointed knife to cut down into the almond filling to a depth of about ¼-inch along the edges of the pastry strips and along the rim, taking care not to cut into the pastry itself. With your finger, press down lightly on the almond filling between the latticed pastry strips to make indentations for the lemon curd. Then let the torte cool completely. Meanwhile, prepare the Lemon Curd. Press down the almond filling again if necessary and carefully spoon the lemon curd between the latticed pastry strips. Cover the top of the springform pan with plastic wrap and refrigerate until chilled, (or as long as 2 days). Before serving, run a knife or a small metal spatula around the edge of the pan and remove the side.

Lemon Curd:

5 large egg yolks
½ cup sugar
6 tablespoons fresh lemon juice
Peel of 1 lemon, grated
4 tablespoons unsalted butter

With a wooden spoon, beat the egg yolks and sugar in a heavy 2-quart saucepan over low heat, until they are thick, creamy and pale yellow, about 8 to 10 minutes. Add the lemon juice and peel and stir until the mixture is thick enough to coat the spoon, about 3 to 4 minutes. With the wooden spoon, beat in the butter, a tablespoon at a time, making sure that each tablespoon is fully incorporated before adding the next. When all the butter has been added, stir the mixture with the spoon until thick. Remove the pan from the heat and immediately transfer the mixture to a 1-quart bowl and let it cool completely before using.

Grandma's Persimmon Pudding with Hard Sauce

Yield: Serves 8 to 10

1 cup cake flour, sifted
1 cup sugar
1½ teaspoons baking powder
2 teaspoons soda
1 teaspoon vanilla
⅓ cup melted butter or margarine
¼ cup milk
1 cup persimmon pulp, well mashed
1 cup California raisins, chopped fine
1 cup walnuts, chopped fine
1 tablespoon rum
1 tablespoon California brandy
Hard Sauce (recipe follows)

Sift flour; measure again and sift with sugar, baking powder and soda. In a separate bowl, mix vanilla, butter and milk. Add flour mixture to persimmon pulp alternately with milk mixture. Add raisins and nuts. Pour into a greased 8-cup pudding mold; cover and steam for 2 hours. When cool, remove from pudding mold. Pour 1 tablespoon of rum and 1 tablespoon of brandy over pudding; wrap in foil and let stand one week, either at a cool room temperature or refrigerate. Before serving, warm persimmon pudding in oven (still wrapped in foil). Unwrap and place on a serving plate. Flame pudding at the table if desired by pouring over ¼ cup warmed brandy or rum which has been ignited. Serve with Hard Sauce.

Hard Sauce:

2 cups sifted powdered sugar
½ cup (1-stick) butter, softened
½ teaspoon vanilla extract
2 teaspoons rum
3 teaspoons California brandy
1 teaspoon bourbon

Cream powdered sugar with butter. Beat in vanilla, rum, brandy and bourbon. (It will be very soft and fluffy.) Cover tightly and chill in refrigerator. The Hard Sauce is better if it ages for 1 week before serving. To serve, let sauce come to room temperature. Pass separately or put a dollop on top of each slice of persimmon pudding.

Variation: Lemon Sauce

1 large lemon
1 cup sugar
½ cup (1-stick) butter
2 tablespoons boiling water
2 eggs, separated

Grate the peel of the lemon. Set aside. Extract the juice from the lemon and put in the top of a double-boiler. Add the sugar, butter, water and egg yolks and cook over simmering water until bubbly. Add lemon peel and cool. In a deep narrow bowl, beat the egg whites until stiff. Fold the beaten egg whites into the lemon mixture. Serve warm over persimmon pudding.

Gateau Aux Noix Et Framboises

(This is an elegant dessert and is perfect for the non-perfect or beginner cook.)

Yield: Serves 8

4 egg whites, room temperature
¼ teaspoon salt
¼ teaspoon cream of tartar
1 cup superfine sugar
1 cup chopped walnuts or pecans
1 cup whipping or heavy cream
2 tablespoons powdered sugar
½ tablespoon Kirsch
2 cups fresh raspberries or blackberries

Beat egg whites with salt and cream of tartar until meringue is beginning to hold its shape; gradually beat in sugar. Continue beating until mixture is glossy and holds a stiff peak. Fold in nuts. Line 2 cookie sheets with parchment paper and spoon meringue into two 8½-inch circles outlined on the paper. Bake in a preheated 275 degree oven for 1 hour or until meringue can be lifted easily. Cool in oven. Beat cream, sugar and Kirsch until stiff. Fold in well-dried berries. Place 1 meringue on a cake plate. Spread with berry-cream mixture. Top with second meringue. Dust with powdered sugar and refrigerate for 6 to 24 hours.

Note:
Garnish the plate with fresh flowers and mint.

Strawberry Meringue

Yield: Serves 8 to 10

Meringue Circles:

3 egg whites, room temperature
1 cup sugar

Chocolate Sauce:

1 (6-ounce) package semi-sweet chocolate chips
3 tablespoons water
2 pints fresh strawberries, washed and drained
3 cups whipping or heavy cream
½ cup sugar

Beat the egg whites until stiff. Fold in the 1 cup sugar. Line 2 cookie sheets with parchment paper and spoon meringue onto sheets, into 3 equal 8-inch circles. Bake in a preheated 300 degree oven for ½ hour; lower heat to 200 degrees and continue baking another 10 minutes or until done. Remove from oven and cool. Meanwhile, make chocolate sauce. In a small pan, melt the chocolate chips with the 3 tablespoons water, over very low heat. Set aside to cool. Slice 2 pints of stemmed strawberries and set aside. Whip cream with sugar; then proceed with assembling dessert. On serving dish, place 1 layer of meringue, 1 thin layer of chocolate sauce, 1 layer of sliced strawberries and 1 layer of whipped cream; repeat layers again. Top with third meringue; decorate with whipped cream and drizzle remaining chocolate sauce over the top.

Pots de Creme Amande

Yield: Serves 12

3 cups light cream or half and half
¾ teaspoon almond extract
9 egg yolks
¾ cup sugar
¾ cup chopped or sliced toasted almonds
Powdered sugar

Preheat oven to 250 degrees. Scald the cream and add the almond extract. Beat the egg yolks and sugar well, using a mixer, until light and fluffy. Slowly add the scalded milk, beating all the time. Strain this mixture into 12 pot de creme cups or custard cups. Set the cups into a baking pan and fill the pan with hot water to about ½ the height of the cups. Cover and put into preheated oven to poach, about 45 minutes. Remove cups from the water bath and chill well after baking. Before serving, top each cup with toasted nuts and a sprinkle of powdered sugar.

Boysenberry Pizza

Yield: Serves 6 to 8

Crust:

1 cup all-purpose flour
¼ cup powdered sugar
½ cup (1-stick) margarine
¼ cup finely chopped walnuts

Mix flour, powdered sugar, margarine and nuts together and spread into a 12-inch pizza pan. Bake in a preheated 350 degree oven for about 10 minutes. Do not overbake. Cool.

Filling:

2 (3-ounce) packages cream cheese, softened
1 egg
⅓ cup sugar
2 baskets fresh boysenberries
⅔ cup sugar
2 to 3 tablespoons cornstarch
¼ cup water

Mix together the cream cheese, egg and ⅓ cup sugar. Pour into the baked shell. Bake at 250 degrees for 10 to 12 minutes. Cool. When cool, cover with 1 basket of whole boysenberries. Crush the remaining basket of boysenberries and add ⅔ cup sugar. Mix cornstarch and water together. Boil berries, sugar and cornstarch mixture until clear bubbles appear. Cool and pour over boysenberries. Serve with whipped cream topping, if desired.

Variation:
Fresh strawberries may be substituted.

Chocolate Mousse L'Orange

Food Processor

Yield: Serves 10 to 12

9 large egg yolks
1 cup sugar
Peel of ½ orange, removed with vegetable peeler
3 (4-ounce) packages sweet cooking chocolate, broken into pieces (Maillard's is preferred, however German Sweet may be used)
¾ cup (1½-sticks) unsalted butter, melted and sizzling hot
1 tablespoon + 2 teaspoons orange liqueur, divided
9 large egg whites, at room temperature
Pinch of salt
2 cups (1-pint) whipping or heavy cream, chilled and divided
¼ cup powdered sugar, divided

Butter an 8-inch springform pan. Preheat oven to 350 degrees; adjust rack to middle of oven. In a food processor work bowl, using the metal blade, process the egg yolks and sugar together for 1 minute until thick and light colored. Transfer this mixture to a small bowl. With metal blade in place again, add the peel and chocolate to food processor; turn machine on/off several times, then let run until the chocolate is finely and uniformly chopped, stopping the machine as needed to loosen any chocolate stuck between the blade and bowl. With machine running, pour the hot butter through the feed tube and process for 10 seconds. Add the yolk-sugar mixture and 1 tablespoon of orange liqueur; process for 5 seconds. Beat the egg whites until frothy with an electric mixer. Add salt and continue beating until they are firm and shiny, not stiff and dry. Spoon ¼ of the whites into the chocolate in the processor bowl; turn machine on/off 4 times. Transfer the chocolate mixture into the whites and fold in gently but thoroughly. Spoon half the mixture into a springform pan, making a slight outer rim to form a shell. Bake for 28 minutes; let crust cool for 20 minutes. Use the metal blade to process 1 cup of the whipping cream until slightly thickened, about 15 seconds. Add 2 teaspoons orange liqueur and 2 tablespoons powdered sugar and process until thick. Fold gently but thoroughly into the remaining uncooked chocolate mixture. Spread over the baked shell. Freeze the dessert. When frozen, wrap well so that it is air-tight. To serve, allow to thaw in the refrigerator for 2 to 3 hours. Whip the remaining 1 cup cream and serve in a separate dish or spread over surface of the dessert or cover with rosettes, using a pastry bag and a medium star tube.

Daiquiri Chiffon Parfait

(This attractive dessert can be used for filling in a pie crust or in small tart shells)

Yield: Serves 12

1 (0.25-ounce) envelope unflavored gelatin
½ cup cold water
¼ teaspoon salt
5 eggs, separated
1 (6-ounce) can frozen daiquiri mix concentrate, thawed
2 or 3 drops green food coloring
½ cup sugar
½ cup heavy cream, whipped
½ teaspoon vanilla or rum extract
Whipped cream for garnish
Fresh mint leaves (optional)
Lime or fresh fruit slices (optional)

Sprinkle gelatin on cold water in the top of a double-boiler. Allow to stand for 5 minutes. Add the salt and egg yolks; mix well. Place over hot, but not boiling water and cook, stirring constantly, for 3 to 5 minutes until mixture thickens slightly and gelatin is completely dissolved. Remove from heat. Add the thawed daiquiri concentrate and food coloring and chill, stirring occasionally, until mixture mounds on a spoon. Beat egg whites until frothy; gradually add sugar and beat until stiff. Take a large spoonful of the beaten egg whites and stir into the gelatin mixture; then fold in whites. Whip cream with extract and fold into mixture. Chiffon filling will make 8 to 10 parfaits or fill a baked 11-inch pie shell or 12 individual tart shells. Chill until firm. Garnish at serving time with additional whipped cream, mint leaves and fruit slices, as desired.

Coffee Eclairs

Yield: 25 to 30 eclairs

Cream-Puff Dough:

½ cup water
¼ cup butter or margarine
⅛ teaspoon salt
½ cup sifted all-purpose flour
2 large eggs

Preheat oven to 400 degrees. In a small saucepan, slowly bring water with butter and salt to a boil. Remove from heat. With wooden spoon, beat in flour all at once. Return to low heat; continue beating until mixture forms a ball and leaves side of pan. Remove from heat. Beat in eggs, one at a time, beating hard after each addition until smooth. Continue beating until dough is shiny and breaks into strands. Force mixture through a pastry tube or shape with a spatula into 2-inch strips. Place about 2-inches apart on an ungreased cookie sheet. Bake for 20 minutes, or until golden brown. Let cool completely on wire rack, away from drafts.

Filling:

½ cup whipping or heavy cream
2 tablespoons powdered sugar
½ teaspoon powdered instant coffee
¼ teaspoon vanilla extract

Beat cream with sugar, coffee and vanilla just until stiff. Refrigerate, covered, until ready to use.

Method:

With a sharp knife, cut a slice from the top of each eclair. Tear out any soft strains of dough from the inside of each eclair. Fill each with a scant tablespoon of filling; replace tops. To decorate: frost tops with coffee frosting.

Chocolate Strawberries

Yield: 20 to 30 strawberries

- 20 to 30 extra large perfect strawberries, with stems
- 1 (8-ounce) package chocolate chips
- 1 tablespoon vanilla extract
- 1 cup Grand Marnier or other orange-flavored liqueur

Wash berries leaving the stems attached. Gently dry the berries. In a double-boiler, melt the chocolate and blend in vanilla. Remove from heat. With a cooking syringe, inject each berry with the Grand Marnier. Dip the berries into the chocolate, leaving the upper quarter of each berry exposed. Place on waxed paper to cool.

Note:
Serve on a doily or as garnish to ice cream.

Crisped Almond Apples

(Also excellent served over vanilla ice cream)

Yield: Serves 6

- 5 large Granny Smith apples, pared, cored and cut lengthwise into 1-inch pieces
- ¾ cup + 2 tablespoons sugar
- 1½ tablespoons fresh lemon juice
- 1 cup all-purpose flour
- ¼ teaspoon ground cinnamon
- ¼ teaspoon salt
- ⅔ cup finely chopped blanched almonds
- ½ cup (1-stick) unsalted butter, melted
- ¾ teaspoon vanilla
- 1½ cups whipping or heavy cream
- 2 tablespoons sugar

Heat oven to 400 degrees. Generously butter a 9x13-inch baking dish. In a large bowl, toss together the apples, 2 tablespoons sugar and lemon juice. Arrange apples, slightly overlapped, in 3 lengthwise rows in the prepared baking dish. Sift together flour, ¾ cup sugar, cinnamon and salt into a medium bowl. Stir in almonds. Stir vanilla into melted butter and drizzle over almond mixture while tossing with fork until crumbly. Spread evenly over apples. Bake until apples are tender and almond topping is well browned; 30 to 35 minutes. Partially cool on wire rack. (At this point, can be covered and set aside for 6 hours. Beat cream if desired, reheat almond apples for 10 minutes at 350 degrees just before serving.) Beat whipping cream with the 2 tablespoons sugar in a small bowl until soft peaks form. Serve Crisped Almond Apples warm or at room temperature. Serve whipped cream separately.

Fresh Peach Ice Cream

Yield: 1 quart

2 cups heavy or whipping cream
⅔ cup sugar
4 egg yolks
2 cups fresh peach purée
2 tablespoons California peach brandy

In a medium saucepan, bring the cream almost to a boil, and remove from heat. In a separate bowl, mix the sugar and the egg yolks together until the sugar is well dissolved. Add ½ cup of the warmed cream to the egg mixture, then add the egg-sugar mixture to the warmed cream. Return to the heat until slightly thickened and add the peach purée to cool the cream. Add the peach brandy and refrigerate until cold. Pour the mixture into an ice cream freezer and process according to manufacturer's instructions.

Fresh Fruit Ices

Food Processor

Basic Formula:
Fresh fruit
Sugar
Lemon juice

Basic Method:

1. Combine all in food processor fitted with steel blade. Purée. 2. Spread mixture in an 8-inch cake pan; freeze until not quite firm. Scoop back into processor and process until fluffy. 3. Transfer to an airtight container and freeze for 2 hours. Allow to soften 30 minutes in refrigerator before serving.

Variations:

Strawberry Sherbet:

Yield: 3¾ cups

2 pints strawberries, washed and hulled
½ cup sugar
1 tablespoon fresh lemon juice

Raspberry Sherbet:

Yield: 3 cups

2 pints fresh or frozen raspberries
½ cup sugar
1 tablespoon fresh lemon juice
After puréeing, sieve.

Peach Sherbet:

Yield: 3 cups

2 pounds fresh peaches, peeled, pitted and cut into chunks
½ cup sugar
2 tablespoons fresh lemon juice

Apple Sherbet:

Yield: 3 cups

2 pounds apples, peeled, cored and cut into chunks
⅓ cup sugar
1 tablespoon fresh lemon juice

Grand Marnier Ice

Food Processor

Yield: Serves 4 to 6

1 cup sugar
1 piece (2-inch square) orange peel
4 cups fresh orange juice
⅓ cup Grand Marnier liqueur

In a food processor with metal blade in place, add about ¼ cup sugar and the orange peel. Process with on/off bursts until peel is well chopped. Add 1 cup of the Grand Marnier and process until well combined. Add 2 cups of the orange juice and process for 2 seconds. Add the processed ingredients to the remaining orange juice and mix well. Pour into 2 ice cube trays and freeze until solid. Just before serving, add the frozen cubes to the processor work bowl, 1 tray at a time, and process into a smooth fine ice. Spoon into serving containers. Serve at once.

Almond Lemon Cookies

Yield: about 36 cookies

2½ cups all-purpose flour
1 teaspoon baking powder
1 cup unsalted butter, softened
1 cup superfine sugar
2 egg yolks
2 teaspoons vanilla extract
2 teaspoons almond extract
1 teaspoon lemon extract
36 whole blanched almonds, or as necessary

Preheat oven to 225 degrees. Sift flour and baking powder in a small bowl. Beat butter and sugar in large mixer bowl on medium speed until light and fluffy. Beat in egg yolks, one at a time, beating well after each addition. Stir in vanilla, almond and lemon extracts until blended. Gradually stir in flour mixture until smooth. Chill for 30 minutes. Roll dough with hands into balls the size of small walnuts, about 1 tablespoon dough each; place 1½-inches apart on ungreased baking sheet. Press center of each ball with thumb to create a small well; place an almond in each well. Bake until undersides of cookies are dry and tops are just beginning to color, about 30 minutes. These cookies remain quite pale, because of the low baking temperature. Do not alter baking time or temperature. Transfer to rack to cool.

Meltaways

Yield: 24 large cookies or
48 small cookies

Pastry:

1 cup (2-sticks) butter or margarine
1 (8-ounce) carton creamed cottage cheese
2 cups sifted all-purpose flour

Mix well with pastry blender, and form into a ball. Refrigerate at least 2 hours or over night.

Filling:

½ cup sugar
½ cup brown sugar, packed
1 teaspoon cinnamon
1 cup chopped walnuts or pecans
¼ cup butter or margarine, melted
1 egg, well beaten

Combine the sugar, brown sugar, cinnamon and nuts in a small bowl. Melt the butter and keep warm. Divide the chilled dough into three equal parts. Roll each part on a well-floured board, into a round circle, approximately 15-inches in diameter. Brush with ⅓ of the melted butter and sprinkle ⅓ of the filling mixture evenly over the entire circle. Cut into either 8 large or 16 small pie-shaped wedges. Roll dough from the outside to inside, forming a crescent shape. Place on a non-stick cookie sheet, point side down. Brush with beaten egg. Bake in a preheated 375 degree oven for 15 to 20 minutes or until golden brown. Continue in the same manner with the remaining 2 parts of dough.

Rosé Sauce

Yield: 1 cup

1 (10-ounce) package frozen raspberries
¼ cup sugar
2 tablespoons cornstarch
½ cup California rosé wine

In a saucepan, heat raspberries until thawed. Combine sugar and cornstarch and stir into berries. Heat for 2 minutes, stirring constantly, or until sauce is transparent. Add Rosé wine and mix well. Heat for 1 minute longer. May be served chilled or at room temperature. Serve over pound cake, ice cream, lime sherbet or fresh peach slices.

Note:
You may wish to substitute strawberries.

Valley Raisin Dessert Sauce

(This sauce is wonderful over pound cake or vanilla ice cream.)

Yield: 1 pint

½ cup dark rum
½ cup California seedless raisins
½ cup sugar
¼ cup water
1 cinnamon stick, broken in half
½ teaspoon vanilla extract
1 tablespoon grated lemon peel
1 tablespoon grated orange peel
½ cup chopped pecans

Place raisins in a bowl and pour rum over them. Set aside. In a heavy saucepan, mix the sugar and water together, then add the cinnamon stick. Bring to a boil and boil hard for 2 minutes. Add the raisins and rum and cook for 5 minutes more. Add the vanilla, lemon and orange peel and the pecans. Spoon into a sterilized pint jar and seal or store in refrigerator.

9-6W

Oil
Coalinga

On a hunting trip to the Coast Range mountains west of Coalinga, in 1864, Frank Dusy and John Clark discovered oil seeping up through the ground. They formed a partnership with W. A. Porter, bought the land, and organized the San Joaquin Petroleum Company They sold their "black gold" on the streets of the county seat at Millerton, and soon the new "gold rush" was under way.

It is the love of the land and the preservation of the landscape which is the watch-word of the timber industry in the Valley. In 1874, the owners of the California Lumber Company secured huge tracts of sugar pine and other timber lands in the Sierras. It was this company who established the town of Madera as a depot for the lumber they sent down the mountains by flume. The manager of the company, W. H. Thurman, laid out the town of Madera, named it Madera, Spanish for lumber, and built the first residence. The first lumber roared down the flume on October 26, 1876.

Some of the early flumes can still be seen in the Sierras, and children delight at the stories of water rushing down the flumes while the huge logs bumped and groaned their way to the Valley below.

A timber harvest today is a much cleaner and more ecologically controlled venture than it once was. The average yield in 1935 was fifty million board feet per year. Today, with conservation and replanting, the yield has increased to seventy-six million, fifteen-thousand board feet per year.

Compliments of **Spencer Enterprises, Inc.** *and An Anonymous Friend*

Brunch

Brunch Chicken with Biscuits

Yield: Serves 4

2 tablespoons vegetable oil
1 small onion, chopped
½ green pepper, finely chopped
⅔ cup sliced fresh mushrooms
2 tablespoons cornstarch
1½ cups milk
1½ to 2 cups cooked chicken, cut into cubes
Salt and pepper

Heat oil in a skillet. Add onion, green pepper and mushrooms; sauté until limp. Add cornstarch and cook for 1 minute stirring constantly. Add milk gradually; stirring until boiling. Add chicken and salt and pepper to taste. Pour mixture into a deep 9-inch pie plate.

Biscuits:

2 cups flour
1 teaspoon salt
2½ teaspoons baking powder
⅓ cup butter or margarine
⅔ cup milk

Sift flour, salt and baking powder together. Cut in butter with a pastry blender until mixture looks like coarse meal. Using fork, stir in enough milk to make a soft but not sticky dough. Knead lightly 8 to 10 times on floured board; roll out dough to about ½-inch thickness. Cut into 1½-inch rounds with a cookie cutter.

Method:

Place rounds on top of chicken mixture around the outer edge of the pie plate. Brush biscuit tops with a little milk. Bake in a preheated 400 degree oven for 10 to 15 minutes, or until biscuits are golden and chicken mixture is bubbling.

Crab Artichoke Casserole

(This dish can be made ahead of time.) Yield: Serves 4 to 6

2 (9-ounce) packages frozen artichoke hearts
¾ pound fresh crab meat
2 tablespoons butter or margarine
¾ pound fresh mushrooms, sliced
¼ cup butter or margarine
¼ cup flour
2 cups milk
1 tablespoon dehydrated chopped onion
1 tablespoon Worcestershire sauce
¼ cup California dry sherry
½ teaspoon seafood seasoning
Salt and pepper to taste
Parmesan cheese

Cook frozen artichoke hearts according to package directions; drain well and reserve several hearts for garnish. Place remaining artichoke hearts in an 8½x11-inch buttered baking dish. Select a few larger portions of crab meat for garnish and reserve; distribute remaining crab over artichoke hearts. In a small skillet, sauté mushrooms in the 2 tablespoons of butter until limp and most of the moisture has evaporated. Place over crab and set aside. In a saucepan melt the ¼ cup butter, add flour and blend in well. Add milk, onion, Worcestershire sauce, sherry, seafood seasoning, salt and pepper, stirring constantly until mixture thickens. Pour mixture over artichoke-crab-mushroom layer. (At this point, dish may be refrigerated until ready to cook.) Before baking, sprinkle top of casserole with Parmesan cheese. Garnish with reserved artichoke hearts and crab. Bake in a preheated 375 degree oven for 20 minutes or until bubbly around the edges. (Baking time needs to be increased if casserole has been refrigerated.)

Egg-Asparagus Brunch Casserole

*(Different and delicious!
Can be made the day before)*

Yield: Serves 4 to 6

1 (10-ounce) package frozen asparagus spears
2 slices bacon, diced
1 cup sliced fresh mushrooms
2 tablespoons butter, melted
¼ cup flour
2 cups milk
Dash white pepper
8 large eggs, beaten
½ cup evaporated milk
½ teaspoon salt
Parsley for garnish

Cook asparagus according to package directions. Drain well and set aside. In a skillet, sauté bacon with mushrooms until limp; drain off liquid and set aside. In small saucepan melt butter; stir in flour and blend. Add milk and pepper and cook over medium heat stirring constantly until mixture thickens. Add reserved mushrooms and bacon. In a separate bowl, beat eggs, evaporated milk and salt together. Scramble egg mixture in 2 tablespoons of butter. In a 7x11-inch buttered baking dish spread one half of the mushroom sauce. Layer the cooked eggs over sauce. Place cooked asparagus over eggs and top with remaining sauce. Refrigerate overnight if desired. Cover and bake in a preheated 275 degree oven for 1 hour. Garnish with parsley and serve with hot rolls and fresh fruit for a special brunch.

Eggs Florentine

Yield: Serves 4 to 6

1 pound fresh spinach
¼ cup water
Pinch of salt

Wash spinach; remove stems and discard. Place clean spinach in a saucepan, with water and salt. Cover and steam over low heat for about 5 minutes; drain and set aside.

Cheese Sauce:

3 tablespoons butter
3 tablespoons flour
Salt
White pepper
1 cup hot chicken broth
½ cup half and half
¾ cup freshly grated Parmesan cheese

Melt butter in medium saucepan. Add flour, salt and pepper to taste; cook until bubbly. Add broth and cream; cook until thickened, stirring constantly. Remove from heat; stir in cheese. Set aside, but keep warm.

Eggs:

Boiling salted water
White vinegar
6 eggs

Heat 1½-inches of salted water to a boiling point in a medium skillet; add a few drops of white vinegar. Poach eggs in water to desired degree of doneness. When eggs are done, place cooked spinach on a warm serving dish. Remove eggs from skillet with a slotted spoon and place on spinach. Pour cheese sauce over eggs and spinach. Serve immediately.

Ousse

Yield: Serves 6

6 slices lean bacon, cut into 1½-inch pieces
6 thin slices Swiss cheese
6 eggs
Salt and pepper to taste
1 tablespoon chopped parsley
¼ cup half and half or light cream

Cook the bacon until crisp; drain on paper toweling. Place bacon in a 9x13-inch shallow dish; layer cheese over the top. Break the eggs onto the cheese, one on each slice; sprinkle with salt, pepper and parsley. Pour the half and half over all. Bake in a preheated 325 degree oven for 15 to 20 minutes or until egg whites are set. Serve immediately.

Harry's Eggs n' Such

(Men love this brunch dish!)

Yield: Serves 6

1 pound bulk pork sausage
¼ pound chopped fresh mushrooms
1 medium onion, diced
Salt and pepper to taste
6 eggs
3 tablespoons dairy sour cream
1 (12-ounce) jar red chili salsa
2 cups (½-pound) sharp Cheddar cheese, grated
2 cups (½-pound) mozzarella cheese, grated
2 cups (½-pound) Velveeta cheese, grated

In a large skillet on medium-high heat, sauté sausage, mushrooms and onion until sausage is browned. Pour into colander and drain well. Salt and pepper to taste; set aside. Put eggs and sour cream into a blender and blend for 1 minute. Pour egg mixture into a 9x13-inch baking dish; bake in a preheated 400 degree oven for 4 to 7 minutes or until eggs are softly set. Remove from oven and spoon salsa evenly over the top of eggs. Sprinkle sausage mixture over top of salsa and top with mixed cheeses. Bake in a preheated 325 degree oven for 30 minutes.

Ham & Broccoli Strata

Yield: Serves 8 to 10

12 slices white bread, crusts trimmed, cut into halves
3 cups grated Cheddar cheese
2 (10-ounce) packages frozen chopped broccoli, cooked and well drained
3 cups diced cooked ham
3 cups milk
6 eggs, beaten
½ teaspoon salt
½ teaspoon dry mustard
2 tablespoons dried chopped onion

Butter a 9x13-inch casserole dish. Layer the ingredients in the following order: 6 slices bread, 1 cup cheese, 6 slices bread, 1 cup cheese, broccoli, ham, 1 cup cheese. In a large bowl, combine milk, eggs, salt, mustard and onion. Pour mixture over casserole. Refrigerate at least 6 hours or overnight. Remove casserole from refrigerator at least one hour before baking. Bake in a preheated 350 degree oven for 50 to 60 minutes or until center is set. Let stand 10 minutes before cutting.

Mexican Eggs

Yield: Serves 6

- 6 fresh corn tortillas
- 2 tablespoons shortening or salad oil
- 4 tablespoons butter or margarine
- ½ cup minced onion
- 1 (4-ounce) can diced green chiles
- 1 cup half and half or light cream
- 8 eggs, beaten
- 1 teaspoon salt
- 10 to 12 pork link sausages, cooked, drained and kept warm
- 2 cups shredded longhorn cheese
- Pitted ripe olives for garnish
- Diced fresh tomatoes
- Green or red chili sauce (optional)

Cut tortillas into matchstick-size pieces. Heat shortening and 2 tablespoons of the butter in an electric frying pan heated to 350 degrees. Fry tortillas until crisp and remove from frying pan. Melt remaining 2 tablespoons butter and sauté onions and chiles for about 4 minutes. In a bowl, gradually stir cream into beaten eggs; add salt. Reduce heat to 250 degrees and pour in egg mixture; sprinkle tortilla strips over eggs and cook until softly scrambled. Turn eggs onto a large serving platter. Garnish with sausage, diced tomato, olives and cheese. You may wish to place in a warm oven until cheese melts. Serve with chile sauce, if desired.

Chile Rellenos Casserole

Yield: Serves 6

- 4 slices firm white bread or sour dough French bread
- 2 tablespoons butter or margarine
- 1½ cups shredded sharp Cheddar cheese
- 1½ cups shredded Jack cheese
- 1 (4-ounce) can green chiles (remove seeds)
- 6 eggs, well beaten
- 2 cups milk
- 2 teaspoons paprika
- 1 teaspoon salt
- ½ teaspoon oregano
- ½ teaspoon pepper
- ¼ teaspoon garlic powder
- ¼ teaspoon dry mustard

Trim crusts from bread and butter on one side. Place in an 8x11-inch casserole buttered side down. Sprinkle Cheddar cheese and Jack cheese on top of bread; place chiles on top of cheese. In a bowl, beat eggs, milk, paprika, salt, oregano, pepper, garlic powder and dry mustard together. Pour milk mixture over casserole. Cover and chill 4 to 6 hours or overnight. Bake uncovered in a preheated 325 degree oven for 50 minutes or until set in center. Allow to stand for 10 minutes before cutting.

Oven Fondue Fantastic

(This is a wonderful and different do-ahead main brunch dish!)

Yield: Serves 6

- 6 slices bread (bakery white)
- 6 eggs, well beaten
- 3 cups grated sharp Cheddar cheese
- 3 cups milk
- 1 (4-ounce) can mushrooms, drained
- 2 tablespoons chopped pimiento
- 1 teaspoon paprika
- 1 teaspoon dry mustard
- 1 teaspoon salt
- 3 tablespoons chopped green pepper
- 1½ cups shrimp or flaked crab meat (optional)

Trim crusts from bread and cut each slice into fourths; place in a buttered 9x13-inch baking dish. Combine eggs, Cheddar, milk, mushrooms, pimiento, paprika, mustard, salt, green pepper and optional shrimp or crab meat; blend well. Pour mixture over bread and mix gently. Cover casserole and refrigerate for at least 4 hours or overnight. Bake, uncovered, in a preheated 350 degree oven for 40 to 45 minutes or until puffy and golden brown.

Hash Brown Omelet

(An easy brunch or quick supper dish) Yield: Serves 4

4 thin slices bacon
2 cups frozen hash brown potatoes, or diced boiled potatoes
½ cup onion, chopped
½ cup green pepper, chopped
4 large eggs
¼ cup milk
¼ teaspoon salt
⅛ teaspoon pepper
½ cup coarsely grated Cheddar cheese

In an 8-inch skillet that can fit under the broiler, cook the bacon until crisp. Remove and crumble bacon; pour off all but 2 tablespoons of fat from the skillet. Increase heat to moderate, add potatoes, onion and green pepper. Press into skillet and cook about 3 minutes until potatoes start to brown. Turn potato mixture over and press firmly into skillet. In a small bowl, beat eggs, milk, salt and pepper until well blended. Pour over potato mixture; sprinkle with cheese and crumbled bacon. Cook 10 to 15 minutes without stirring, until most of the egg is set. Place in oven and broil 2 to 3 minutes as close to heat source as possible, until top is set and bubbly. Turn omelet out onto a warm plate and cut into wedges to serve.

Note:
Finely chopped cooked ham or chicken may be substituted for the bacon.

Italian Frittata

(This is great for a light supper!) Yield: Serves 4

3 hot Italian-style sausage links
½ cup butter or margarine
¼ cup olive oil
3 medium-sized potatoes, pared and cut into ⅛-inch thick slices
1½ teaspoons salt
½ cup chopped onion
5 eggs

Prick sausages with a fork and parboil for 5 minutes. Remove from water and place on rack, under broiler, for 10 minutes or until cooked through. Remove from oven and cut into ¼-inch thick rounds. Set aside. In a large skillet melt ¼ cup of the butter with 2 tablespoons of the olive oil. Add potatoes, sprinkle with 1 teaspoon salt and turn them several times until they are well coated with the butter and oil mixture. Cook over medium heat for 10 minutes or until potatoes are lightly browned. Push potatoes to one side of the pan; add onions and cook 5 minutes. Add sausages and mix all ingredients in the pan together and cook 5 minutes longer. Drain off fat. In a large bowl, beat eggs with ½ teaspoon salt; add vegetables and sausage mixture. Heat remaining butter and oil in a 9-inch skillet over medium heat. When very hot, pour in egg mixture, spreading it so that it will cook evenly. From time to time remove the skillet from the heat and give it a vigorous shake to prevent the eggs from sticking. When eggs become firm, remove skillet from heat. Place a large warmed plate over the skillet; flip the egg cake onto the plate and then slide back into skillet. Cook another 3 minutes. To serve, cut into wedges.

South of the Border Quiche

Yield: Serves 6

⅔ to ¾ pound lean ground beef
¼ cup chopped onion
2 tablespoons taco seasoning mix
1 can (4-ounces) diced chiles
1 cup grated sharp Cheddar cheese
½ cup Monterey Jack cheese
4 eggs, slightly beaten
1 to 1½ cup half and half
Few dashes Tabasco sauce
¾ teaspoon salt
¼ teaspoon white pepper
Unbaked, single pastry shell
Guacamole (see following recipe)
Shredded lettuce
Chopped tomatoes

In a skillet, combine ground beef and onions; cook, stirring occasionally, until beef is browned and onions are tender. Drain ground beef mixture well of all excess fat; blend in taco seasoning mix and chiles. In the pastry shell, layer cheeses and then beef mixture. In a medium bowl, combine eggs, half and half, Tabasco sauce, salt and white pepper. Beat with a fork or whisk until well mixed but not frothy. Pour egg mixture through a sieve, over the beef mixture; allow about ¼-inch head room when filling quiche. Position oven rack in lower one-third of oven. Bake in a preheated 375 degree oven for 45 to 55 minutes, or until quiche tests done. Let quiche stand for 10 minutes, or until set, before serving. Garnish quiche with shredded lettuce, chopped tomatoes and guacamole.

Guacamole:

Food Processor

1 to 2 ripe avocados
½ cup dairy sour cream
1 tablespoon fresh lemon juice
½ to 1 teaspoon salt
¼ teaspoon garlic powder
¼ teaspoon onion powder
Tabasco sauce to taste

In a processor work bowl, fitted with metal blade, combine ripe avocado (peeled and seeded), sour cream, lemon juice, salt, garlic powder, onion powder and Tabasco sauce to taste. Process until smooth.

Quiche Le Grand

Yield: Serves 8

- 1 unbaked (9-inch) deep dish pie shell
- 2 tablespoons grated Parmesan cheese
- 2 cups grated Swiss cheese
- 1½ cups cooked turkey breast, cut into ½-inch cubes
- ¼ cup butter
- 1 small onion, finely chopped
- 1¼ cups chopped broccoli, blanched and well drained
- 2 tablespoons butter, melted
- ¼ teaspoon dried Fine Herbs, crumbled
- ⅛ teaspoon cinnamon
- ⅛ teaspoon garlic powder
- ⅛ teaspoon salt
- ⅛ teaspoon cumin or comino
- ¼ teaspoon basil, crumbled
- ¼ teaspoon Worcestershire sauce
- ¼ teaspoon tarragon, crumbled
- ⅛ teaspoon ground coriander
- Dash of paprika
- 2 eggs
- 1½ cups half and half, or light cream
- ¼ cup Parmesan cheese
- 1 teaspoon nutmeg
- Salt and pepper to taste

Position rack in lower one-third of oven and preheat to 350 degrees. Sprinkle 2 tablespoons grated Parmesan in the bottom of unbaked pie shell. Layer Swiss cheese and turkey over Parmesan cheese. Set aside. Melt ¼ cup butter in small skillet over low heat. Add onion and cook until soft. Set aside. In a large bowl, combine broccoli, melted butter, Fine Herbs, cinnamon, garlic, salt, cumin, basil, Worcestershire sauce, tarragon, coriander, paprika and onion and toss lightly until thoroughly mixed. Arrange broccoli mixture over turkey in the pie shell. In a small bowl, beat eggs on high speed until light and fluffy. Reduce speed to medium and blend in half and half, ¼ cup Parmesan cheese, nutmeg, salt and pepper. Pour the egg mixture over filling in pie shell, allowing about ¼-inch of head room when filled. Bake for 35 to 45 minutes or until quiche tests done. Let quiche stand for 10 minutes, or until set, before cutting.

Mexican Quiche

Yield: Serves 6 to 8

1 tablespoon oil
1 pound boneless lean chuck roast
1½ teaspoons paprika
¼ teaspoon chili powder
1 large onion, diced
1 clove garlic, crushed
1 unbaked (10-inch) pastry shell
1 egg white, lightly beaten
1½ cups grated Monterey Jack cheese
1 cup dairy sour cream
¾ cup chopped green onion
1 (4-ounce) can chopped green chiles
3 eggs, beaten
1 teaspoon salt
¼ teaspoon pepper

Heat oil in a large skillet over medium-high heat. Pat chuck roast with mixture of paprika and chili powder. Add meat, onion and garlic to skillet and brown meat well. Reduce heat and braise, tightly covered, for 1½ hours or until meat shreds easily. Let meat cool; then shred. Meanwhile, preheat oven to 400 degrees. Brush pastry shell with egg white and bake for 5 minutes. Cool. Reduce oven to 325 degrees. Combine meat, cooked onion and garlic, cheese, sour cream, green onion, chiles, eggs, salt and pepper and mix well. Pour mixture into partially baked pastry shell. Bake 60 minutes or until filling is set and crust is nicely browned. Cool slightly, then spread top with sour cream and decorate with avocado slices. Serve with salsa, if desired.

Portuguese Omelet

Yield: Serves 4

½ cup half and half or light cream
½ teaspoon salt
¼ teaspoon white pepper
8 egg whites
8 egg yolks
2 tablespoons chopped parsley
2 tablespoons butter
1 tomato, cut into wedges
1 green or red bell pepper, sliced ¼-inch thick
8 ripe olives
1 clove garlic, minced
1 tablespoon olive oil
2 tablespoons California white wine
2 tablespoons grated Parmesan cheese

In a large bowl, combine salt, pepper and egg whites and beat with electric mixer until egg whites are stiff but not dry. In a separate bowl, beat egg yolks until thick and lemon-colored. Fold yolks and parsley into egg whites. Melt butter on medium-high heat in a large 9 to 10-inch skillet. Pour mixture into skillet and cook slowly until lightly browned, approximately 5 minutes. Remove from top of stove and bake in a preheated 350 degree oven for 10 to 12 minutes. In another skillet sauté the tomato wedges, green or red pepper slices, olives and garlic in olive oil. When vegetables are tender, add wine and remove from heat. Take omelet out of oven and sprinkle top with cheese and serve with sautéed vegetables.

Blintzes

Yield: Serves 6 to 8

Batter:

2 eggs
¾ cup milk
2 tablespoons butter, melted
¼ teaspoon salt
½ cup flour, sifted

In a bowl lightly beat the eggs and milk together. Add the melted butter, salt and flour and mix well. Lightly butter a small 6-inch skillet and spoon in a little batter, tilting the pan in a circular pattern, to spread it thinly and evenly. Cook over medium heat until the batter is set and begins to brown. Turn out onto a dish, browned side up. Continue until all batter is used.

Filling:

1 large carton (1-pound) large curd cottage cheese
2 tablespoons dairy sour cream
2 egg yolks
3 tablespoons sugar
1 teaspoon vanilla
½ teaspoon salt
1 cup California raisins (optional)

Combine all ingredients in a medium sized bowl and mix well. Spread mixture over the crepes and fold over into a fan shape or roll up and tuck in the ends of each crepe. (If you have done it correctly, then mixture will be spread on cooked side of crepe.) Brown each Blintz in margarine and transfer to a warm serving dish, or individual plate. To serve, top with sour cream, whipped cream, honey or stewed berries.

Main-Dish Crepes

Yield: 10 to 12 Crepes

1 cup cold milk
4 eggs
1 cup water
1 tablespoon California brandy
¾ teaspoon salt
2 cups + 1 tablespoon sifted all-purpose flour
4 tablespoons melted butter or margarine

Put milk, eggs, water, brandy and salt into a blender and process. Add flour and butter. Cover and blend at full speed for 1 minute. Scrape mixture off sides of jar and blend a few seconds more. Cover and refrigerate mixture for 2 to 3 hours or overnight. When ready to make crepes, stir mixture with a spoon. Batter should be thick enough to coat the spoon; if too thick, add a little water to batter.

Crepes Ensenada

Yield: Serves 4 to 6

12 thin slices cooked ham
1 (4-ounce) can green chiles, washed and seeded
12 slices Monterey Jack cheese
12 (8 to 10-inch) flour tortillas
4 tablespoons butter or margarine
⅓ cup flour
½ teaspoon dry mustard
4 cups (1-quart) milk
4 cups (1-pound) Cheddar cheese, grated

Place one slice ham (about ⅔ size of tortilla), one chile and one piece Jack cheese (about the size of chile) on the flour tortilla; roll up together and place, seam side down, in a shallow, greased casserole, making sure that they do not touch. In a large saucepan, melt butter. Mix flour and dry mustard together and blend mixture into butter to form a paste. Slowly add milk, stirring constantly and cook over medium heat until mixture thickens. Add Cheddar cheese slowly, stirring until melted. Pour sauce over rolled tortillas. Bake in a preheated 350 degree oven for 40 minutes or until hot and bubbly.

Metropolitan Museum Of Art, History and Science Fresno

"Dedicated to the enrichment of lives through education, inspiration and experience and to the preservation of the rich heritage of the magnificent San Joaquin Valley"; this museum, a five-story brick Italian Renaissance building with arched windows, terra-cotta ornaments, and a recessed porch and balcony, is truly a community labor of love, and the answer to the long-time dream of bringing the major collections in the Valley under one roof.

With the opening of the museum, Fresno received a precious gift, sixty paintings, making up one of the most comprehensive collections of its kind. The collection of mid-seventeenth century Dutch subjects to an early twentieth century American illusory piece was the gift of well-known collectors, Maria and Oscar Salzar.

Fresno has long been the home of some beautiful, yet diverse works. Each group brought with them the treasures of their lives before; magnificent Persian carpets, paintings, porcelains, fabrics and other object d'art. Modern day artists are represented everywhere, and the list of accomplished and well-known Valley creators is a long one. From the Hispanic murals of John Sierra to the lovely watercolors of "The Tuesday Group", local art is thriving.

There are craft groups, fabric groups, pottery groups and sculpture groups. The Fresno Art Center (founded in 1959 by the Junior League) offers classes, produces shows and features a hands-on gallery devoted entirely to exhibitions for children.

Compliments of An *Anonymous Friend*

Crepe Manicotti

Yield: Serves 8

½ pound ground beef
½ cup chopped onion
1 small clove garlic, minced
1 (8-ounce) can tomatoes, cut up (do not drain)
1 (6-ounce) can tomato paste
1½ teaspoons dried basil, crushed
½ teaspoon sugar
¼ teaspoon fennel seed, crushed
½ cup water
½ teaspoon salt
2 eggs, beaten
3 cups ricotta or cream-style cottage cheese
¼ cup grated Parmesan cheese
1 tablespoon dried parsley flakes
¼ teaspoon salt
¼ teaspoon pepper
16 basic "Main-dish Crepes" (see page 304)
1 cup shredded mozzarella cheese

For sauce, brown ground beef with onion and garlic. Drain off fat. Add undrained tomatoes, tomato paste, basil, sugar, fennel, water and ½ teaspoon salt. Simmer, uncovered, about 15 minutes, stirring often. For filling, mix eggs, ricotta, Parmesan, parsley, ¼ teaspoon salt and pepper. To assemble, spoon about 3 tablespoons of filling along center of unbrowned side of crepe. Fold two opposite edges so they overlap on top of filling. Place seam side down in a 9x13x2-inch baking dish. Repeat with remaining crepes. Spoon sauce over crepes. Cover; bake in a preheated 375 degree oven for 25 minutes. Uncover; sprinkle crepes with mozzarella. Bake until cheese melts.

Chicken Divan Crepes

Yield: Serves 6

1 (10-ounce) package frozen chopped broccoli
1 (10¾-ounce) can cream of chicken soup, undiluted
½ teaspoon Worcestershire sauce
¾ cup grated Parmesan cheese
2 cups cooked chicken, cut into strips
12 Main-dish Crepes (see page 304)
⅓ cup mayonnaise
½ teaspoon curry powder
1 tablespoon milk

Cook broccoli according to package directions; drain well. Combine broccoli with soup, Worcestershire sauce, ½ cup of the Parmesan cheese and chicken. Divide mixture into 12 portions and place 1 portion on each crepe. Roll the crepe up and place in a shallow baking dish. Combine mayonnaise and curry, then add milk and stir; spread over crepes. Sprinkle with ¼ cup cheese; broil until cheese bubbles.

Creamy Ham & Egg Crepes

Yield: Serves 6 to 8

¼ cup finely chopped onion
4 tablespoons butter or margarine
¼ cup all-purpose flour
2 teaspoons prepared mustard
2 cups milk
1 cup shredded sharp Cheddar cheese
½ cup dairy sour cream
2 cups diced cooked ham
1 (4-ounce) can mushroom stems and pieces, drained
4 hard-cooked eggs, chopped
18 to 20 Main-dish Crepes (see page 304)

In a saucepan, sauté the chopped onion with butter, until onion is tender. Blend in flour and mustard. Add milk and cook, stirring constantly, until mixture thickens and bubbles. Add cheese and stir until melted. Remove from heat and reserve. In a large bowl, blend ⅔ cup of the cheese sauce into the sour cream; stir in ham, mushrooms and hard-cooked eggs. Spoon about ¼ cup of the mixture into center of each crepe. Roll up crepes and place, seam side down, in a 9x13x2-inch baking dish. Pour reserved cheese sauce over crepes. Bake in a preheated 375 degree oven for 20 to 25 minutes.

Crabmeat Crepes

Yield: 10 to 12 crepes

- 1 (7½-ounce) can king crabmeat, drained
- 1 teaspoon butter
- 1 teaspoon chopped green onion
- ½ cup dry California white wine
- ½ teaspoon Worcestershire sauce
- ⅛ teaspoon pepper
- Dash of cayenne
- 2 cups white sauce
- 1 recipe of Main-dish Crepes (see page 304)

Separate crabmeat, removing membrane and bones; set aside. In a medium skillet, sauté green onion in butter for 1 minute. Add crabmeat, sauté for 2 minutes longer. Add wine, Worcestershire sauce, pepper and cayenne. Cook over medium heat, stirring for 3 minutes. Stir in 1 cup of the white sauce until just blended. Remove mixture from heat and divide evenly between the crepes, rolling each crepe and placing seam side down in a 9x13-inch baking dish. Pour remaining 1 cup of white sauce over crepes. Bake in a preheated 350 degree oven for 20 minutes or until warmed through and bubbly.

Enchiladas Verdes

(Can be frozen) Yield: Serves 12

Enchiladas:

1 cup vegetable oil, more if needed
24 fresh corn tortillas
2 pounds Jack cheese, grated
2 pounds Cheddar cheese, grated
1 large onion, chopped

Heat oil in frying pan; dip tortillas in hot oil to soften. Combine Jack and Cheddar cheese together and generously spread over each softened tortilla. Sprinkle with onions. Roll up and place, seam side down, in one of two 9x13-inch casserole dishes. Cover with Verde Sauce (recipe follows).

Verde Sauce (or green sauce):

1 (10-ounce) package frozen chopped spinach
2 (10¾-ounce) cans cream of chicken soup
3 to 4 green onions, chopped
2 (4-ounce) cans diced green chiles
¼ teaspoon salt
1 pint dairy sour cream
1½ cups grated Jack and/or Cheddar cheese for topping

Cook spinach and drain well. Add soup, green onions, chiles and salt. Put in blender and process; add sour cream. Pour over enchiladas. Top with grated cheese. Bake in a preheated 350 degree oven for approximately 25 minutes, until bubbly.

French Toast with Apple Custard Sauce

Yield: Serves 6

Oil
4 eggs
1 cup whipping cream
¼ teaspoon salt
3 large thick slices egg bread, (crusts trimmed, cut diagonally into 6 triangles)
Powdered sugar
Apple custard sauce (see recipe below)

Heat ½-inch oil in electric skillet to 325 degrees. Preheat oven to 400 degrees. Beat eggs, cream and salt in medium bowl. Dip each slice of bread, allowing it to soak up as much liquid as possible. Fry in hot oil until browned, turning only once. Transfer to baking sheet and bake until puffed, about 3 to 5 minutes. Drain on paper toweling. Arrange on heated platter. Sprinkle with powdered sugar and serve immediately with Apple Custard Sauce on the side.

Apple Custard Sauce:

1 cup milk
2 eggs
2 tablespoons sugar
1 teaspoon vanilla
Pinch of salt
½ cup applesauce
1 teaspoon minced lemon peel

Heat milk in top of double boiler, over gently simmering water, until small bubbles form around edge. Combine eggs, sugar, vanilla and salt in mixing bowl and beat well. Slowly beat warm milk into egg mixture, beating constantly until well blended. Return to double boiler and continue cooking over low heat until sauce is thickened, stirring constantly. Mix in applesauce and lemon peel, and heat through.

French Toast Grand Marnier

(Make the night before - an elegant way to serve French Toast)

Yield: Serves 4

8 slices French bread (no sourdough), sliced ¾-inch thick
4 eggs
1 cup milk
2 tablespoons Grand Marnier or other orange-flavored liqueur
1 tablespoon sugar
½ teaspoon vanilla
½ teaspoon salt
2 tablespoons butter or margarine

Arrange bread in a single layer, in a 9x13-inch baking dish. In a medium bowl, beat eggs with milk, using a rotary beater. Add Grand Marnier, sugar, vanilla and salt; stirring until well blended. Pour mixture over bread, turning slices to coat on both sides. Cover dish with plastic wrap and refrigerate overnight. To cook, sauté bread in a hot buttered skillet until golden brown, about 4 minutes on each side. Sprinkle each slice with powdered sugar and serve with butter, syrup or preserves.

Cherry French Toast

Yield: Serves 4

3 eggs
¾ cup milk
1 tablespoon honey
½ teaspoon vanilla
8 slices bread

Beat eggs, milk, honey and vanilla until well mixed. Dip bread slices in mixture and place on a greased cookie sheet. Bake in a preheated 400 degree oven for 5 to 7 minutes on each side. Serve hot, with Sweet Cherry Sauce.

Sweet Cherry Sauce:

2 cups pitted fresh sweet cherries
½ cup sugar
1 cup water
2 tablespoons fresh lemon juice
½ teaspoon ground ginger
1 tablespoon cornstarch

In a saucepan, combine cherries, sugar, water, lemon juice and ginger. Mix well and cook gently until cherries are tender. Dissolve cornstarch in small amount of water; add to cherry mixture and cook until thickened and clear. Keep warm and serve over hot French toast. Sprinkle with powdered sugar, if desired.

Apple Pancakes

Microwave

Yield: Serves 6

¼ cup butter or margarine
1½ cups thinly sliced, peeled apple
½ cup sugar
½ teaspoon cinnamon
¼ teaspoon nutmeg
1 cup buttermilk complete pancake mix
½ teaspoon cinnamon
¼ teaspoon nutmeg
¾ cup water
1 teaspoon vanilla
1 tablespoon sugar
¼ teaspoon cinnamon

In a 9-inch, microwave-safe pie plate or round cake pan, melt butter on High (100% power) for 30 to 45 seconds or until butter is melted. Stir in apples, ½ cup sugar, ½ teaspoon cinnamon and ¼ teaspoon nutmeg. Cover; microcook on High (100% power) for 3 to 4 minutes or until apples are tender. In a medium bowl, blend together pancake mix, ½ teaspoon cinnamon, ¼ teaspoon nutmeg, water and vanilla. Pour evenly over cooked apples. In a small bowl, combine 1 tablespoon sugar and ¼ teaspoon cinnamon; sprinkle over batter. Microcook, uncovered, on High (100% power) for 3 to 5 minutes or until wooden toothpick inserted 1½ to 2-inches from edge comes out clean. Let stand for 5 minutes. Cut into wedges, and invert wedges to serve.

Oatmeal Pancake Mix

(This mix can be made ahead and stored in refrigerator.)

Yield: Makes 4 recipes of 16 pancakes each

2 cups oatmeal
2 cups whole wheat flour
½ cup wheat germ
1 cup instant non-fat dry milk solids
2 teaspoons baking soda
½ teaspoon salt
2 tablespoons brown sugar

Combine oatmeal, whole wheat flour, wheat germ, dry milk, baking soda, salt and brown sugar in a large mixing bowl. Cover tightly and store in refrigerator until ready to use.

For 16 Pancakes:

Combine...
1 cup Oatmeal Pancake Mix
1 egg
1 cup buttermilk
2 tablespoons melted butter

Country Store

Caramel Pecan Roll

Yield: Makes 4 dozen ½-inch slices

2 tablespoons butter or margarine, softened
1 (7-ounce) jar marshmallow creme
1 tablespoon vanilla
4½ cups (1-pound) powdered sugar, sifted
1 (14-ounce) package vanilla caramels
¼ cup milk
1½ cups chopped pecans

In a small mixer bowl, beat together, with electric mixer, butter, marshmallow creme and vanilla until combined. With mixer on low speed, gradually add in about half of the powdered sugar. By hand, stir in enough of the remaining sugar to make a stiff mixture. Turn out onto a clean surface and knead in the remaining powdered sugar. Wrap and chill until firm, about 2 hours. In the top of a double-boiler, combine caramels and milk. Place over, but not touching, boiling water; heat until melted, stirring occasionally. Cool slightly. Form chilled marshmallow mixture into four 6-inch logs. Sprinkle nuts on a sheet of waxed paper. With knife, spread melted caramel over the top and sides of one log; invert onto nuts. Spread uncoated side with caramel; coat with nuts. Repeat with remaining logs. Wrap, and store in refrigerator.

Coconut Bon Bons

Yield: 80 to 100 bon bons

1 stick butter, melted
1 (14-ounce) can condensed milk
2 (6-ounce) cans flake coconut
3 cups chopped nuts (use your favorite nuts)
1½ boxes powdered sugar
1 teaspoon vanilla

In a large mixing bowl, combine all of the ingredients. Cover and store in refrigerator overnight. The next day, form mixture into ½-inch balls (use a melon scoop) and put the formed balls on a waxed paper-lined cookie sheet.

Chocolate Dip:

½ block paraffin

3½ cups chocolate chips

Melt the paraffin and chocolate chips together in a double-boiler, blending well. (Do not allow paraffin to touch burner at any time!) When melted and smooth, dip bon bons into mixture by inserting a toothpick into ball and dipping into warm chocolate. Place each dipped ball on waxed paper until chocolate is set.

Chocolate Fruit Balls

Yield: 3 to 4 dozen

⅓ cup dried apricots
1 cup pitted prunes
¼ cup California raisins
¼ cup walnuts
⅓ cup sugar
1 pound candy-making chocolate, finely chopped

Place apricots in a bowl and pour boiling water over them until they are covered; let stand until water is cool. Drain well. Grind the apricots, prunes, raisins and walnuts through a coarse blade of food grinder or process in the food processor with a metal blade. Transfer mixture to a mixing bowl and combine mixture with the sugar. Form into ½-inch balls using all the mixture. Set aside. Place water in bottom of double-boiler to within ½-inch of bottom of smaller pan; bring to boiling point. Remove from heat and add chocolate in top of double-boiler, stir until melted. Dip fruit balls into chocolate to coat well. Remove ball from chocolate and dry on waxed paper until candy is set. Store candy, covered, in a cool, dry place.

Nut-Stuffed Figs

Yield: Makes 2 dozen

1 (12-ounce) package dried whole figs (24 figs)
1 cup orange juice
1 tablespoon grated lemon peel
1 tablespoon lemon juice
3 tablespoons sugar
24 pecan halves
Sugar

Remove stem end from figs. Combine orange juice, lemon peel, lemon juice and sugar. Place figs in a large saucepan and pour the juice mixture over them. Heat to boiling. Cover, and reduce heat. Simmer until figs are tender, about 45 minutes. Drain well and cool. Insert knife into stem-end of each fig to form a pocket. Fill each pocket with 1 pecan half. Roll figs in sugar, and let dry overnight.

Mocha Fudge

Yield: 1 pound

3 cups sugar
½ cup unsweetened cocoa powder
1 cup strong coffee
3 tablespoons butter or margarine
1½ teaspoons vanilla
Pecan halves

Butter sides of a heavy 3-quart saucepan. In prepared pan, combine sugar and cocoa powder. Stir in coffee. Cook over medium heat, stirring constantly, until sugar dissolves and mixture boils. Cook to soft ball stage (238 degrees) stirring only as necessary. Immediately remove from heat; add butter and vanilla. Cool to lukewarm (110 degrees) without stirring. Beat vigorously until mixture thickens and loses it gloss. Turn into a buttered 9x5x3-inch pan. Score in squares while still warm. Press a pecan half into each square. Cover and refrigerate. Cut when firm.

White Walnut Fudge

Yield: 2 pounds

2 cups evaporated milk
6 cups sugar
1 teaspoon salt
6 tablespoons butter
1½ teaspoons vanilla
1 cup marshmallow creme
1½ cups chopped walnuts

Combine milk, sugar, salt and butter in a 4-quart saucepan. Mix well; cook over medium heat, stirring constantly, to 236 degrees on a candy thermometer (soft ball stage). Remove from heat. Cool at room temperature without stirring, until lukewarm. Blend in vanilla. Work in marshmallow creme and nuts, stirring until not glossy. Spread in a greased 12x7-inch pan. Cut into small squares.

Munching Almond Brittle

Microwave

Yield: 1 pound

1 cup sugar
½ cup white corn syrup
1 (16-ounce) jar dry roasted almonds
2 teaspoons vanilla extract
1 teaspoon baking soda

In a 1½-quart casserole, stir together sugar and syrup. Microwave at high temperature for 4 minutes. Stir in almonds and microwave at high temperature for 3 to 5 minutes, until light brown. Add vanilla extract to syrup, blending well. Microwave at high temperature 1 to 2 minutes more. Add baking soda and gently stir until light and foamy. Pour mixture onto a lightly greased cookie sheet, or buttered non-stick cookie sheet. Let cool for ½ to 1 hour. When cool, break into small pieces and store in an airtight container.

Easy Toffee

Yield: 3 pounds

1 cup butter, melted
1 cup sugar
1 cup chopped, canned, salted almonds
1 (8-ounce) chocolate bar without nuts
1 small (6-ounce) package chocolate chips
½ cup ground walnuts

In a medium saucepan, combine butter and sugar and bring to a boil. Boil for 3 minutes and add almonds. Cook until nuts are light brown and then pour onto a buttered cookie sheet with 1-inch sides. Let mixture cool slightly. In another saucepan combine the chocolate bar and chocolate chips. Stirring constantly, melt the chocolates and then pour over the surface of the nut mixture. Cover with ground walnuts. Put cookie sheet with candy on it in the refrigerator and cool. When cool, remove from refrigerator and break candy into small pieces.

Microwave English Toffee

Yield: About 1 pound

1 cup butter
2 cups sugar
1½ cups chopped almonds
1 (12-ounce) package semi-sweet chocolate chips

In a large heatproof glass bowl, melt the butter on high in the microwave. Remove from oven and add sugar, stirring constantly. Return to microwave and cook on high for 9 minutes, stirring every 3 minutes, or until mixture reaches hard-crack stage. Stir in a small handful of chopped almonds. Pour syrup onto a cookie sheet with 1 to 2-inch sides. Sprinkle on chocolate chips. When chocolate has melted, spread over the candy, and then sprinkle remaining chopped almonds on top. Refrigerate until cool. Remove from pan and break into pieces.

Candied Violets

(A lovely garnish!)
(This recipe takes 2 days to make.)

Yield: As many as needed

Violets (as many as needed);
pick the violets on a dry day
2 ounces Gum Arabic (available
at any pharmacy)
½ pint water
½ pound sugar

Gently wash and stem the violets. Place on a waxed paper-lined cookie sheet. Dissolve the Gum Arabic in the water. Paint the flowers with the Gum Arabic solution and then sprinkle with sugar. Let dry for 24 hours. At the end of the 24 hours, make a syrup of sugar and water in a non-metal pan. Bring to a boil. Add a few drops of food coloring (purple) to make a violet-colored syrup. Remove the waxed paper from the cookie sheet and re-arrange the violets in a shallow baking pan. Do not crowd the blossoms. Gently cover with the hot syrup. Let them soak for 24 hours. At the end of the 24 hours, drain off the excess syrup and place flowers in a cool oven to dry.

Serving Suggestions:
Use on top of cheesecakes, candy, cakes, tarts or ice cream.

Variation:
You may want to substitute your favorite rose petals for the violets.

Fresno Almond Paste

Food Processor Yield: 1¼ cups

1⅔ cups blanched almonds
1½ cups powdered sugar
1 egg white
1 teaspoon almond extract

Insert metal chopping blade in food processor work bowl. Process for about 45 seconds until almonds are ground fine. Add the powdered sugar, egg white and almond extract. Process for 30 seconds or until almond mixture forms into a ball.

Note:
If you are not going to use almond paste immediately, wrap tightly in plastic and store at room temperature for up to 1 week or in refrigerator for up to 3 weeks.

Whole Wheat Granola

(Great as a snack or for breakfast—as well as in bread) Yield: 3 quarts

7 cups oatmeal
1 cup wheat germ
1 cup unsweetened coconut
1 cup chopped walnuts
1 tablespoon brewers yeast
½ cup raw, unsalted, shelled sunflower seeds
¼ cup sesame seeds
½ cup honey
1 cup brown sugar
¾ cup vegetable oil
½ cup hot water
¾ tablespoon salt
½ cup soy flour
1 cup whole wheat flour

In a 6-quart bowl, mix together oatmeal, wheat germ, coconut, walnuts, yeast, sunflower seeds and sesame seeds. In a 1½-quart saucepan, mix together the honey, brown sugar, oil and hot water. Heat (do not boil) and add to oatmeal mixture. Add salt, soy flour and whole wheat flour and mix well. Spread on 2 (10x15-inch) jelly-roll pans. Bake at 225 degrees for 60 to 75 minutes, stirring occasionally. Store in airtight container.

WARNER

Warnor's Theatre
Fresno

Built as part of the famous Pantages theater chain in 1928, at a cost of $750,000.00, this Italian Renaissance building boasts an interior "sunburst" dome some one hundred feet in diameter. This beautiful Movie Palace equipped for both vaudeville and movies included one of the first Vita-phone sound systems. In 1929 the Warner Brothers purchased the theater for $1,000,000.00, and it became the first Warner theater outside of Hollywood. The first motion picture shown at the new Warner's was "The Hottentot", starring Edward Everett Horton. The theatre's premier included appearances by such contract players as Monte Blue, Douglas Fairbanks, Jr., Myrna Loy and Loretta Young. In 1967 the theater was sold and its name was changed to the Warnor's. In 1973 it passed into private ownership and has been operated as a special purpose theater ever since.

The Fresno Philharmonic Orchestra was founded in 1954 and has played to "packed houses" ever since. It is classified as a Metropolitan Orchestra, and through the years has played host to some of the most illustrious musical talents.

In 1959, the Junior League of Fresno inaugurated the Young Artists Award. It is a scholarship program for aspiring young musicians from the western states and Hawaii. Each year a different category is chosen and the college-age students compete for the prize. The world-class judges make their decision and along with the prize, the young musician appears as the guest performer with the Fresno Philharmonic.

In the hope that there is another VanCliburn, Beverly Sills, or Toscanini out there, we offer this information: The Young Artists Award, Suite 201B, 1300 North Fresno Street, Fresno, California 93703.

Compliments of Wallace and Maxine Quinlisk, Mike and Ladean McCormick, John and Lollie Horstmann, Charles Tingey Associates

Cinnamon Nuts

(Eat one and you can't stop till the bowl is empty.)

Yield: 3 cups

½ cup water
1 cup sugar
1 teaspoon cinnamon
1½ teaspoons vanilla extract
3 cups shelled walnuts or pecans, preferably halves

In a 2-quart saucepan, combine the water, sugar and cinnamon. Bring to a boil over medium heat stirring constantly until thick. Add vanilla and stir. Fold nuts into mixture and remove from heat immediately. Spread nuts out on a large piece of waxed paper to cool. Separate nuts and store in tightly covered container.

Glazed Walnuts

(These make a wonderful gift for someone at holiday time.)

Yield: 3 cups

¼ cup margarine
½ cup sugar
¼ cup light corn syrup
½ teaspoon vanilla extract
3 cups shelled walnuts, preferably halves

In a 2-quart saucepan, melt margarine. Stir in sugar and corn syrup. Bring to a boil over medium heat stirring constantly. Boil without stirring for 5 minutes. Remove from heat; stir in vanilla. Place walnuts in a 13x9x2-inch pan. Pour syrup over nuts, stirring constantly to coat evenly. Bake in a preheated 250 degree oven for 1 hour, stirring several times while baking. Remove from pan immediately. Cool. Store in a tightly covered container.

Smoked Almonds

1 cup almonds, natural or blanched
¼ teaspoon smoked salt
¼ teaspoon seasoned salt
⅛ teaspoon garlic salt
2 teaspoons vegetable oil

Place almonds in a single layer of a shallow baking pan. Roast 18 to 20 minutes in a preheated 300 degree oven, turning every 4 to 5 minutes to prevent burning. In a small bowl mix smoked salt, seasoned salt, onion salt, garlic salt and vegetable oil. Pour over almonds and roast an additional 8 to 10 minutes longer, stirring frequently. Remove almonds from oven and spread on paper towels to cool. Store nuts in an air tight container.

Party Popcorn

(Great gifts for children) Yield: 14 cups

Up to 1 week ahead:
1 cup pecan halves
1 cup whole blanched almonds
12 cups popped corn (about ¾ cup popcorn)
½ cup dark brown sugar, firmly packed
½ cup butter or margarine, softened
½ teaspoon salt

In 10½x13-inch roasting pan, spread pecans and almonds in single layer. Bake in a preheated 350 degree oven for 10 to 15 minutes, stirring occasionally, until nuts are lightly browned. Remove pan from oven; add popped corn. Meanwhile, in a small saucepan over medium heat, melt sugar and butter or margarine; stir into popcorn mixture along with salt. Toss well to coat. Bake 10 minutes longer or until golden, stirring once. Cool in pan. Store in tightly covered container.

Apricot Ambrosia Jam

Yield: Approximately 4 pints

5½ cups granulated sugar
2 cups cut-up fresh apricots
½ cup quartered maraschino cherries
1½ cups drained canned pineapple chunks
⅓ cup lemon juice
2 (3-ounce) pouches liquid pectin

Stir sugar, apricots, cherries, pineapple and lemon juice together in a large kettle. Bring mixture to a full rolling boil, and cook for 2 minutes. Add pectin. Skim and stir for 2 minutes. Seal in hot sterilized jars.

Blue Ribbon Peach-Orange Jam

Yield: Approximately 6 to 7 pints depending on fruit size used.

18 large ripe peaches
1 to 3 oranges
Sugar

Wash and pit peaches; do not peel. Wash the oranges. Coarsely grind the peaches and oranges. (Use the three oranges if they are quite small or you like a pronounced orange flavor.) Measure the ground fruit mixture into a large non-metal kettle. For each measure of fruit, add one measure of sugar. Bring the fruit-sugar mixture to a boil. Cook for 20 minutes, maintaining a gentle boil, stirring frequently. Ladle jam into hot sterilized canning jars; cover with two-piece lids and process in a boiling water bath for 10 minutes.

Spiced Pear Jam

Yield: Approximately 2 pints

3¾ cups peeled, ground or sliced pears
3¼ cups sugar
¼ cup fresh lemon juice
1 teaspoon cinnamon
1 teaspoon nutmeg
⅛ teaspoon salt
2 (3-ounce) pouches of liquid pectin

Stir pears, sugar, juice, cinnamon, nutmeg and salt together in a large non-metal kettle. Bring mixture to a rolling boil and boil for 2 minutes. Remove and add pectin. Skim and stir for 5 minutes. Seal in hot, sterilized jars.

Frozen Kiwi Jam

Microwave

Yield: Approximately 5 half-pints

3½ cups kiwi fruit pulp
1 cup light corn syrup
4½ cups sugar
1 (1¾-ounce) package powdered pectin

Cut kiwi fruit in half crosswise and scoop out the pulp with a spoon or peel the fruit. Place the fruit in a microwave-safe bowl and place in microwave oven. Cook on high heat for 2½ minutes. (May heat in a 4-quart saucepan for 4 minutes.) Crush the fruit with a potato masher and place in a non-metal 4-quart saucepan. Add corn syrup, and mix well. Stir in sugar and heat mixture to 100 degrees, if fruit is not warm enough to dissolve sugar. Do not overheat, as fruit will not retain its bright green color. Stir until sugar is dissolved. Add pectin and mix well. Pour into sterilized (freezable) ½-pint containers and cover tightly. Store in the freezer until use.

Cranberry Port Jelly

Yield: About 5 (8-ounce) jars

2 cups cranberry juice cocktail
3½ cups sugar
1 (3-ounce) package liquid pectin
¼ cup California port wine

In a large saucepan, combine cranberry juice cocktail and sugar. Bring to a full rolling boil, stirring constantly. Add pectin and return to a full rolling boil; boil hard for 1 minute. Remove from heat and stir in port wine. Skim off foam. Immediately ladle into hot sterilized jars, leaving ⅛-inch head space. Seal with 2-piece metal lids. Invert jar for a few seconds, then stand upright to cool.

Red Pepper Jelly

Yield: 6 to 8 (6-ounce) jars

2 cups red bell peppers, finely chopped (about 4 large peppers)
1 medium white onion, chopped fine
7 cups sugar
1½ cups cider vinegar
1 teaspoon salt
2 teaspoons cayenne pepper
2 (3-ounce) packages liquid pectin

In a large kettle, cook peppers, onion, sugar, vinegar, salt and cayenne pepper for 2 minutes at a full boil. Remove from heat and add pectin. Cook an additional 5 minutes. Pour into hot sterilized jars and seal with 2-piece metal lids. Invert jar for a few minutes, then stand upright to cool.

Serving Suggestion:
Spoon the jelly over an 8-ounce block of cream cheese and serve with crackers.

Hawaiian Nectar Jelly

Yield: 6 to 12 (6-ounce) jars

1½ cups unsweetened pineapple juice
½ cup fresh lemon juice
2 cups California Burgundy wine
2½ pounds sugar (2-pounds, 8-ounces)
2 (3-ounce) pouches liquid pectin

Combine ingredients in a non-metal double-boiler. Bring mixture to a full rolling boil, stirring constantly, until sugar is dissolved completely. Remove from heat and add liquid pectin. Stir until dissolved and then skim off foam. Seal in hot sterilized jars.

Fig Conserve

Yield: Approximately 4 pints

3 pounds fresh California Black Mission figs
1 cup water
1 (1¾-ounce) package powdered pectin
9 cups sugar
2 lemons - ½ cup juice and all grated peel
1 cup coarsely chopped walnuts

Wash and grind figs (do not peel). Using 5 cups of ground fruit, add 1 cup water, ½ cup fresh lemon juice and grated peel of the lemons. Place in a 6 to 8-quart kettle; add pectin to fruit, stirring well. Bring to a boil over high heat, stirring constantly. Add sugar and continue stirring. When mixture reaches a rolling boil, continue to stir at rolling boil stage for 3 minutes. Add nuts and boil for 1 minute more. Remove from heat. Place mixture in hot, sterilized ½-pint jars, filling to within ⅛-inch from top. Seal with 2-piece metal lids and invert jar. Leave inverted for ½ hour before turning right side up.

Spiced Grapes

(Try to make the syrup 1 day before processing the grapes.)

Yield: 7 (1-pint) jars

Syrup:

2¼ cups sugar
3 cups water
1 cup white vinegar
2 (2½-inch) sticks cinnamon
8 whole allspice berries
10 whole cloves
1 slice of ginger (about the size of a quarter)

Combine sugar, water and white vinegar in a non-aluminum pan, and boil for 5 minutes. Remove from heat, add spices, cover and let sit over night at room temperature.

Grapes:

7 to 10 pounds California Thompson seedless grapes

Clean and scald 7 (1-pint) canning jars. Leave jars in hot water until ready to fill with grapes. Wash the grapes and remove stems. Be selective; pack only whole unblemished grapes in the jars. Tightly pack the jars, but do not crush the grapes. Fill to within ½-inch of the top. Bring the syrup to a boil while packing the grapes in the jars. Pour the boiling syrup over the grapes, again filling to ½-inch of the top. Seal with the sterilized lids and screw on tight. Submerge the jars in the hot water bath and process for 20 minutes. Remove and cool.

Note:
These grapes are excellent served cold in salads or used as a curry condiment.

Baked Cranberry Walnut Relish

Yield: 4 cups

1 pound fresh cranberries
2½ cups sugar
1 cup coarsely broken walnuts
1 cup tart orange marmalade
Juice of 1 lemon or lime

Wash and drain cranberries; put in shallow baking pan and stir in sugar. Cover tightly with lid or foil and bake in a preheated 350 degree oven for one hour. Put walnuts on a separate baking sheet in the same oven to toast during the last 10 minutes of baking. Add walnuts, marmalade and lemon or lime juice to cranberries. Mix well and chill. Keep cranberries refrigerated because they do not have preservatives added.

Candied Cranberries

Yield: Approximately 3½ cups

(Use the ruby-red candied berries as a garnish for ham, turkey or fruitcake; or place some of the berries in small paper cups and serve them like after-dinner mints.)

2½ cups sugar
1½ cups water
4 cups cranberries
Sugar

In a saucepan, combine 2½ cups sugar and water; bring to a boil, stirring occasionally. Place cranberries in a 10x6x2-inch baking dish. Pour boiling syrup over cranberries. Place in a preheated 300 degree oven; bake, uncovered, for 40 minutes, stirring occasionally. Cover loosely and cool overnight. The next day, drain off syrup and bring syrup to a boil in a medium saucepan. Boil for 2 minutes. Pour syrup over cranberries and cool without stirring. Repeat last process 2 more times. Remove the berries and cover loosely; let dry for 3 days. Turn several times for an even drying. Roll in sugar and store in a tightly covered container.

Cranberry Chutney

(Should be made 2 or 3 days before serving)

Yield: About 6 cups

- 1 pound fresh cranberries, washed and picked over
- 1 cup sugar
- 1 (13-ounce) can sliced cling peaches, drain and reserve juice
- ½ cup chopped onion
- 2 tablespoons fresh lemon juice
- 1 teaspoon salt
- Dash cayenne pepper
- ½ teaspoon ground ginger
- 1 cup California raisins

In a large saucepan, combine cranberries and sugar. Drain peaches and add the syrup to the cranberries in the saucepan. Set the peaches aside. Place the cranberry mixture over medium heat and cook, uncovered, for 15 minutes, stirring occasionally. Add peaches and continue cooking for 5 minutes more. Cool, then chill in the refrigerator until ready to serve.

Cranberry Orange Relish

Food Processor
(A refreshing alternative to cranberry sauce)

Yield: 1¼ cups

- ½ pound or 2 cups fresh cranberries
- ½ small navel orange, washed, quartered with peel intact
- ½ cup granulated sugar
- 1½ tablespoons bourbon (option: Grand Marnier)
- ¼ cup chopped walnuts

Clean cranberries. Process cranberries and orange in food processor until evenly chopped to whatever texture you desire. Add sugar and bourbon and process. Mix in walnuts. This relish will keep for several weeks in the refrigerator or several months in the freezer.

Bread & Butter Pickles

(A family treasure)

Yield: 6 to 7 pints

25 to 30 medium-sized cucumbers, sliced
8 large onions, chopped
2 large green peppers, chopped
½ cup salt
5 cups apple cider vinegar
5 cups sugar
2 tablespoons mustard seed
1 teaspoon tumeric
½ teaspoon cloves

Wash cucumbers and slice thin. Chop onion and peppers and combine with cucumber and salt. Let stand 3 hours and then drain. Combine vinegar, sugar and spices in large non-metal kettle; bring to a boil. Add drained cucumbers and heat thoroughly until transparent. Pack while hot into hot sterilized jars and seal.

Red Pepper Relish

Yield: 10 half-pints

24 sweet red peppers (about 8 cups)
7 medium onions
3 cups sugar
3 cups vinegar
2 tablespoons salt

Cut peppers and onions in half lengthwise; slice thinly. In a saucepan, combine peppers, onions, sugar, vinegar and salt. Simmer uncovered for 30 minutes. Pour mixture into hot sterilized jars. Seal.

Grape Leaves

In the spring, pick the large tender Thompson seedless grape leaves. Pick them before chemical spraying begins in the vineyard. Wash them and stack them in bundles of 20 to 25. Tie each bundle with string. Dip each bundle into a brine solution and pack in sterilized jars and seal.

Brine Solution:

½ cup non-iodized salt (or so)
2 quarts cold water

In a large pot, add the salt to the water. Stir until the salt is dissolved. (Hint: To know if there is enough salt in the water, place an egg in the bottom of the liquid. When it rises to the top and a dime-sized portion of the egg emerges above the water, then there is enough salt. If the exposed area is smaller than a dime add more salt; if it is larger than a dime add more water.) Bring solution to a boil. Cover the leaves in each jar with the brine.

Pickled Anything
(Pickled Vegetables)

Almost any vegetable can be used. Layer zucchini, broccoli, celery, carrots, onions, cauliflower, cucumber, green beans, turnips, green cherry tomatoes - or whatever. Cut in healthy bite-size chunks and place in a 1½-quart jar with closely fitted top. Pack vegetables firmly into jar.

Combine the following ingredients and heat to boiling; pour over vegetables:

2 cups sugar
2 cups white distilled vinegar
2 cups water
2 teaspoons mustard seed
2 teaspoons salt
4 cloves garlic
1 dried chili

Make at least 1 week ahead. Keeps 3 weeks in refrigerator.

Zucchini Relish

Food Processor Yield: 8 pints

10 cups zucchini, processed unpeeled (Each vegetable may be chopped separately in a food processor using the metal blade or in a food grinder.)
4 cups onions, chopped
2 cups celery, chopped
2 large green bell peppers, chopped
5 tablespoons salt

Mix the vegetables in a large non-aluminum kettle. Add salt and enough cold water to cover. Let stand overnight at room temperature. Drain through a large colander and rinse 3 or 4 times. Return to kettle.

1 tablespoon cornstarch
2½ cups distilled white vinegar
6 cups sugar
1 tablespoon tumeric
1½ teaspoons black pepper

Dissolve cornstarch in a small amount (2 to 3 tablespoons) of the vinegar. Mix with the rest of the vinegar, sugar, tumeric and pepper. Add to the vegetables. Cover and simmer 30 minutes. Pack into hot, sterilized jars. Seal with hot lids. Process in boiling water bath for 5 minutes.

Flavored Butters

(A great gift by themselves or with loaves of homemade bread) Yield: ½ to 1 cup

Make up to 1 week ahead of serving time:
Soften ½ cup of butter or margarine; stir in the desired seasonings (recipes follow). Transfer to a small bowl or crock. Cover and chill.

Honey Butter:
In a small bowl, stir ¼ cup honey and ½ teaspoon finely shredded lemon peel into the softened butter or margarine.

Orange Butter:

In a small bowl, stir 1 tablespoon powdered sugar and ½ teaspoon finely shredded orange peel into the softened butter or margarine.

Parsley Butter:

In a small bowl, stir 1 tablespoon snipped parsley, 1 tablespoon fresh lemon juice, ¼ teaspoon dried crushed savory, ⅛ teaspoon salt and a dash of pepper into softened butter or margarine.

Garlic Butter:

In a small bowl, stir 2 or 3 cloves minced garlic into the softened butter or margarine.

Herb Butter:

In a small bowl, stir ½ teaspoon dried crushed thyme and ½ teaspoon ground sage into the softened butter or margarine.

Tarragon Butter:

In a small bowl, stir 2 teaspoons fresh lemon juice and 1 teaspoon dried crushed tarragon into the softened butter or margarine.

Mustard Butter:

In a small bowl, stir ¼ cup prepared mustard and 2 tablespoons snipped parsley into the softened butter or margarine.

Bleu Cheese Butter:

In a small bowl, stir ¼ cup crumbled bleu cheese into the softened butter or margarine.

Caviar Butter: (Can use to garnish fish)

In a small bowl, stir 1 tablespoon fresh lemon juice and ¼ cup black caviar into the softened butter or margarine.

Note:

You may want to add salt to taste.

Maitre D'Hotel Butter: (Can use to garnish broiled steak)

In a small bowl, stir ½ teaspoon salt, ¼ teaspoon white pepper and 2 teaspoons chopped parsley. Stir constantly. Add 2 tablespoons fresh lemon juice and mix well into the softened butter or margarine.

Nut Butter:

In a small bowl, stir 1 cup ground pecans or walnuts and 2 tablespoons Worcestershire sauce into the softened butter or margarine.

Food Processor Date Peanut Butter

Yield: Approximately 1½ cups

2 cups cocktail peanuts
1 tablespoon honey
¾ cup pitted dates, quartered (4-ounces)

In food processor bowl process peanuts with metal blade 3 to 5 minutes or until butter forms, scraping sides of bowl occasionally to make sure all of the mixture is evenly blended. Add the honey and continue processing for about 2 minutes more or until butter is smooth. Add the quartered dates; process with on-off motion several times or until dates are finely chopped. Place the butter in small covered jars or crocks. Refrigerate to store.

Mulled Seasoning for Wine

(A nice gift)

Yield: 1 packet seasoning

½ teaspoon allspice
6 whole cloves
½ teaspoon ground orange peel
2 (½-inch) pieces cinnamon stick
Dash nutmeg
1 (3-inch) square cheesecloth
String

Place the ingredients in a little mound on the cheesecloth. Pull up into a small bag and tie with the string.

Hot Mulled Wine:

1 packet Mulled Seasoning
1 (750-milliliter) bottle
California dry red wine
½ cup sugar

In a medium saucepan, combine Mulled Seasoning, wine and sugar. Simmer for 20 minutes, then remove the Mulled Seasoning packet. Pour wine mixture into serving container or wine cups to serve.

Pâté in Mold

Yield: Serves 16 to 20

½ pound sweet butter
2 large onions, sliced
2½ pounds chicken livers
3 hard-cooked eggs
¼ cup cognac
1 teaspoon salt
Pepper

In a frying pan, melt ¼ cup butter and sauté onions, then remove. Melt half of the remaining butter and sauté half of the chicken livers, until pink in the middle. Remove, then repeat with the other half of the butter and livers. Place ⅓ of the onions, ⅓ of the livers, 1 egg, cut up, ⅓ of the cognac in the food processor or blender and process until smooth. Repeat twice with the rest of the ingredients. Stir in salt and pepper to taste. Turn into a 1½-quart mold, brushed with salad oil. Chill overnight. Turn out onto a platter to serve.

Homemade Dog Biscuits

Yield: about 8 dozen biscuits

3½ cups all-purpose flour
2 cups whole wheat flour
1 cup rye flour
1 cup cornmeal
2 cups bulgur
½ cup powdered non-fat dry milk
4 teaspoons salt
1 package active dry yeast
¼ cup warm water (105 to 110 degrees)
2 cups chicken stock
1 egg
1 tablespoon milk

In a large bowl, combine the flours, cornmeal, bulgur, dry milk and salt; set aside. In a separate bowl, dissolve yeast in ¼ cup warm water. Add chicken stock and mix. Add the liquid to the dry ingredients. Knead the mixture about 3 minutes (dough will be quite stiff), and roll out dough on a floured board to ¼-inch thickness. Immediately cut into shapes with cookie cutters (a doggy bone shape is fun), or cut into small rectangles with a knife and place on an ungreased cookie sheet. In a small bowl, beat egg and 1 tablespoon milk. Brush this mixture on the top of each biscuit. Bake in a preheated 300 degree oven for 45 minutes. Then turn off heat and leave biscuits in the oven overnight to get "bone hard".

Sparrow Supper

1½ cups wild bird seed
1 cup bread crumbs
1 cup graham crackers, crumbled
Raw beef suet
½ teaspoon sand

In a medium sized bowl, add 1½ cups wild bird seed, 1 cup bread crumbs, 1 cup graham crackers, set aside. Put suet through a meat grinder, then melt down in a double-boiler. Allow suet to cool and slightly harden. Reheat and while in liquid form, pour 1 cup over the dry ingredients. Add ½ teaspoon sand for grit; mix well and spoon into a 5x3x1-inch loaf pan. Refrigerate until firm. Cut into small pieces and place on feeder tray.

Cityscape Fresno

Triple exposure: downtown Fresno.

Tomorrow holds only promise for the Valley and its citizens. Every year new arrivals bring with them the hopes and the dreams of a bright future, and the Junior League of Fresno will continue to support and participate in that future.

From the beginning, the Junior League has been an active participant in the community and dedicated to the principle of voluntarism. Along with the area, the projects that this group has undertaken, through the years, have grown in scope. It was the early projects and the example set by our pioneer members that laid the ground for our present-day successes.

1948-1950 Aid for children left orphaned and destitute by the war, pediatric donations to hospitals, public information about tuberculosis, originated the Dental Health Council.

1951-1960 Dental Health education in schools, junior art classes, hospital donations, campership program, participated in formation of the Fresno Junior Museum, originated the Young Artists' Awards for the Fresno Philharmonic, helped form the Fresno Arts Center.

1961-1970 Built "Mr. McGregor's Cabbage Patch" for Fresno Storyland, worked with the Council of Jewish Women to organize the Volunteer Bureau, built a room for Valley Children's Hospital, worked with women of Fresno's Mexican-American community to present Fresno Fine Arts Festival, sponsored and won the All-American City Award for Fresno.

1971-1980 Opened Pediatric Playroom at Valley Medical Center, sponsored the Volunteen and Volunteer of the Year Award programs, drug education project for elementary schools, television "spots" on drug abuse, International Visitors Program, wrote "How To Organize an Organization" for the community, shelter care for dependent, abused and neglected children, College Arts Competition, Rape Information Booklet, co-sponsored District Desegregation Workshop for city schools, Parlier-Fantz Outdoor School, produced three television programs on "Learning Disabilities," Criminal Justice Coalition.

1981- Co-sponsored seminars and forums on sex education in the schools and teenage pregnancy, "Youth Model Options" course for children in grades 8 to 12, Originated the Senior Girls Athlete of the Year Awards, created and produced the film "All The Special Children" on handicapped children, Parents Aware education program on drug abuse, Juvenile Justice coalition building project for local agencies, Built the Fresno Ronald McDonald House, promoted the campaign for "Chemical People," sponsored an education project for children at the Fresno Metropolitan Museum.

The above are just a few of our community endeavors over the years; and what is coming, in the future, looks very exciting!

Compliments of ***Octavia Diener***

Bluebird Surprise

(A special treat for Bluebirds)

2 cups flour
½ teaspoon baking powder
1 teaspoon baking soda
1 cup sugar
1 cup California raisins
½ cup shortening
½ cup water
⅓ cup nutmeats

In a medium bowl, combine flour, baking powder and baking soda and set aside. In a saucepan, add sugar, raisins, shortening and water and bring to a boil and cook 5 minutes. Remove from heat and add the liquid to the dry ingredients; mix well. Add nutmeats. Spoon into a well greased 8x8-inch cake pan. Bake in a preheated 350 degree oven for 20 to 25 minutes. Serve in pieces on a feeder tray or ground feeder.

Sachets

(A nice gift for friends or a "homey" touch for your house)

Yield: 4 small bags

1 ounce (4½-tablespoons) powdered cloves
1 ounce (3½-tablespoons) caraway seed
1 ounce (3½-tablespoons) nutmeg
1 ounce (3-tablespoons) mace
1 ounce (4½-tablespoons) cinnamon
6 ounces (⅔-cup) powdered orrisroot (Florentine Iris), available at your local apothecary

In a small bowl, combine all of the ingredients. Mix thoroughly. Spoon into small decorative cloth bags. Use in drawers and closets to freshen the pretties.

Bath Salts

(An inexpensive gift idea for children to make for special occasions)

Yield: Enough bath salts to last a life-time!

10 pound sack rock salt
Food coloring, any color you fancy
⅛ ounce (a few drops) of essence oil or you may use your favorite perfume or bath oil
1 large glass jar with lid (do not use a plastic container as this mixture will "eat up" the sides)
Decorative glass bottles with glass lids or corks

Fill the large glass jar ¾ full with the rock salt. Add 1 or 2 drops of the food coloring. Add 3 to 4 drops of the essence oil or your favorite perfume. Put the lid on the jar and shake! Shake well until the color is evenly distributed throughout the salt. Open the jar and check to see if you want to add any more perfume or food coloring. If everything is "just right", then pour the mixture into the decorative bottles. Put the lids on. You might want to tie a pretty ribbon around the neck of the jar.

Note:
This is a good rainy-day project. Fun for Girl Scouts, Boy Scouts, Blue-birds, Campfire Girls, Indian Guides, or any other group activity!

Menus

IMPERIAL DYNASTY
HANFORD, CALIFORNIA

Richard C. Wing, C.E.C., Chef/Owner of the Imperial Dynasty restaurant, is a Certified Executive Chef who has received numerous awards and accolades through the years. His awards include; Chefs' de Cuisine Association of California (Honored Chef of the Month), California Wine Patrons (Achievement Award), International Wine and Food Society (Cordon Bleu Award, Best Dinner, 1960, 1966 & Best Dish, 1960, 1966), Mobil Travel Guide Four Star Award, Wine Spectator's Top 100 Grand Award, Golden Wok Award and the Holiday Magazine Award (1966 thru 1978). His affiliations include: the American Academy of Chefs, Les Amis D'Escoffier Society, Chevaliers Du Tastevin, Society of Bacchus and the International Institute For Dining Excellence.

In submitting these recipes, Mr. Wing stated, "The interesting aspect about these recipes for a gourmet dinner is that one is served many courses, yet no taste is repeated. This, of course, is what one must aim in planning menus for gourmet dining.

To have variety and to avoid repetition is a proof of one's skill as a good cook. It is also the result of good menu planning. One achieves variety by applying different methods of cooking, different ingredients, and by cooking these ingredients so that they all taste different. . . ."

". . . Fortunately for us living here in the far west California, we are blessed by our acceptance of new ideas, new expressions, new experiences and our friendly eagerness to absorb the culture and cuisine from other lands. No wonder it is so natural for East and West to meet happily and to join together in good spirit around the gracious international dining table for the grand pleasure of good food, wine, taste and bon appetit . . . Through this wonderful interchange of good food, wine and taste we learn to understand and to appreciate each other better; and in a grand culinary style we are promoting goodwill and good faith among nations. Good food is the essence of good living."

IMPERIAL DYNASTY CHINESE PAGODA

Continental
Chinoise Dinner
Menu

COLD APPETIZER
Sliced Salmon Sashimi
and
Filet Mignon Steak Tartare
California Champagne

HOT APPETIZER
Escargots à la Imperial Dynasty
California Chardonnay

SOUP
Pheasant Consommé

SEAFOOD ENTREE
Jade Scampi and Abalone with Sauce Soubise
California Chardonnay

GAME ENTREE
Quail in Paradise à la Chinoise
California Pinot Noir

MEAT ENTREE
Medallions of Veal with Chinese Mushrooms
California Cabernet Sauvignon

SALAD
Fresh Lotus Root and Watercress Salad

DESSERT
Carabao Mango with Grand Marnier
California Cremant
California Spumante

THE FIRST COURSE: COLD APPETIZER

Sliced Salmon Sashimi and Filet Mignon Steak Tartare

Yield: 4 Servings

Fresh Salmon:

¼ pound fresh salmon filet

(Only very fresh salmon in season may be eaten as sashimi; frozen fish simply will not do. Only salmon from the ocean water should ever be eaten raw. Freshness is the paramount requirement in the preparation of this delicacy. Without it there can be no thought of eating fish raw. Season is important, too. The red-fleshed salmon is best in spring and in early summer. When it is in prime condition, the flesh should be firm, glistening and bright salmon red. The fresh salmon selected should have a clean, fresh smell and there must be no unpleasant odor.)

With a sharp knife, slice salmon filet on a slant angle into very thin slices. Keep the filet well chilled at all times, both to preserve it and to make it easier to slice. Arrange and mount salmon sashimi slices on top of beef slices, about 4 to 6 slices per serving. Try to handle the fish as little as possible while slicing since the warmth of the hands can spoil the freshness. It is good to keep washing your hands in cold water and drying them while slicing raw salmon and beef.

Fresh Beef:

¼ pound fresh beef tenderloin

(Only the very fresh beef tenderloin without age may be eaten raw.) Trim the meat by removing all fats, sinews and tendons. With a very sharp knife, slice beef into thin slices; arrange beef slices in a fan-like manner, about 4 to 6 slices per portion on sheet pan.

Beef Dipping Sauce or Marinade:

1 cup beef au jus or beef boullion, chilled
¼ cup thin soy sauce "sang-chau" (sold in Chinese grocery stores)
2 tablespoons garlic-ginger oil (crushed garlic and fresh ginger root cooked together in peanut oil; strained and chilled)
1 tablespoon fresh lemon or lime juice
½ cup California white wine (sweet sauterne)
1 teaspoon dry mustard
Freshly ground black pepper to taste

Combine all above ingredients and taste, and adjust any and all of the ingredients as you wish to your taste.

Shredded Lettuce and Onion Salad:

1 medium-sized onion, peeled and thinly sliced
1 heart of lettuce, washed and finely shredded

Toss and mix together to be used as foundation for steak tartare.

Garnish Topping:

1 tablespoon pickled scallions, finely cut (sold in Chinese grocery stores)
1 teaspoon parsley, washed and finely chopped
½ teaspoon sesame seeds, toasted
1 boiled egg, shelled and chopped
1 lime, cut in quarter wedges

These garnishes will help the presentation to please both the eyes and the palate.

Last Minute Assembly and Serving:

Pour dipping sauce over salmon and beef slices, arranged on sheet pan for about 10 to 15 seconds of soaking, no longer, so the fresh salmon and fresh beef retain their fresh red color. With a spatula or turner, transfer the marinated salmon and beef slices over individual mounds of shredded lettuce and onion salad foundation on chilled plate. Sprinkle with garnish topping: chopped parsley, pickled scallions, boiled chopped egg and sesame seed. Lime wedges on the side.

Save marinade, keep in refrigerator for future use.

Please note:
Appetizers, hot or cold, should be spicy and tasty in order to perform their tantalizing function.

THE SECOND COURSE: HOT APPETIZER

Escargots à la Imperial Dynasty

Yield: 4 Servings

French snails in the shells on hot gridiron. Delectably flavored with garlic-ginger butter, cornish hen purée, cashew spread and fragrance of chablis wine; bedecked with garlands of thinly sliced onions. Dig into this dish of culinary mystique and be in a savory mood.

24 empty imported French snail shells
24 imported French snails in can from Burgundy, France
1 tablespoon baking soda (bicarbonate soda)
1 tablespoon garlic salt
1 pot of peanut oil for deep frying (keep for future use)

Sauce Mixture:

½ cup butter, melted
2 garlic cloves, peeled and mashed
2 ginger root slices, peeled and mashed
1 tablespoon shallot, cleaned, peeled and chopped
1 teaspoon purée of cornish hen (or strained chicken baby food)
1 teaspoon cashew-spread (or peanut butter)
1 teaspoon Dijon mustard
½ cup California white wine (dry chablis)
1 teaspoon chopped parsley
Salt and pepper to taste
Pinch of nutmeg
Juice of ½ fresh lemon
1 tablespoon bread crumbs
1 small-sized onion, peeled and thinly sliced

Wash and clean the shells in a wire basket and parboil in boiling water with baking soda for 5 minutes; rinse and drain. Deep fry the shells in a wire basket in hot peanut oil (350 degrees) for 1 minute. Drain the shells by shaking the wire basket; sprinkle the inside of each shell with garlic salt. Place shells on a baking pan and bake in hot oven for 3 minutes; do not brown. Now the shells are processed and ready to give a good flavor to the snails.

Remove the snails from can and place in wire basket; wash and blanch in boiling water for 10 seconds and drain. Plunge into the hot peanut oil (350 degrees) for about 5 seconds and drain.

Heat the butter in a wok or saucepan and stir-fry the garlic, ginger and shallots, but do not brown. Then add all the other ingredients and stir-fry until the sauce mixture begins to bubble.

Add the processed snails to the sauce mixture. Do not let sauce reach to boiling point (or butter sauce will separate). Remove from heat.

With a pair of bamboo chopsticks or a cocktail fork, stuff each snail into a shell by placing the soft part in first; then fill each shell with the butter sauce mixture and place in snail gridirons.

Sprinkle the top of each snail with bread crumbs and bedeck with garlands of thinly sliced onions.

When ready to serve, bake in preheated 450 degree oven for 8 to 10 minutes or until the butter sauce begins to bubble. Serve at once, piping hot with plenty of French sour-dough bread to soak up the butter sauce.

Please Note:
The snails in the shells may be prepared in advance and kept in the refrigerator until ready to serve. The fresh ginger root will deodorize the garlic when cooked together in the same pot.

THE THIRD COURSE: SOUP

Pheasant Consommé

Yield: 4 Servings

Please Note:
In preparation of this rich consommé of pheasant, be sure to cook enough to provide a sufficient reserve as stock to make numerous soups, sauces or other culinary preparation.

(Remember that in making the nutritious liquid known as soup, one is basically trying to extract flavors from the natural solid ingredients. Slow cooking is desirable. Do not hurry [I do not mean laziness]; allow the rich liquid to simmer gently in order to bring out the natural flavors that are in the meat and bone. Also, remember to always start the water and the meat or poultry at the same temperature; thus both water and meat will be heated at the same rate, and the natural juices are able to flow out of the ingredients to enrich the water into a rich broth.)

4 quarts (or more) cold water
1 whole pheasant (3 to 4-pounds), cleaned and cut
1 whole chicken hen (4 to 5-pounds), cleaned and cut
2 carrots, washed and cut
3 celery stalks, washed and cut
3 leeks, washed and cut
2 medium-sized onions, peeled and cut
1 small-sized garlic bulb
1 small-sized (olive-sized) fresh ginger root
3 dried jujubes (sold in Chinese grocery stores)
1 small can Chinese straw mushrooms (sold in Chinese grocery stores)

Put cold water, pheasant, chicken, carrots, celery, leeks, onions, garlic bulb, ginger root and jujubes together in a soup pot. Place soup pot with cover on in a steam cooker, and steam-cook for 8 hours or more. By steam-cooking the soup stock, there will be no evaporation and no agitation of the rich broth, which will remain naturally clear and retain all the essence, nutritive value and natural flavors of the blending ingredients. At the end of cooking time, strain through a fine sieve (since vegetables cause rapid spoilage in the stock, this will keep the soup fresh longer). To obtain a clear consommé, degrease it, and strain again through the strainer with a filter cone. Let soup cool without covering or place soup pot in bath of ice water in order to shorten the cooling period. Keep reserve consommé in refrigerator to be used to make numerous soups, sauces, or other preparation.

(Cooking by steam which is called "jeng" in Chinese cooking technique, has been holding its place for centuries both in home cooking for its simplicity, and in the most elaborate banquet of Chinese "haute-cuisine" for the delight it offers to the discriminating diners. Steam-cooking is a triumph of simplicity. One wonders why the rest of the world has largely ignored this culinary art of cooking. Anything cooked by steam preserves its original flavor, and yet it affords a taste so distinct from any other that the Western palate instantly identifies it as "Chinese".)

When ready to serve, reheat the rich consommé; charm the rich broth with a touch of brandy; taste for seasoning; garnish each cup with Chinese straw mushrooms . . . all of which will enhance the consommé to perfection. This is indeed a provocative, nourishing and rich consommé to stimulate the appetite for the grand entree.

THE FOURTH COURSE: SEAFOOD ENTREE

Jade Scampi and Abalone with Sauce Soubise

Yield: 4 Servings

(This is truly a stunning seafood dish which conveys all the romance and excitement of culinary artistry. Two scampi and jade green florets in embrace, nestle on top of an abalone medallion and caress lovingly with sauce soubise.)

Scampi:

8 scampi or large raw prawns
2 tablespoons salt (to be added
to 1-quart of water)

Shell and de-vein scampi, leaving tails on. With a sharp knife, make a slit along the vein-side of scampi; soak in salt-water for 5 minutes and rinse thoroughly.

Jade Florets:

1 head firm fresh broccoli

Wash broccoli, divide into florets, taking care to keep a two-inch length of tender green stalk on each piece of floret. If florets are large, cut into small size.

Scampi and Broccoli Assembly:

With the curve underside of the scampi, wrap-around the stem of each floret; hold together with a toothpick; poach in hot water for about 5 minutes. Do not overcook. The scampi should be ivory-white in color and the broccoli florets should be jade green.

Abalone:

4 abalone steaks (center cuts only)
2 eggs, lightly beaten
2 tablespoons peanut oil
Salt and pepper to taste

Trim and pound abalone steaks; season with salt and pepper to taste; dip in lightly beaten eggs; pan-fry in peanut oil for less than 10 seconds on each side. Do not overcook, because overcooking will harden and toughen the abalone.

Sauce Soubise:

2 tablespoons butter
1 medium-sized onion, peeled and finely chopped
2 cups consommé (from Third Course consommé)
1 cup white wine sauce (veloute)
2 tablespoons cream
Salt and pepper to taste
2 tablespoons sherry wine
2 teaspoons pickled scallions, finely chopped (sold in Chinese grocery stores)

Melt butter in a saucepan; add chopped onions and stir—cook for about 2 minutes, do not brown onions; add 2 cups consommé and stew slowly for about 20 minutes; add 1 cup white wine sauce and cook slowly for about 15 minutes or more, then strain through sieve, pushing through the onions to make a purée. Bring to a boil again and finish the sauce with cream and taste for seasoning with salt and pepper; wire whip the sauce to creamy smooth texture; charm with sherry wine and finally add chopped pickled scallions to give it a Chinoise touch.

Garnish and Serving:

1 teaspoon toasted seaweeds mixture (sold in Chinese grocery stores)
1 bunch watercress, washed
1 cucumber, washed and sliced
1 lemon, sliced

Transfer the cooked jade scampi on top of the pan-fried abalone medallions and embrace with sauce soubise; sprinkle with toasted seaweeds on the top and garnish with watercress, cucumber slices and lemon slices on the side.

THE FIFTH COURSE: GAME ENTREE

Quail in Paradise à la Chinoise

Yield: 4 Servings

(Behold this magnificent dish! The tender and delicate quail floating on a succulent grapefruit cup to paradise.)

Quail:

4 fresh quails, cleaned and de-boned
2 tablespoons thin soy "sang chau"
1 tablespoon sesame oil, toasted
2 tablespoons California sherry
2 tablespoons water chestnut powder (sold in Chinese grocery stores)
2 tablespoons peanut oil
2 cups game consommé (from Third Course consommé reserve)
½ cup California Madeira wine

Prepare and clean quails. The quails must be fresh, young and plump. With a sharp knife split the birds lengthwise through their backs and do not separate the two halves of each bird. Debone the breast and leave the thighs and legs with bone in; flatten each bird. Moisten each bird with a mixture of thin soy, sesame oil and sherry wine; coat each bird lightly with water chestnut powder; pan-fry in peanut oil for about 2 minutes on each side to golden brown. Transfer the birds to a roasting pan; add 2 cups game consommé and ½ cup Madeira wine; finish roasting in a preheated 450 degree oven for about 15 minutes; remove the birds from roasting pan and save the pan juices for the preparation of the sauce.

Sauce (Glace de Gibier with Chestnut):

This is a superlative sauce prepared from the rich game extract (pan juices) combined with purée of French chestnut and Madeira wine.

2 tablespoons imported French chestnut purée (natural, not with syrup)
Juice of 1 medium-sized orange
2 tablespoons California Madeira wine
Reserve pan juice (from roasting quails with game consommé)
Salt and pepper to taste

Pour the rich pan juices (extract) in a saucepan and bring to boil again; add French chestnut purée, juice from fresh orange and Madeira wine; wire whip into a creamy sauce. If the sauce is too thin, re-adjust by adding more French chestnut purée. If the sauce is too thick, re-adjust by adding more Madeira wine or game consommé (from Third Course consommé reserve). Taste for seasoning with salt and pepper.

Broiled Grapefruit Cups:

2 large-sized grapefruit, cut in halves
2 tablespoons brown sugar
½ teaspoon nutmeg
2 tablespoons butter

Cut the grapefruit into halves; cut out the center parts and separate the sections from the membranes of each half; sprinkle grapefruit halves with brown sugar, dash of nutmeg and dot with butter. Broil the grapefruit halves to golden brown.

Garnish and Serving:

- 4 whole imported French chestnuts (natural, not with syrup)
- 1 tablespoon toasted sliced almonds

Mount one bird on top of each broiled grapefruit cup; place one whole French chestnut on top of each bird. When ready to serve, warm in oven, glaze with chestnut sauce and sprinkle toasted sliced almonds on top . . . really an exciting presentation with a touch of exotic flavor to delight the appreciative gourmets.

THE SIXTH COURSE: MEAT ENTREE

Medallions of Veal with Chinese Mushrooms

Yield: 4 Servings

(This East and West culinary combination of the fragrance of Chinese mushrooms with the delicacy of Provimi veal is truly sumptuous and superlative . . . because they both absorb and blend together with each other's natural flavors so readily and so gloriously.)

Veal:

Provimi veal is a delicately flavored meat and almost white with very little fat. The medallions are small cutlets from the veal rib-eyes with all the sinews and tendons removed.

- 4 medallions of veal (2 to 3-ounces in weight and lightly flattened)
- 2 tablespoons almond powder
- 1 tablespoon butter
- 1 tablespoon peanut oil

Sprinkle the veal slices lightly with almond powder on both sides. Melt the butter in a skillet over a fairly high heat and add peanut oil. Sauté the veal slices quickly in the combined hot peanut oil and butter until golden brown on both sides (for about 1 minute on each side.) Do not overcook the veal. Add the mushrooms and the sauce; simmer gently for 5 minutes. The almond powder from the coated veal slices will help thicken the sauce slightly. Remove the mushrooms and the veal slices from the skillet.

Dried Chinese Mushrooms:

(The best Chinese mushrooms come from South China where they are harvested in the winter and dried by sun and air. When buying dried Chinese mushrooms in a Chinese grocery store, choose the large and thick mushrooms which have curled edges and bursted caps. They are the most delicious, succulent and delicate food. Also, they are highly treasured for their bouquet. Dried Chinese mushrooms, which must be soaked before they are used in cooking, often serve both as ingredient and as condiment. They have a rich woodsy flavor like fresh truffles, and a meaty taste as concentrated as a bite of beef next to the rib-bone. Chinese mushrooms are not cheap, but worth it. Here are mushrooms that make you say "ah" in good eating.)

8 large-size dried Chinese mushrooms (sold in Chinese grocery stores)
2 cups game consommé (from Third Course consommé reserve)
½ cup California white wine (sherry wine)
1 tablespoon thin soy "sang chau"
½ teaspoon sesame oil

Wash dried mushrooms quickly in several changes of cold water; then soak mushrooms in 3 cups water until softened (for about 30 minutes or longer.) When the mushrooms have softened, squeeze out the water and cut off the tough fibrous stems. Leave each mushroom in whole piece and save the water which has been flavored by the mushrooms. Put the mushrooms in a saucepan and pour in consommé, white wine, thin soy and sesame oil; and bring to boil. Lower the heat and stew the mushrooms for 1 hour or longer until the liquid is reduced to half. Set aside.

Asparagus:

1 bunch large-sized asparagus (4 to 5 spears for each serving)

Wash the asparagus well in several changes of cold water, making sure all the fine sand has been removed from the tips. Snap off the tough ends of the stalks and keep only the tender spears. Place the asparagus in a wire basket and blanch in boiling water for only 3 minutes; remove and quickly plunge in cold water; drain and set aside until ready to serve. When ready to serve, lower the partially cooked asparagus into a pot of boiling water for another 2 minutes; remove quickly and transfer to serving plates. In order to keep the texture of the asparagus crisp and tender, do not overcook. They should never be permitted to become soft and soggy.

Assembly and Garnish:

4 radishes (washed and sculptured into radish roses)

Cap two mushrooms on top of each veal slice and mount over the asparagus spears. Reduce the wine sauce slightly and grace the wine sauce over the combination of veal, mushrooms and asparagus. Garnish with a crest of radish rose on top of each medallion of veal.

THE SEVENTH COURSE: SALAD

Fresh Lotus Root and Watercress Salad

Yield: 4 Servings

(This salad is designed to refresh the palate with a distinct contrast of flavors and textures.)

Oil and Vinegar Salad Dressing:

1 cup olive oil
2 tablespoons white wine vinegar
½ teaspoon dry mustard
½ teaspoon sesame oil
1 clove garlic, peeled and crushed
Salt and pepper to taste

Combine and blend together all the ingredients in mixing bowl. Cover and chill in the refrigerator. (About 1¼ cup of dressing.)

Watercress:

1 bunch fresh watercress

Remove and discard the larger stems from the watercress and wash. Drain and dry the watercress thoroughly. Chill them in refrigerator for 1 hour or longer before serving time. The watercress has a peppery taste to it that will add a bit of tang to the salad.

Lotus Root Slices:

1 fresh lotus root, 5 to 6-inches in length, peeled, washed and sliced (sold in Chinese grocery stores)

Lotus root is a root of the lotus plant or water lily and resembles a sweet yam in texture. The lotus root, when cut straight across, has a pretty lacy pattern and adds design as well as taste and texture to the salad. Wash the fresh lotus root under cold running water and peel off the skin. Trim off both ends of the root and slice into thin slices (about ⅛-inch thickness), dropping the slices as you proceed into a pan of cold water to prevent them from discoloring. Boil 1 quart of water in a pot and add lotus root slices to boil for about 5 minutes. Drain and rinse the par-boiled lotus root slices with running cold water and dry them thoroughly. Chill the lotus root slices in the refrigerator until ready to serve. The lotus root will add a crunchy texture to the salad.

Assemble and Serving:

Stir and strain the oil-vinegar dressing and discard the garlic. Combine lotus root slices, watercress and oil-vinegar dressing in a salad mixing bowl and toss gently. Serve on chilled salad plates.

THE EIGHTH COURSE: DESSERT

Carabao Mango with Grand Marnier

Yield: 4 Servings

Mango Halves:

4 fresh, ripe mangoes, peeled and cut in halves
1 medium-sized fresh orange, extracted juice
1 ounce Kirsch

Peel away the skin and divide each mango into halves by cutting carefully around the large oblong and rather flat pit. Soak the mango in fresh orange juice and Kirsch liqueur. Allow the mango halves to mellow in the liqueur-juice, and chill in refrigerator for 1 hour or longer before serving time.

Grand Marnier Mango Sauce:

2 ounces Grand Marnier

Put 4 mango halves in the liqueur juice in a blender; purée them by running the machine for about 10 seconds; then add the Grand Marnier and let the machine run for another 3 seconds. The mango purée becomes a smooth and velvet fruit sauce.

Assembly and Serving:

1 tablespoon coconut, finely grated

Arrange each mango half on an individual chilled dessert dish and glaze with freshly made Grand Marnier mango sauce. Sprinkle with finely grated coconut on the top . . . for a delightful conclusion to an enchanting gourmet expedition.

THE AHWAHNEE HOTEL
YOSEMITE NATIONAL PARK

THE AHWAHNEE

Hear you all!

At the sound of horns throughout the Manor,
you will assemble in the Great Hall
and await the entrance of Squire Bracebridge and his Family.
You will stand to greet the Squire and his Family
as they enter the Great Hall.
The Squire will welcome you most heartily,
and you will then partake of the Christmas Dinner in Bracebridge Hall,
which shall be served with Songs and Merriment, and you shall all—
". . . Lord and Lady, Youth and Maid,
Give rein to Mirth and let not fade
The tumult of unceasing joy;
Nourish laughter, Gloom destroy."

Thus begins Christmas Dinner at Bracebridge Hall, The Ahwahnee Hotel, Yosemite. This world-famous hotel takes on the trappings of Elizabethan England for this special event, and each visitor to the Squire's table, leaves full of the bounty of the land and the joy of the season.

The only event more splendid than dinner at Bracebridge Hall is the still, white blanket of snow that covers Yosemite Valley in Winter.

THE AHWAHNEE

Christmas Dinner At
Bracebridge Hall
Menu

THE RELISH
Ahwahnee Pâté Maison, Cumberland Sauce

THE SOUP
Scottish Barley Soup

THE FISH
Fresh Norwegian Salmon en Croute

THE PEACOCK PIE
Boned Duckling, Naturale Sauce

THE BOAR'S HEAD AND THE BARON OF BEEF
Roast Sirloin of Beef, Bordelaise Sauce
Yorkshire Pudding
Artichoke with Carrot Mousse
Duchess Potato

THE SALAD
Hearts of Palm and Asparagus Vinaigrette

THE PUDDING AND THE WASSAIL
Plum Pudding with Rum Sauce
Hot Mulled Wine
Assorted Cheeses
Freshly Ground Coffee
Mints

FIRST COURSE: THE RELISH

Ahwahnee Pâté Maison

Yield: Serves 8

½ pound forcemeat
½ pound pheasant meat
4 ounces bacon
3 ounces Madeira
2 ounces poultry livers
Salt and pepper to taste
1 pound pie pastry
Egg—for egg wash

Remove sinews from all meats. Marinate the forcemeat, pheasant meat and bacon in Madeira overnight in refrigerator. Drain. Season the meats with salt and pepper to taste. Process the marinated meats and poultry livers in a food processor or meat grinder until homogenously ground. Line a 9-inch pie plate with pie pastry and fill with processed meat mixture. Cover with pie pastry and crimp edges. Brush on an egg wash. Bake in preheated 400 degree oven for one hour.

SECOND COURSE: THE SOUP

Scottish Barley Soup

Yield: Serves 2

1½ ounces pearl barley
2 ounces mixed vegetables, diced
2 ounces lean lamb, diced
Fat
4 cups lamb or beef consommé

Wash and blanch the barley thoroughly. In a small frying pan, sauté the lamb until lightly browned in a little fat; drain. In a saucepan bring barley, vegetables, sautéed lamb and lamb or beef consommé to a boil. Lower heat and simmer for 1½ hours.

THIRD COURSE: THE FISH

Fresh Norwegian Salmon en Crout

Yield: Serves 1

Fresh salmon filet (6 to 8 ounces)
Puff pastry (your own favorite recipe or frozen dough)
Hollandaise sauce (see page 128)

Wrap fresh salmon filet in puff pastry. Seal or crimp edges securely. Bake on parchment-lined pan in preheated 425 degree oven for 25 minutes or until golden brown. Slice and serve with hollandaise sauce.

FOURTH COURSE: THE PEACOCK PIE (Boned Duckling, Naturale Sauce)

Choose your favorite holiday dish for this course.

FIFTH COURSE: THE BOAR'S HEAD AND THE BARON OF BEEF

Roast Sirloin of Beef

Yield: Serves 8 to 10 ounces per person

New York strip (loin)
Salt, pepper, paprika and minced garlic to taste
Unsalted butter

Purchase one solid piece of New York strip (loin) allowing 8 to 10 ounces of meat per person. Sprinkle with salt, pepper, paprika and minced garlic to taste. Sauté in a large frying pan in melted unsalted butter for two minutes on each side; then bake in a preheated 375 degree oven until medium-rare.

Yorkshire Pudding

Yield: Makes 10 to 12

5 eggs
½ pound all-purpose flour
2 cups milk
Salt and nutmeg to taste
Butter

In a blender combine eggs, flour, milk and salt and nutmeg to taste. Process until thoroughly mixed. Pour mixture into buttered muffin pans. Bake in a preheated 450 degree oven about 20 to 25 minutes or until browned and puffy.

Artichoke with Carrot Mousse

Yield: 8 servings of 3 artichokes each

2 pounds carrots, peeled
2 egg yolks
¾ cup whipping or heavy cream
Pinch of minced fresh tarragon
24 artichoke bottoms

Cook carrots in a small amount of water; drain. Place cooked carrots, egg yolks, cream and tarragon in a blender and blend until thoroughly mixed. Fill artichoke bottoms with carrot mousse mixture. Bake in a preheated 350 degree oven for ½ hour.

SIXTH COURSE: THE SALAD

Choose your favorite holiday salad for this course.

SEVENTH COURSE: THE PUDDING AND THE WASSAIL

Plum Pudding with Rum Sauce

Yield: 4 cups

1 pound powdered sugar, sifted
1 pound unsalted butter, softened
4 ounces Meyer's rum
1 teaspoon vanilla
Plum pudding

Beat sugar, butter, rum and vanilla until well-blended. Spoon over your favorite plum pudding.

Wassail or Hot Mulled Wine

Yield: 3½ to 4 quarts

¼ cup brown sugar, packed
1 teaspoon ground ginger
5 whole cloves
1 stick cinnamon
2 quarts apple cider
2 cups water
2 cups Madeira
2 cups brandy

Bring all ingredients to a boil in a large soup pan or kettle. Reduce heat and simmer for 10 minutes. Remove cinnamon and cloves. Drink and have a great Christmas!

THE BOGHOSIAN'S
FRESNO, CALIFORNIA

A Lavish Old-World Dinner

When Nicholas Boghosian was a young bachelor his father gave him some advice: "After you're married you can budget and skimp on everything else but never cut back on food."

". . . The Boghosians have not spared time, effort, love or the budget in their preparations. As Nic explains, 'Armenians are a party waiting to happen. We're fun-loving and we love good food.'

"Ten years ago, when Nancy and Nic were married, they discovered they shared a keen interest in cooking and a desire to retain the cultural traditions that were so much a part of the Armenian community in Fresno, California, where they grew up. Many of the recipes they remembered from childhood were disappearing because modern cooks were using shortcuts or giving up traditional foods entirely. They decided to go back to the source for guidance, and so they consulted their grandmothers.

"Before we talked to them we did research and worked out a recipe that we both thought came pretty close to the dish we remembered. Then one of our grandmothers would come over and watch us cook it to be sure we had it right. Of course each added her own ideas," Nic says. 'My grandmother was amazed when I showed her I could make phyllo dough. It was a real accomplishment, but it takes years of practice to get it as thin as professional bakers do, so now Nancy and I buy it packaged just like everyone else.'

". . . While the Boghosians revere their rich culinary heritage, they happily integrate it with modern technology, using up-to-date appliances to accomplish in minutes what might have taken their grandmothers hours to complete. 'For one of our big parties we freeze as much ahead as we can,' Nancy says, 'and I've found that most Armenian dishes freeze very well. We also depend on the food processor for much of the chopping and cheese grating that Armenian recipes require.' "

Excerpts reprinted by permission: "*Bon Appétit*", Bon Appétit Publishing Corporation, Los Angeles, California, September 1980, Volume 25, Number 9.

Armenian Dinner for Twelve Menu

APPETIZERS

Dried Armenian Olives
Cheese Boeregs
Lahmajoon
String and Monterey Jack Cheeses
Toorshi
Yalanchi Dolmas
Cocktails

ENTREE

Sou Boereg
Imam Bayeldi
Dolmas
Kufta
Shish Kebab
Bulgur Pilaf
Armenian Wedding Pilaf
California Petite Sirah

DESSERT

Halvah with Cheese
Kadayif
Shakarishee
Bourma
Demi Tasse Coffee

Cheese Boeregs
(Cheese Triangles)

Yield: 30 appetizers

1 pound Monterey Jack cheese, grated
1 egg, beaten
Salt
1 pound phyllo pastry sheets
1 cup (2-sticks) unsalted butter or margarine, melted

Combine cheese, egg and salt and mix well. Set aside. Unroll phyllo dough and place one sheet on work surface. (Keep remainder covered with waxed paper and damp towel to prevent drying.) Brush phyllo with melted butter. Top with second sheet and brush with butter. Cut into lengthwise strips about 5-inches wide. Place about 1 tablespoon of the cheese mixture at one end of phyllo strip. Fold over to form triangle, then continue folding like a flag. Brush end with a little butter and carefully tuck into fold to seal. Repeat with remaining phyllo and filling.

Preheat oven to 400 degrees. Place triangles on ungreased baking sheet and brush again with butter. Bake until crisp and golden, 12 to 15 minutes. Serve warm.

Note:
Cheese Boeregs can be frozen before baking. Flash-freeze on baking sheets until solidly frozen. Stack between layers of foil in large box. Bake without thawing in 400 degree oven for about 15 to 18 minutes.

Lahmajoon
(Armenian Pizza)

Yield: about 100 appetizers

Filling:

2 pounds lean ground meat (1½ pounds beef and ½ pound lamb)
½ cup all-purpose flour
1 large onion, finely chopped
1 green pepper, finely chopped
½ bunch parsley, finely chopped
1 (14½-ounce) can whole peeled tomatoes, drained and chopped
½ cup tomato sauce
6 tablespoons tomato paste
1 (2-ounce) jar diced pimiento
3 garlic cloves, minced
Ground red pepper
Salt and freshly ground pepper

Combine ground meats and flour and mix well. Add remaining ingredients and blend thoroughly.

Crust:

3 (1-pound) loaves frozen bread dough, thawed
Flour

Place 1 pound of dough on well-floured work surface. Sprinkle rolling pin and dough with flour. Roll dough into large circles about ⅛-inch thick, adding flour as needed to prevent sticking.

Method:

Cut circles 3 to 4-inches in diameter, using a jar lid on tuna can. Place 1 tablespoon meat mixture on each circle, spreading to edges with fork to prevent burning. (Filling will shrink a bit during cooking, but if too much is added, excess juices will cause crust to become soggy.) Preheat oven to 400 degrees. Place Lahmajoons on ungreased baking sheets and bake for 15 to 20 minutes. Serve warm or at room temperature.

Note:
Lahmajoons can be frozen. To reheat, arrange without thawing on baking sheet, tent with foil and heat through, about 10 to 15 minutes at 375 degrees.

Toorshi
(Pickled Vegetables)

Yield: 4 quarts

2 quarts water
1 quart white vinegar
⅓ cup coarse salt
12 celery stalks, peeled and sliced into thin 3-inch long sticks
6 carrots, peeled and sliced into thin 3-inch long sticks
1 head cauliflower, separated into florets
1 medium head cabbage, cut into small wedges, about 2-inches
12 to 16 garlic cloves, peeled

Sterilize four 1-quart jars. Combine water, vinegar and salt in a large saucepan and bring to full boil; keep hot. Divide vegetables and garlic among jars. Add boiling brine, filling to within ½-inch of top. Seal and store for at least 1 to 2 weeks before serving.

Note:
Vegetables can also be layered in a crock. Weight with a plate to keep vegetables submerged in brine and store in refrigerator. Toorshi will keep indefinitely if well sealed and stored in cool, dark place.

Yalanchi Dolmas
(Stuffed Grape Leaves)

Yield: Approximately 100 appetizers

Filling:

2 cups corn oil
6 large onions, finely chopped
1 (16 or 17-ounce) can stewed tomatoes
1 celery stalk, finely chopped
1 green pepper, finely chopped
2 garlic cloves, minced
Dash of ground red pepper
Salt and freshly ground black pepper
2 cups long-grain rice
1 cup water
½ cup tomato sauce
Juice of 1 lemon
1 (16-ounce) jar grape leaves, rinsed and drained
3 cups water
½ cup tomato sauce
Juice of 2 or 3 lemons
Pinch of garlic salt

Heat oil in large skillet or Dutch oven. Add onion and cook until transparent. Stir in tomatoes, celery, green pepper, garlic, red pepper, salt and black pepper and cook about 5 minutes. Add rice, 1 cup water, ½ cup tomato sauce and lemon juice. Cover and cook over medium heat until all water is absorbed, about 20 to 30 minutes. Transfer to bowl, cover and chill overnight.

Place 1 tablespoon filling on veined side of each leaf at its base. Fold in sides of leaf over filling and roll tightly toward leaf's tip. Arrange compactly in Dutch oven or heavy large saucepan that has been lined with grape or lettuce leaves. Add water, tomato sauce, lemon juice and garlic salt, then cover with layer of grape leaves. Top with heavy plate (this prevents Yalanchi from moving and losing shape during cooking). Diffuse heat by setting trivet over burner. Simmer Yalanchi until most of the liquid is absorbed, about 30 minutes. Taste and add more lemon juice if more tartness is desired. Refrigerate overnight. Arrange on platter and serve chilled.

Note:
Yalanchi Dolmas can be frozen.

Sou Boereg
(Baked Cheese Squares)

Yield: 18 to 24 squares

"Outstanding first course . . . place square on plate and garnish with a sprig of mint or parsley. For the daring, sprinkle a tad of sugar on your square."

- 2 to 3 cups (½ to ¾-pound) Monterey Jack cheese, grated
- ½ cup parsley, chopped (optional)
- 1 pound phyllo dough
- 1 cup unsalted butter or margarine, melted
- 1 to 1½ cups milk
- 2 eggs, well beaten

Butter a 12x16-inch baking pan. Mix grated cheese and parsley together in a bowl; set aside. Place 1 sheet phyllo dough in bottom of pan and brush lightly with melted butter. Repeat layers of dough and butter until you have ½ the dough used (12 to 16 sheets). Spread cheese-parsley mixture evenly over the dough. Then repeat layering the phyllo dough and brushing with butter until all the dough is used. Brush top layer with butter. Cut UNCOOKED pastry into the number of serving pieces desired. Mix milk and beaten eggs together and pour over uncooked pastry. Bake in a preheated 400 degree oven for 20 to 30 minutes or until golden brown.

Note:
It is necessary to work quickly with phyllo dough because it dries quickly and becomes brittle. Cover unrolled phyllo dough with wax paper and then with a damp towel. Also, do not worry if the dough crumbles a bit as you layer it, just continue to work as quickly as possible. Phyllo can be cut in half and put in a smaller baking dish for making a smaller quantity. Excess dough can be wrapped completely and refrozen.

Imam Bayeldi
(Armenian Eggplant Salad)

Yield: Serves 4

1 large eggplant
Salt
Olive oil
½ cup olive oil
1 large onion, chopped
1 medium-sized green pepper, chopped
1 clove garlic, minced
Pinch of basil
1 medium tomato, chopped
¼ cup chopped fresh parsley
Salt and freshly ground pepper
½ cup tomato sauce
Lettuce
Green pepper rings
Lemon wedges
Parsley sprigs

Discard top stem from eggplant; cut eggplant into 4 wedges. Sprinkle each wedge liberally with salt and let stand 30 to 60 minutes. Rinse and drain thoroughly. Pat dry with paper toweling. Preheat oven to 450 degrees. Arrange eggplant on a rimmed baking sheet and brush lightly with olive oil. Bake until light golden brown, about 20 minutes. Meanwhile, heat ½ cup olive oil in a large skillet. Add onion, green pepper, garlic and basil and sauté until onion is wilted (do not overcook). Add tomato and parsley and cook 5 minutes longer. Season with salt and pepper to taste. Reduce oven temperature to 375 degrees. Slash eggplant diagonally being careful not to pierce skin. Divide filling mixture over wedges, pressing into cuts. Pour tomato sauce over top. Bake until eggplant is fork tender, about 30 minutes. Let cool, then chill thoroughly. To serve, arrange chilled eggplant over bed of lettuce and garnish with green pepper rings, lemon wedges and parsley.

Dolmas
(Stuffed Vegetables)

Yield: Serves 8 to 10

1 (16-ounce) jar grape leaves, rinsed and drained, or substitute parboiled cabbage leaves
1½ to 2 pounds lean ground meat (use any proportion of beef and lamb)
1 (8-ounce) can tomato sauce
¾ cup long-grain rice
1 medium onion, finely chopped
½ cup chopped fresh parsley
1 teaspoon salt
½ teaspoon freshly ground pepper
½ teaspoon allspice
3 zucchini, trimmed and cut into sections about 3-inches long, each hollowed on one end (leave about ¼-inch base)
2 Japanese eggplants, unpeeled and cut like zucchini
3 medium tomatoes, tops cut off and reserved, pulp removed and reserved
2 red or green peppers, tops cut off and reserved, seeded
Juice of 1 fresh lemon
1 (8-ounce) can tomato sauce
Water

Line bottom of 6-quart Dutch oven with some of grape (or cabbage) leaves. Combine meat, 1 can tomato sauce, rice, onion, parsley, salt, pepper and allspice in large mixing bowl and blend well. Fill zucchini and eggplant shells with meat mixture. Lay vegetables on their sides over leaves, placing open end of one against closed end of another. Fill tomatoes and peppers; replace tops and pack, upright, tightly into pan. Use remaining meat mixture to stuff grape leaves, placing 1 tablespoon of meat on veined side of each leaf at its base. Fold in sides of leaf over filling and roll tightly towards leaf's tip. Place filled grape or cabbage rolls over other vegetables. Squeeze lemon juice over top and cover with remaining tomato sauce and reserved tomato pulp. Cover with any remaining grape leaves and place heavy plate on top.

Add just enough water to cover Dolmas. Cover with lid and bring to a boil over medium heat. Reduce heat to low and simmer 45 minutes. Remove from heat and let stand for 30 minutes. Transfer vegetables to platter using slotted spoon. Boil broth until reduced and full-flavored. Pour over Dolmas.

Note:

1. Amounts of vegetables can vary according to seasonal availability—for example, use more tomatoes when they are at their peak.
2. Pack stuffed vegetables and grape leaves tightly so they do not float and lose their shape or any of the filling during cooking.
3. Grape leaves will vary in size. Use larger ones for stuffing and any smaller or torn leaves for lining bottom of pan.
4. Lining casserole with grape or lettuce leaves prevents vegetables from sticking to pan.

Kufta
(Filled Meatballs)

Yield: 12 to 18 meatballs

Filling:

½ pound ground lamb
2 large onions, finely chopped
¼ green pepper, finely chopped
¼ cup minced fresh parsley
¼ teaspoon (each) salt, freshly ground pepper and paprika

Sauté meat in large skillet until browned. Add onion and cook slowly for 30 minutes. Add green pepper and parsley and cook 10 minutes longer. Stir in seasoning and cook for 5 minutes. Chill until ready to use.

Broth:

Lamb bones
1 (8-ounce) can tomato sauce

Boil lamb bones in salted water (broth need not be rich), removing scum as it accumulates. Stir in tomato sauce and blend well.

Outer Layer:

1 pound very lean lamb, ground twice
¼ to ½ pound very lean ground beef
1 cup fine bulgur
1 egg
Dash of ground red pepper
Salt and freshly ground pepper

Combine all ingredients. (Keep small bowl of ice water handy and continue dipping hands as you mix. This helps blend ingredients, makes meat easier to mold and expands the bulgur.) Knead like dough for about 15 minutes, dipping hands into ice water periodically until meat is sticky. Mold into balls about the size of an egg. Form indentation using thumb and forefinger (rotate ball in palm of hand as you press sides to form an even cavity) to make wall as thin as possible, about ¼ to ½-inch. (Cavity should be about 1½ to 2-inches deep and 2½-inches wide.)

Method:

Place 1 tablespoon filling in each meatball; bring edges around and seal opening to make it as smooth as possible. Add Kufta, a few at a time, to broth and boil until they float to surface and are cooked through, about 10 minutes. Serve with or without broth.

Note:

For a quicker broth, half-fill a 6-quart casserole with water; add 1 can tomato soup and salt to taste, and bring to a boil.

Ingredients for outer layer also can be formed into balls about the size of large olives and boiled in broth. Serve as soup course. (An Armenian matza-ball soup.)

Meatballs and broth can be frozen separately. Boil meatballs after freezing.

Shish Kebab

Yield: Serves 6 to 8

Marinade:

1 large onion, minced
½ to ¾ cup minced fresh parsley
½ to 1 cup vegetable oil
½ to 1 cup California dry red wine
2 to 3 garlic cloves, minced
Garlic salt and freshly ground pepper to taste

For marinade, combine minced onion, parsley, oil, wine, garlic, garlic salt and pepper in a glass bowl.

Meat:

Leg of lamb varies in size; as a rule of thumb, plan on ½ pound per serving before boning and trimming. One leg should serve 4 to 6 generously, with 4 cubes of meat for each skewer.

3 pounds boned, trimmed leg of lamb, cut into 2 to 2½-inch cubes
1 large onion, cut into 8 to 10 pieces
1 large green pepper, cut into 8 to 10 pieces
8 to 10 large mushrooms
Salt

Method:

Add meat to marinade and stir to coat well. Cover and refrigerate overnight. Prepare barbecue (or use broiler). Drain meat and alternate on skewer with 1 piece onion, 1 piece green pepper and 1 mushroom. Grill or broil to desired doneness. Salt just before serving.

Note:

3 legs of lamb will serve 15 generously.

Bulgur Pilaf

Yield: Serves 4 to 6

- 2 tablespoons solid vegetable shortening
- ½ cup crushed coil vermicelli
- ¼ cup butter or margarine (½-stick)
- 1 onion, finely chopped
- ½ green pepper, finely chopped
- 1 cup coarse bulgur
- 1 (10½-ounce) can chicken broth combined with water to make 2 cups liquid
- Salt

Heat shortening in large saucepan. Add vermicelli and sauté until lightly browned. Add butter and let melt. Stir in onion and green pepper and sauté until onion is transparent. Blend in bulgur. Bring liquid to boil in small saucepan; stir into bulgur and return to boil. Reduce heat, cover, and simmer until liquid is absorbed, about 20 minutes. Add salt to taste. Remove from heat, and let stand, covered, for about 20 minutes before serving.

Armenian Wedding Pilaf

Yield: Serves 4 to 6

- 1 tablespoon solid vegetable shortening
- ½ cup crushed coil vermicelli
- ¼ cup (½-stick) butter
- 1 cup long-grain rice
- 2 cups chicken broth, preferably home made
- Salt

Topping:

- ¼ cup (½-stick) butter
- ½ cup blanched slivered almonds
- ½ cup coarsely chopped dried apricots
- ½ cup California raisins
- ½ cup coarsely chopped dates (optional)
- ½ cup firmly packed brown sugar
- Dried apricot halves studded with blanched whole almonds (garnish) or julienne strips of dried apricots

Heat shortening in medium saucepan. Add vermicelli and sauté until browned. Add butter and rice and sauté 5 minutes. Bring broth to boil; pour over rice mixture and return to boil. Reduce heat, cover and let simmer until all liquid is absorbed, 15 to 20 minutes. Add salt to taste. Let stand covered, about 20 minutes, then transfer to heated platter.

For topping: Heat butter in skillet. Add almonds and sauté until lightly browned. Add apricots, raisins, dates and brown sugar and cook 2 to 3 minutes. Pour topping over rice and garnish with dried apricot halves.

Kadayif
(Walnut or Cheese-Filled Dessert Squares)

Yield: 12 to 15 pieces

1 pound Kadayif dough*
¾ cup (1½-sticks) unsalted
butter or margarine, melted

Filling No. 1:

1½ cups chopped walnuts
1½ tablespoons sugar
1 teaspoon cinnamon

Filling No. 2:

¾ pound Monterey Jack cheese,
sliced

Syrup:

2 cups sugar
1½ cups water
1 teaspoon fresh lemon juice

Preheat oven to 400 degrees. Pull dough apart and fluff in large bowl. Toss lightly with melted butter or margarine. Spread half into 9x13-inch baking dish.

For filling: Combine walnuts, sugar and cinnamon, or use cheese, and spread over first layer of dough. Cover filling with remaining dough, distributing evenly. Bake until top is golden brown, about 40 minutes.

Meanwhile, prepare syrup. Mix sugar, water and lemon juice in saucepan and bring to boil. Pour half of the syrup over warm Kadayif. Cut while warm. Pass remaining syrup in pitcher for those who prefer sweeter flavor. Syrup can be made well in advance. Add wedge of lemon to prevent crystallization and store, covered, in refrigerator.

*Kadayif is a shredded dough that can be purchased at Armenian or Greek markets.

Bourma
(Walnut-Filled Pastry Rolls)

Yield: About 3 dozen 4-inch pieces

3 cups finely chopped walnuts
¼ cup sugar
1 teaspoon cinnamon
1 pound phyllo pastry sheets
1 cup (2-sticks) unsalted butter or margarine, melted
½ cup (1-stick) unsalted butter or margarine, melted

Syrup:

3 cups sugar
2 cups water
1 tablespoon fresh lemon juice

Combine walnuts, sugar and cinnamon in mixing bowl; set aside. Unroll phyllo; remove 2 sheets and place on work surface. (Keep remainder covered with waxed paper and damp towel to prevent drying.) Brush top sheet lightly with butter. Sprinkle about 4 tablespoons of nut mixture over lengthwise half of the phyllo.

Using a wooden dowel about ¾-inch in diameter and at least 24-inches long, and starting it along the nut-filled side of phyllo, roll phyllo loosely around dowel. Lay dough seam side down on work surface. Lift one end of dowel and, using hands, gently push dough together from each end to form a crinkled roll about 10 to 12 inches long. Slide dough off dowel. Insert index finger in each end of Bourma to transfer to an ungreased jelly roll pan (11x17-inches), or slide off dowel directly onto pan. Let stand uncovered so phyllo dries slightly while making remaining Bourma.

Preheat oven to 300 degrees. When Bourma have dried slightly, pull ends out accordion-fashion until they touch the 11-inch edges of pan. Pour remaining ½ cup melted butter over top and bake until lightly browned, about 35 to 40 minutes.

For syrup, combine sugar, water and lemon juice in saucepan and boil until slightly thickened. Keep warm.

After removing Bourma from oven, drain excess butter from jelly roll pan. Using serrated knife, immediately cut pastries into pieces about 4-inches long. Pour warm syrup over warm pastries and allow it to soak in completely.

CHIHUAHUA MERCADO
FRESNO, CALIFORNIA

In 1944, the Villegas family came to the San Joaquin Valley from Chihuahua, Mexico. It was in 1947 that they opened a small restaurant, and the Chihuahua Cafe soon became well-known for its homemade tortillas. The popularity of the little restaurant resulted in the founding of the Chihuahua tortilla factory.

Today, this large corporation not only manufactures tortillas, but they supply a diverse selection of Mexican food products at the Chihuahua Mercado "market" and "Mexicatessen".

This menu, created by Senora Corina Villegas, represents a hearty Mexican dinner.

To those of us priviliged to live in the San Joaquin, these dishes and related recipes have been a treasured part of our everyday lives.

Mexican Dinner Menu

SALAD
Shrimp and Abalone
California Brut Champagne

ENTREE
Corinàs Chili Verde Con Carne De Res
Calabasas Con Maiz
Mexican Fried Rice
Fresh Corn and Flour Tortillas
California Cabernet Sauvignon
California Zinfandel

DESSERT
Capirotada
Fresh Brewed Coffee
California Cognac

Shrimp and Abalone Salad

Yield: Serves 6 to 8

1 (15-ounce) can whole abalone, well drained and rinsed
¾ cup fresh lemon juice
½ cup diced carrots
20 large shrimp, cleaned, boiled, peeled and cut into thirds
1 medium white onion, sliced
½ cup dill pickles, diced
3 small fresh tomatoes, cut into wedges
2 pickled jalapeño peppers, diced
1 tablespoon of the pickled jalapeño juice
½ teaspoon salt
Romaine lettuce leaves

Cut abalone into ¼-inch squares. Place in glass bowl, cover with 6 tablespoons of the lemon juice. Layer ingredients starting with carrots, then shrimp, onion, pickles, tomatoes and jalapeños. Pour the rest of the lemon juice and jalapeño juice over salad and sprinkle with salt. Stir two or three times to blend juices; cover and refrigerate until ready to serve. Serve well-chilled on a bed of romaine lettuce. May be made a day or two in advance.

Corina's Chile Verde Con Carne De Res

Yield: Serves 6 to 8

2½ pounds sirloin tip or T-bone steak, cut into ½-inch cubes (bite-size pieces)
3 cloves of fresh garlic, chopped
Vegetable oil
2 teaspoons salt
1 teaspoon flour
4 cups prepared chile verde salsa (see recipe, page 382)

In a large non-stick skillet on medium heat, fry meat and garlic until brown and slightly crisp; add oil only as needed, stirring meat to keep from burning. Sprinkle on salt and flour; stir until absorbed completely. Slowly stir in prepared chile verde salsa. If sauce appears too thick, add extra water, but be careful not to make too watery. Let simmer for 10 minutes. Serve hot.

Calabasas Con Maiz

Yield: Serves 6 to 8

5 medium zucchini
1 small white onion, finely chopped
1 clove fresh garlic, minced
1 teaspoon vegetable oil
1 (17-ounce) can whole kernel corn, drained
2 large tomatoes, diced
8 ounces Monterey Jack cheese, cut into ½-inch slices

Slice zucchini approximately one-inch thick and steam in ¼ cup water on low to medium heat until tender but not overcooked. Drain and set aside. In another saucepan, sauté the onion and garlic in the vegetable oil until limp but not brown. Add corn, tomatoes and zucchini and cook covered about 5 minutes, draining off any excess liquid.

Place cheese slices around top of vegetables and let stand, covered, over low heat for five minutes. Serve hot.

Mexican Fried Rice

Yield: Serves 6 to 8

1 small onion
1 clove garlic
2 cubes chicken bouillon
2 cups boiling water
1 tablespoon vegetable oil
1 cup long-grain rice
2 large tomatoes, diced
Salt to taste

Chop onion and garlic together; set aside in small bowl. Dissolve bouillon cubes in two cups of boiling water. In a large frying pan heat oil; add rice, stirring constantly as rice is browning. When rice is evenly browned, add onion, garlic and tomatoes. Sauté together until onion and tomato is tender. Add the 2 cups of chicken bouillon to pan. Cover; let come to a boil, then lower heat and let simmer on low until all liquid has evaporated (approximately 25 minutes) and rice is nice and fluffy. Salt to taste.

Chile Verde Salsa

Yield: 4 cups

2 to 3 green chili peppers (see note below)
1 (28-ounce) can whole tomatoes
3 cloves garlic, chopped
½ cup water
1 teaspoon salt
Pepper

Note:
Chili peppers vary in degree of spiciness. Jalapeño peppers are the first choice of Señora Corina for this dish. They are a meaty, dark-green pepper and very hot. Since she has always been the thoughtful hostess, consideration is given to the more sensitive palates of guests who are not accustomed to eating extra-hot chiles. Therefore, she recommends mixing 2 jalapeño chiles with 3 Fresno chiles, for a milder, yet tangy salsa.

Toast chile peppers on a hot plate burner (medium heat) until skins are slightly charred. Place peppers in a plastic bag, let sit for approximately 10 minutes (this helps the skin to separate from the meat of the peppers). Using rubber gloves, peel and stem peppers. Place peppers in blender along with the tomatoes, garlic, water and salt. Cover, and process on-off quickly about 3 times on chop. This should give the desired texture. Do not over-process. This should make approximately 4 cups of salsa.

Capirotada

Yield: Serves 6 to 8

- 1 (16-ounce) loaf of French bread, sliced
- 4 ounces slivered almonds
- 4 ounces whole peanuts
- 4 ounces halved walnuts
- 1 cup California raisins
- 2 ounces Cheddar cheese
- 12 ounces Monterey Jack cheese
- 12 cups water
- 1½ pounds pilloncio (whole brown sugar which can be found in Mexican delicatessens)
- 6 whole cloves (Black Rose)
- 3 sticks whole cinnamon
- ½ cup (1-stick) butter or margarine

This dish may be prepared a day or two ahead of time and served warm or cold. Toast bread until dry, set aside. Mix almonds, peanuts, walnuts and raisins together in small bowl; reserve. Slice cheeses about ½-inch thick, reserve for layering. Bring water to a boil, add brown sugar, cinnamon and cloves. Let boil until sugar dissolves, approximately 15 minutes. Remove from heat, set aside. Use medium to large Dutch oven with double-handles and lid. Butter bottom of pan generously, to prevent sticking. Layer bottom of pan with bread, breaking pieces to cover pan evenly. Sprinkle with ⅓ of the nut-raisin mix. Then cover with ⅓ of the cheeses. Butter one side of bread to be used for second layer, then repeat with nut-raisin mix and cheeses. Repeat layering one more time finishing up with cheese on top. Place pan over low heat. Slowly add warm sugar-spice mixture along sides of pan; should take about 10 cups of prepared liquid. Reserve remaining two cups for topping. Cover pan and let simmer on very low heat, about ten minutes until liquid is absorbed by bread (but not dried). Dish is ready to serve or may be placed in a warm oven and served later. Serve topped with whipped cream or vanilla ice cream and a light sprinkling of the sugar liquid as a topping.

Bibliography

Americans and the California Dream 1850-1915, by Kevin Starr, Peregrine Smith, Inc., Santa Barbara, California, 1981.

Garden Of The Sun, by Wallace Smith, Fresno, California, 1939.

Fresno County, The Pioneer Years, From The Beginnings To 1900, by Charles W. Clough & William B. Secrest, Jr., edited by Bobbye Sisk Temple, Panorama West Books, Fresno, California, 1984.

Vintage Fresno, Pictorial Recollections of a Western City, by Edwin M. Eaton, The Huntington Press, Fresno, California 1965.

Stagecoach Heyday, In The San Joaquin Valley 1853-1876, by William Harland Boyd, Kern County Historical Society, Bakersfield, California, 1983.

Madera, by Charles W. Cough, Madera County Historical Society, Panorama West Books, Fresno, California, 1983.

The Call of Gold, True Tales On The Gold Road To Yosemite, by Newell D. Chamberlain, Valley Publishers, Fresno, California, 1977.

The Yosemite, by John Muir, Doubleday & Co., Inc., Garden City, New Jersey, 1962.

Our Yosemite National Park, by John Muir, Outbooks, Golden, Colorado, 1980.

Illustrated Guide To Yosemite, by Virginia & Ansel Adams, Sierra Club, San Francisco, California, 1963.

The Life and Adventures of John Muir, by James Mitchell Clarke, Sierra Club, San Francisco, California, 1980.

The Chinese Of America, by Jack Chen, Harper & Row, San Francisco, California, 1980.

"The Archeological Zone Of Tula", by Raul Guerrero Guerrero, Archaeological Conference, Fresno, California, 1982.

"The Head of Joaquin Murrieta", by Richard Rodriquez, "California", California Magazine, July 1985, Volume 10, number 7, pp. 55-62,89.

A *Rocky Road, The Pilgrimage of the Grape,* by Charles W. Bonner, edited by John G. Taylor, illustrated by Doug Hansen, Pioneer Publishing, Fresno, California, 1983.

"Agricultural Crop and Livestock Report 1984", by the County of Fresno Department of Agricultural Commissioner, Fresno, California, 1984.

"Community Economic Profile", Fresno County & City Chamber Of Commerce, Fresno, California, 1960-1983.

References

Sr. Hipolito Santillan, Mexican Consul, Geneve, Switzerland.
The Honorable Armando O. Rodriguez, Fresno, California.
Mr. Frank Del Real, Fresno, California.
F. John Sierra, Curator, Centro Bellas Artes, Fresno, California.

A special thank you to:

Richard C. Crossman, for his generous donation
Laurie Bolger Sonneman, for her secretarial skills
Hills, Renaut, Homen & McCormick, for their generous donation
Glenda Parsley, Nancy Koontz and Roxanne Flores, for their computer skills

Friends of Junior League

Harriet Beach
Nicholas Boghosian
Carol Boos
Lynn Cammack
Lucille Demes
Linda Denham
Marcia Falk
Mark Frandsen
Jan Gerdts
Mercina Glenn
Sarah Hagopian
Iva Hansen
Mary Kachadoorian
Eloise King
Betty Kitts
Robert Oliver
Verlinda Olson
Jim Pardini
Agnes Pelous
Peggy Perkins
Mary Lou Schaaf
Zephyr Shekoyan

Underwriters

BANK OF FRESNO

SAULSBURY ORCHARDS AND ALMOND PROCESSING
SUN-DIAMOND CORPORATION

Fresno Equipment Company
Gottschalks
Spalding Wathen
Harris Ranch Beef Company
Donaghy Sales, Incorporated
Octavia Diener
Western States Administrators
San Francisco Floral Company
Campbell's Soup
Spencer Enterprises and
Anonymous donors

Susan Bonner Martin
Gus and Greti Bonner
Mike and Ladean McCormick
John and Lollie Horstmann
Tiny's Olive Branch Restaurant
Edwin and Kristan O'Neill
Charles B. Bonner
Nicholas and Nancy Boghosian
Wallace and Maxine Quinlisk
Charles Tingey Associates
Hestbeck's Foods, Incorporated
Robert and Stephanie Oliver
American Paving Company

Index

Index

-M-

-Y-

-Z-

Recipes From The Junior League of Fresno

To order "California Treasure", fill out the following information and mail it to:
Junior League of Fresno Publications
P.O. Box 16278, Fresno, California 93755

Name ______

Address ______

City ______

State ______ Zip ______

Phone (   ) ______

Allow 30 days delivery with each order

Method of Payment:

Visa # ______

Expiration Date ______

Master Card # ______

Expiration Date ______

Master Card Bank Number ______

Personal Check ______ Money order ______

Make Checks payable to J.L.F. Publications

Number of books $17.50 each $ ______

Shipping & Handling add $2.50 each ______

Gift Wrapping add 50¢ each book (Holiday or other?) ______

Sales tax add 6% each (Calif. residents only) ______

Total Amount of order $ ______

Recipes From The Junior League of Fresno

To order "California Treasure", fill out the following information and mail it to:
Junior League of Fresno Publications
P.O. Box 16278, Fresno, California 93755

Name ______

Address ______

City ______

State ______ Zip ______

Phone (   ) ______

Allow 30 days delivery with each order

Method of Payment:

Visa # ______

Expiration Date ______

Master Card # ______

Expiration Date ______

Master Card Bank Number ______

Personal Check ______ Money order ______

Make Checks payable to J.L.F. Publications

Number of books $17.50 each $ ______

Shipping & Handling add $2.50 each ______

Gift Wrapping add 50¢ each book (Holiday or other?) ______

Sales tax add 6% each (Calif. residents only) ______

Total Amount of order $ ______

Recipes From The Junior League of Fresno

To order "California Treasure", fill out the following information and mail it to:
Junior League of Fresno Publications
P.O. Box 16278, Fresno, California 93755

Name ______________________

Address ______________________

City ______________________

State ______________ Zip ________

Phone (   ) ______________________

Allow 30 days delivery with each order

Method of Payment:

Visa # ______________________

Expiration Date ______________________

Master Card # ______________________

Expiration Date ______________________

Master Card Bank Number ______________

Personal Check ______ Money order ______

Make Checks payable to J.L.F. Publications

Number of books $17.50 each $ __________

Shipping & Handling add $2.50 each __________

Gift Wrapping add 50¢ each book (Holiday or other?) __________

Sales tax add 6% each (Calif. residents only) __________

Total Amount of order $ __________

- -

Recipes From The Junior League of Fresno

To order "California Treasure", fill out the following information and mail it to:
Junior League of Fresno Publications
P.O. Box 16278, Fresno, California 93755

Name ______________________

Address ______________________

City ______________________

State ______________ Zip ________

Phone (   ) ______________________

Allow 30 days delivery with each order

Method of Payment:

Visa # ______________________

Expiration Date ______________________

Master Card # ______________________

Expiration Date ______________________

Master Card Bank Number ______________

Personal Check ______ Money order ______

Make Checks payable to J.L.F. Publications

Number of books $17.50 each $ __________

Shipping & Handling add $2.50 each __________

Gift Wrapping add 50¢ each book (Holiday or other?) __________

Sales tax add 6% each (Calif. residents only) __________

Total Amount of order $ __________

Reorder Additional Copies

AUREL WOODS ADAMO LORRAINE ZULIM ANDERSON ROSE MUIR ANDERSO

DY BALDWIN NANCY STAPLES BARR SUSAN WORTHINGTON BARTLETT

JANCY CHOOLIJIAN BOGHOSIAN LINDA DAVIS BOYAJIAN NANCY MITCHELL

EBECCA MILANO CAMPODONICO CAROL ROBERTSON CHANDLER ELAINE SILVE

KIMBERLY PROBASCO COLEMAN ROBIN SIMONET COLMAN RUTHANNE COOKE

OAN CRAWFORD NANCY CROSSLAND JOAN ALLER CROSSMAN BARBARA BLUM

AROLINE DICKSON JANIS HELMICK DONAGHY JANE MCLEOD DUZI PAMEL

INDA AVENT ESTEP CAROL FLINT FERBER SUSAN LILES FISHER BARBARA ZIK

AULA GOOGOOIAN GANIMIAN CAROL BROWER GARDNER KRISTINE JENSEN

IAUREEN FLANNERY GREGG CHRISTINE HOVEY HALLAIAN

HARLOTTE WESTFALL HIRASUNA MARGARET GEARY HOFF ELIZABETH MCL

ANET JOHNSON JOHNSON DEBORAH JORDON JONES WENDY SMALL JONES MAURINE

EBRA KAZANJIAN CATHERINE KAZARIAN MARY MCKEIGHAN KINTER

RACE HOAGLEND LEESON PAULA LANGENBERG LOWRY SUSAN HOUG

ADEAN QUINLISK MCCORMICK KRIS IMOBERSTEG MCGANN TERESE CENCI MC

IANE FRIES MERRILL ELIZABETH ROWLAND MEUX SHERYLL MOLINARI MARGARET

YNDRA ROWLAND MORROW LISA PALMO MOSS JONEL MACRIS MUELLER SUZAN

IARY KAY WEBBER OROSCO ELLEN DAVIS PATTON BETSY MILES PAVICH

ALLY STOCKING PORTER AUDREY PUNNETT VERA DOLLARD PURCELL GAYL

ATHY SOUTHFIELD ROBINSON LESLIE SPEAR RUBEL ELLEN WIMER RUSSELL

UDITH JENSEN SCHUBERT KATHLEEN LAWLER SCOTT CAROL FLOGSTAD SHANAHAN

IICHELLE GAMBER STRACHAN LOUISE HYDE SUSSMAN MONA FLORA SWAN

LIZABETH TOOKOIAN TAYLOR LYNN WEIDMANN TAYLOR PATRICIA STOCKING T

KAREN JONES TRAPNELL BARBARA CHALLSTROM VAN ROZEBOOM CHRIS

UGENIA STEINHAUER WAUGH DEBORAH DUNNE WEINER KATHLEEN MCCANN

SUZANNE CHOOLJIAN YENGOYAN LINDA LANEY ZENNER TERRY FALKE ZUBER LYNN B

LLOYD BRINKER LINDA ANN DENHAM JACQUELINE GIGGERIAN DOUMAN

ATHERINE DESMOND FRANDSEN ANN VONNE GETZ PAULETTE BOGHOSIAN

KATHERINE BISHOP STOKES DENISE WALTERS TWEED LORRIE WINTHER AILEEN

UDY KNAPP ANDREEN PAULA HANSEN ANDREWS KATHY BOOME ANGELI

ESTER WEAKLEY ASPERGER KATHIE RUSTIGAN BABIGIAN LAUREL ROBY B

MARY ELIZABETH JOHNSON BARTLETT JANE PIPPERT BAXTER ANNE RUSH BENNI

CAROL BLASINGAME BARBARA RUBY BLICKENSTAFF PATRICIA RYAN BLOSSE

WANDA TRUAX BRADFORD LYLA TILSTON BREWER MARILYN GOODWIN BRICKE

ANN SHOWALTER BUCHANAN MAYBETHE RHODES BUCK SUE ELLEN THORNTO

BETSY HEAD CASILLAS CAROL WENDT CASWELL TAY NOSSAMAN CHERRY SHELLY N

ANE ROBINSON COYLE FAYE TURNBAUGH COYLE PHYLLIS WHITE CRIBARI LLOY

ANN DELLAVALLE WENDY DIAMOND OCTAVIA REID DIENER MARSHA MO

VICTORIA ECHEVERRIA DONALD JUDIE CLEARY DOWLING FRANCES KIRKPA

OAN JACOBSEN EMERSON FRANCIS FROST ERMOIAN GLEE MITCHELL EWELL V

MARTY DEMES FLAMING SYLVIA MCLEOD FORAKER ALYCE BERNADICOU F

KAY WILLIAMS FURGURSON LYNNE ENDERS GLASER ANN MOORELAND GRA

CORALEIN SMITH HALLOWELL PATRICIA HAMMAR JANELEE VOLKMANN HAMME

GERALDINE GILLIS HAYDEN VIRGINIA COUCH HAYS BILLIE JEAN CRANSTON HENDE

BARBARA KING HICKS EVELYN ROTH HIGGINBOTHAM JANICE HELMUTH HILL

LOLLIE ZWETZIG HORSTMANN GAIL KENNEASTER HOWARD GERALDINE WEIRICH

ETHEL KIMZEY JORDAN SALLY BRECKENRIDGE KADELL CAROL SMITH KEMP

PEGGY BUNTON LANG LOREE MACKAY LARSEN JUDITH TIEN LAU B

JOANNE BIERBAUM LIPPERT ROSALIE CAINE LOONEY NEL ABERNATHY LORE

FRANCES GRAY MACLEOD ELEANOR WATSON MACMICHAEL MARILYN MANN C

SHIRLEY BROWN MCGRATH SHERI CLARK MCKEIGHAN KAREN JACOBSEN ME

FLORENCE BISCEGLIA OLSEN PAMELA OLSEN DAGNE NORDHOLM OLSON MA

OYCE TAYLOR PARR HELENE CORDER JOHNSON PEARD HARRIET STOREY PERKI

UDY JOHNSON PIERROT NANCY FOREMAN POLHEMUS BARBARA WYNNE POPOVI

BETSY WEBB REEVES HARRIET RUFF ROBERTS JILL BLOSSER ROBINSON

BETTY MAXWELL ROTH AMANDA HICKMAN RUBY SHIRLEY COWAN RUFF

BETSEY DIMOCK RYAN ANN HOLLINS SADLER BARBARA CALVERY SAMPLE

ALICE BENADOM SCHAFER MARTHA WALROND SEARS JACQUELINE BIEN SHAVES

KAREN ADAMS SHEPARD MARIA SANCHEZ SIMI JOANN TAUL SLINKARD ELIZABET

CONNIE HARGROVE STAMOLIS PATRICIA ROGERS STARK CAROLYN V

BARBARA HARMON STRACHAN CAROLYN STUART SANDY SPEERS STUBBLEFIELD

VALDENE ROBINSON THOMASON MARGARET CARPENTER THORBURN RO

BETTY LOBREE TOLLADAY ROSE ADELLE GIANELLA TUSCHKA BABET

BETTY SMALL WATSON ELAINE MUZIO WEINER JUNE PORTER WILD

BERNICE MCKINLEY WOOLF